Grow
FRUIT
Naturally

A Hands-On Guide to Luscious, Home-Grown Fruit

Lee Reich

The Taunton Press

I DEDICATE THIS BOOK TO MY PARENTS, JOSEPH AND AIDA REICH.

The Taunton Press
Inspiration for hands-on living®

The Taunton Press, Inc., 63 South Main Street, PO Box 5506, Newtown, CT 06470-5506
e-mail: tp@taunton.com

Editors: Jessica DiDonato and Peter Chapman
Copy editors: Seth Reichgott and Candace B. Levy
Indexer: Heidi Blough
Cover design: Rita Sowins / Sowins Design
Interior design: Rita Sowins / Sowins Design
Layout: Rita Sowins / Sowins Design
Illustrator: Vicki Herzfeld Arlein
Photographer: Lee Reich, except where noted
Cover photographers: Front cover (top): Jerry Pavia; (bottom): David T. Gomez/istockphoto.com;
Back cover (left): Lee Reich; (right): Matthew Benson

Fine Gardening® is a trademark of The Taunton Press, Inc., registered in the U.S. Patent and
Trademark Office.

The following names/manufacturers appearing in *Grow Fruit Naturally* are trademarks: Agroneem®,
AZA-Direct®, AzaMax®, Azatrol®, Cadillac®, Cyd-X®, Deerchaser™, DiPel®, Ecosense®, Entrust®,
Fig Newtons®, Green Light®, Greencure®, K+Neem™, Kaligreen®, Kocide®, Kool-Bot™, Listerine®,
Lysol®, Milorganite®, M-Pede®, Neemix®, NimBioSys™, Organica®, Pine-Sol®, Remedy®, Safer®,
Sluggo®, Stylet-Oil®, Sunspray®, Surround®, Sweet Tarts®, Tangle-Trap®, Thuricide®, Triact®, Trilogy®,
Vicrosoft®

Library of Congress Cataloging-in-Publication Data
Reich, Lee.
  Grow fruit naturally : a hands-on guide to luscious, home-grown fruit / author: Lee Reich.
      p. cm.
  Includes bibliographical references and index.
  ISBN 978-1-60085-356-2
1. Fruit-culture--United States--Handbooks, manuals, etc. 2. Organic gardening--United States--Handbooks,
manuals, etc. I. Title. II. Title: Hands-on guide to luscious, home-grown fruit.
  SB355.R444 2012
  634.0973--dc23
                              2011049718

Printed in the United States of America
10 9 8 7 6 5 4 3 2 1

Acknowledgments

What wondrous life is this I lead!
Ripe apples drop about my head;
The luscious clusters of the vine
Upon my mouth do crush their wine;
The nectarine and curious peach
Into my hands themselves do reach;
Stumbling on melons as I pass,
Insnared with flowers, I fall on grass.

—*The Garden*, Andrew Marvell
(17th century)

A number of people helped mature and ripen this book. For this, I offer thanks to the editors, designers, and other staff at The Taunton Press. Thanks also to the following people for helpful commentary on selected chapters, or portions thereof, of the manuscript draft: Jana Beckerman, Bruce Bordelon, Tom Burford, Ed Fackler, Julie Frink, Jim Gilbert, Jeff Moersfelder, Marvin Pritts, Robert Purvis, and Lon Rombough. And special thanks to Vicki Herzfeld Arlein for her many insightful comments on the text and design, as well as for her artful and lucid illustrations.

Contents

PART 2: THE FRUITS

Introduction

I am an avowed fruit nut. I love to eat (good) fruit. I love to grow fruit. I regret not being able to live and garden in more than one place, to enjoy 'Macoun' apples at their best in the Northeast, 'Navel' oranges at their best in southern California, 'Celeste' figs in Texas, and…I could go on. For now, I settle for the best-tasting 'Macoun' apples I've ever eaten harvested only a stone's throw across the lawn from my back door as well as spicy, sweet 'Swenson's Red' grapes that dangle from a vine-draped arbor above my terrace, and kumquats, black mulberries, and pineapple guavas harvested in albeit limited quantities from large pots that winter in sunny windows or the basement. And much more, of course.

This book is not for fruit nuts. This book is for every man, woman, and child. It's for anyone who has at least a bit of area—even a sunny balcony—to plant. It's for anyone who wants to enjoy the rewards, gustatory and otherwise, of home-grown fruits. Pick up a fruit and look at it. What perfection. Nature's original dessert. Nature's healthful snack. Nature's refreshment. Pretty good packaging, too.

Home-grown fruits bring other benefits besides top-notch flavor. Caring for your plants is an opportunity to get outside in the fresh air and sunshine and move your body (productively). When *you* plant a fruit, *you* get to choose which variety tickles *your* palette, not necessarily what variety sells well and can withstand the rigors of shipping and please the palettes of someone in Pasadena, Pensacola, or Portland. Avoiding foods that have been shipped long distances means using and burning less fossil fuels, so it's good for the environment. For the localvore, what could be more local than food harvested a few steps from your back or front door?

Many people plant flowers, shrubs, and vegetables, but consider fruits too difficult to grow. Fruit growing presents a challenge to commercial growers, who must eke maximum yields from every branch of a 100 acres of trees. However, as I'll show you, growing fruit at home is enjoyable and easy, especially if you begin by selecting appropriate types and varieties of fruits for your climate and site.

The emphasis in this book is on growing fruit naturally. "Naturally" is an admittedly loosely defined word not yet restricted by legal definition (as is the term organic) or by dogma, but here is the general sense: Naturally grown fruits develop high flavor, are rich in nutrients and other healthful components, and naturally resist pests and diseases, so don't need regular dousing with toxic pesticides.

The emphasis here is also on simplicity, making fruit growing feasible within the constraints of time and space that today's gardeners and homeowners face. I'm familiar with such constraints, for the past 30 years having juggled my love of fruit growing with graduate school (in pomology; that is, fruit growing), salaried employment (agricultural research with the U.S. Department of Agriculture and Cornell University, in fruit growing), and then self-employment (garden writing and consulting focused, of course, on fruit growing). This book will give you what you need to know to most easily grow the most luscious, healthful fruits you've ever tasted. Following nature's lead will keep things simple and successful.

Of course, simplicity goes only so far when you keep expanding your fruit plantings, as I have done. But then, I'm a fruit nut.

HOW TO USE THIS BOOK

The first part of this book will guide you, beginning where you would begin, with where to plant, what to plant (based on your climate and site), how to plant, and how to care for your plants. The second part of the book details growing, pruning, pests and diseases, and harvesting information for individual fruits, including extensive lists of plants and varieties and descriptions of their unique characteristics. Make sure also to check the back of the book for USDA Hardiness Zone and AHS Heat Zone maps and an extensive list of resources, including suppliers, organizations, and suggested reading.

So let's go outside and begin the journey to enjoying (quoting A. J. Downing in his 1845 classic *Fruits and Fruit Trees of North America*), "fruit…the flower of commodities…the most perfect union of the useful and the beautiful that the earth knows. Trees full of soft foliage; blossoms fresh with spring beauty; and, finally, fruit, rich, bloom-dusted, melting and luscious—such are the treasures of the orchard and the garden, temptingly offered."

The Basics

CHAPTER 1

Planning Your Fruit Garden

The weather is springlike, and fruit plants in color-splashed mail-order catalogs and at local nurseries tempt you with possibilities of luscious harvests for years to come. You pay your money, you dig holes, and you plant, but will you realize your tasty dream? Yes, if you plan before planting!

What requires attention in planning is sunlight, climate (including temperatures and rainfall), pollination needs, plant spacing, and how much of particular kinds of fruits you'd like to harvest. The most straightforward approach is to plan your fruits around the existing conditions in your yard and the varieties of plants that can flourish there.

Sunlight Requirements

One of the most important considerations in determining where to plant and what to grow is sunlight, which you *can* influence to some degree.

Most fruit plants need full sunlight, which means 6 hours or more of unobstructed sunlight each day from spring through autumn. If your yard lacks this much sunlight, consider your options for gaining more light. For example, are there trees you can cut down or back? Or go ahead and plant, realizing that there will be some sacrifice in yield and your plants will be more susceptible to diseases. Another alternative is to plant fruits such as gooseberries or currants, which thrive in shade.

Soil

Surprisingly, perfect soil is not all that important in site selection. Fruit plants do thrive best in soil to their liking, which is especially important with naturally grown fruits that are going to be rich in nutrients and able to naturally resist pests. At the scale of home-grown fruit, though, you can feasibly, if necessary, modify the soil right at the planting site to suit the needs of a specific tree, bush, or vine. That is, unless you are trying to grow fruits on such "terra-ble" soils (for cultivated plants, that is) as exposed bedrock or bog. In that case, the more practical approach is to select a site with reasonably good soil, the kind of soil in which you might plant a lilac bush or a vegetable garden.

Climate

The influences of climate—the weather conditions prevailing over a general area over a long period of time—are manifold. Climate dictates what fruit plants will thrive, even survive. Climate is one factor in the potential for disease. And finally there's the fruit itself; climate can hold sway over a fruit's appearance, even its flavor.

COLD-HARDINESS

Fruit plants vary in their tolerance for cold. Low temperatures may kill only fruit buds (in which case you lose the forthcoming season's crop), may kill occasional

branches, or may kill the whole plant. For a general idea of the average minimum winter temperatures where you live, consult the USDA Plant Hardiness Zone Map on p. 224. Wavy lines overrunning this map bracket each zone, from 1 through 11, delineating the average annual minimum temperature within each zone. As you look through nursery catalogs and read tags on plants in local nurseries, note the USDA Hardiness Zones listed for the fruits. Peaches, for example, are generally adapted from Zones 5 to 9, corresponding to regions experiencing average winter lows of about –15°F to about 25°F. Specific varieties may have narrower adaptation; 'Desert Gold' peach, for example, is adapted to only warmer regions, Zones 8 and 9. Knowing the cold-hardiness zone where you live and the hardiness limits for plants helps you decide which plants will thrive and bear well in your yard.

The USDA map covers the whole country, so it cannot help but generalize average low temperatures over relatively large areas. If you are new to an area or haven't before kept tabs on the weather, rely on what neighbors have to say about winter minimums as well as advice from your local Cooperative Extension office (find yours at www.csrees.usda.gov/extension). Even better, back up your own and others' experience with some hard facts by using a minimum/maximum thermometer (see p. 8).

A minimum/maximum thermometer, besides telling the current temperature, registers the minimum and maximum temperatures that were reached since the thermometer was last reset. If the mercury plummets some blustery winter morning to –20°F at 3 a.m., then "warms" to –5°F when you awaken at 6 a.m., you will know the actual low temperature. (Your plants already knew!)

Keep in mind that the actual low temperature during any winter will not necessarily be the same as the "average minimum" temperature as spelled out on the USDA map. If you live in Vermont or North Dakota, do not let a string of atypically warm winters lull you into planting nectarines. Use the USDA map along with your own observations and those of your neighbors. Then again, winters have been warming, so, depending on your gambling spirit, you may want to try to push some limits. Try growing citrus in Georgia, perhaps?

CHILLING HOURS

Winter temperatures are as important to gardeners in warm regions as they are to gardeners in cold regions, not for absolute cold temperatures but for duration of cool weather. Deciduous fruit plants (plants that lose their leaves and go dormant in winter) will not resume growth in spring until they experience an accumulation

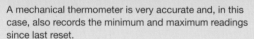

A mechanical thermometer is very accurate and, in this case, also records the minimum and maximum readings since last reset.

Temperatures measured by this digital thermometer can be conveniently read on an indoor digital display.

Minimum/Maximum Thermometers

Minimum/maximum thermometers come in two "flavors": mechanical and digital. Mechanical min/max thermometers have two sliding indicators that are pushed by either the temperature-reading needle of a dial thermometer or by the expanding fluid in a liquid in glass thermometer. One indicator stays where it is pushed to its high point, the other at its low point. High and low temperatures are indicated for the period since the sliders were last reset by being slid back against the needle or fluid.

Digital minimum/maximum thermometers work by . . . who knows? They do essentially the same thing as the mechanical min/max thermometers, except they are reset with a push of a button. One advantage of digital thermometers is that some can transmit readings wirelessly to an indoor reader. I read the minimum, maximum, and present temperatures from the warmth of my bedroom while still in my pajamas. Still, mechanical thermometers are reassuringly simple and reliable. I have both kinds.

I don't reset my minimum/maximum thermometers daily, except during a period when each night's minimum is very important, such as in spring when fruit plants are in bloom. I also like to know the depth of each winter's cold so it can possibly be compared to winter damage and plant performance the subsequent growing season. Resetting a min/max thermometer at the beginning of each winter will supply this information.

of a certain number of hours of cool—not cold—weather, commonly known as "chilling hours." Such chilling occurs, for most plants, between 30°F and 40°F. Temperatures much higher or lower than this amount do not put hours into the cumulative chilling "bank."

The amount of chilling required varies with both the type and variety of fruit. Most apples, for example, need a total of 1,000 to 1,500 hours of chilly temperatures before they will again begin growth in spring. So consider that chilling bank if you want to grow deciduous or temperate-zone fruits and live in an area with short, mild winters, such as in northern Florida, southern California, or a rough belt connecting those regions. If winters where you live are short and mild, plant fruits such as figs, pomegranates, and grapes, which need little or no chilling. If you must have apples or other fruits of colder regions, plant "low-chill" varieties such as 'Beverly Hills' apple and 'Desert Gold' peach that require fewer than 300 chilling hours.

This chilling business also works the opposite way, farther north. Where winters are moderately cold, chilling requirements of low-chill plants are fulfilled early in winter. The result: Overeager blossoms, held back by cold and now waiting only for warmth, are liable to open too early and be nipped by subsequent frosts. Therefore, do not plant low-chill fruits in northern regions.

Not all low-chill fruits come from warm winter regions. Plants native to places where winters are long and steadily cold are also genetically programmed to begin growth after only a short amount of chilling. In their native habitats, the chilling requirements for such plants are not fulfilled until late spring, because cold temperatures are generally below the 30°F to 40°F range for the duration of the long winter. In these regions, spring growth must be quick for the fruits to ripen within the relatively short growing season.

Where winter temperatures fluctuate, with many days in the 30°F to 40°F range, as occurs over much of the continental United States and Canada, chilling hours slowly accumulate through the winter. As a result, if plants such as apricot, which come from regions with long and steadily cold winters, are planted in these regions, they bloom early and their blossoms are often nipped by late frosts.

HEAT ZONES

How cold your winters get—the actual depth of cold—may be the most important consideration about your climate for fruit growing, but it's not the only consideration. If you live in a high-mountain or far-north location where growing seasons are short or if you live in a coastal region where summer temperatures remain relatively cool, you may also have to take your summer weather into account. Heat-loving fruits such as pawpaw, pomegranate, and late-season varieties of grapes may not ripen in such climates.

Pushing the Fruit-Growing Limits

The ideal in growing fruit is to match the plant perfectly to site conditions, but gardeners seem always to be trying to stretch the limits of what they can grow. So the gardener in New York tries to grow figs and the gardener in Georgia tries to grow citrus. New York is generally too cold for figs and Georgia is generally too cold for citrus. The quest for good flavor and, perhaps, the challenge of growing a fruit that your neighbors do not spurs such people on. (I am one such person.) Microclimates, once again, make such endeavors feasible.

Where more heat is needed in winter than is afforded by a south-facing slope, a south wall, or near paving, here are some options:

- Wrap a plant in burlap.
- Build a wire cage around the plant, stuff it with autumn leaves, and cover it to prevent moisture from leaking in.
- After a deciduous plant's leaves drop, dig a trench anywhere from a few inches to a few feet deep right next to the plant, pull the limbs down, and bury them and\or cover them with mulch; the deeper the trench or mulch, the greater the protection from cold. Uncover and pull up the stems before buds start to swell in late winter or early spring.
- Grow a plant in a pot so you can move it to a warm location when necessary.
- Build or buy a greenhouse.

One or more of these techniques have allowed me to grow figs, kumquats, guavas and other fruits in northern regions, most recently in wintry cold upstate New York.

Working with Microclimates

PLANT ON NORTH SIDE OF BUILDING

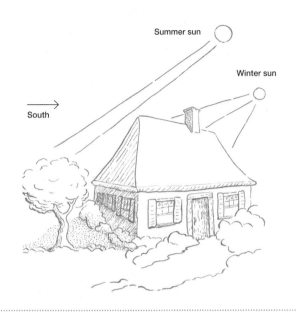

Summer sun

Winter sun

South

PLANT ON NORTH AND SOUTH SIDES OF SLOPES

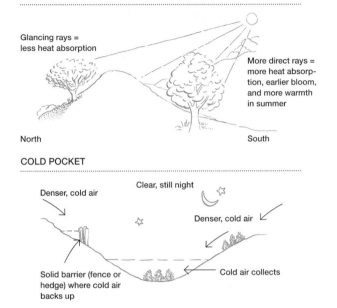

Glancing rays = less heat absorption

More direct rays = more heat absorption, earlier bloom, and more warmth in summer

North

South

COLD POCKET

Clear, still night

Denser, cold air

Denser, cold air

Solid barrier (fence or hedge) where cold air backs up

Cold air collects

On the other side of the coin, too much heat can be detrimental to any plant. Heat damage doesn't result in the dramatic wilted flowers or leaves that follow immediately on the heels of a freezing night. Heat damage is more gradual and cumulative. Plant growth may be stunted, leaves may turn pale or brown, and root function may suffer.

The American Horticultural Society's Plant Heat Zone map (see p. 224), like the USDA's Hardiness Zone map, is overrun with wavy lines that divide the country into zones. On this map, the zones indicate the average number of days per year that the temperature is above 86°F, the temperature at which heat damage might occur. The zones range from Zone 1, with an average of less than one day above 86°F each year, to Zone 12, with an average of more than 210 days above 86°F each year. This map was developed relatively recently and, as such, should be considered a work in progress, useful to tell you where and which fruit plants might suffer "heat stroke" or be unable to ripen thoroughly.

Plants' recommended heat zones are generally listed following their recommended cold-hardiness zones. So sweet cherry, for example, is 5–9, 8–1, with 5–9 being its range of cold-hardiness zones and 8–1 being its range of heat zones.

RAINFALL

Rainfall is less limiting to what you can grow than is temperature. Most plants need a steady supply of water throughout the growing season, but you can water your plants if rainfall amounts are inadequate (see "Watering" on p. 29). Pomegranates and sweet cherries tend to split if it rains as these fruits are ripening, but you can get around these problems with timely harvest and choice of nonsplitting varieties.

Microclimate

"Everyone talks about the weather, but no one does anything about it." Mark Twain, who penned that line, must not have grown fruits. Winter cold zones, summer heat zones, and Mark Twain's statement notwithstanding, you *can* do something about the weather, by seeking out or creating microclimates.

If you've ever leaned back against a sunny brick wall to enjoy its warmth on a winter day, you've experienced the effect of a microclimate, which is a small area where the climate is different from that of the general climate. In this case, the wall caught and held the heat and kept you warmer than you would have been standing in the cold air a few yards away. Microclimates aren't dramatically different from the general climate but may be different enough to benefit your fruit.

PREVENTING FROST DAMAGE

Microclimate comes into play with spring frost hazard. Most fruit plants bloom in late winter or spring, making their blossoms vulnerable to subsequent, hazardous spring frosts. Such frosts rarely kill the plant, but can kill blossoms and the chance of fruit for that year. A difference of a few degrees of temperature can spell the difference between a bountiful harvest and just a few, or no, fruits. Hence the importance of a microclimate.

The way to get your fruit plants to sidestep late frosts is to keep them from rushing into bloom; that is, keep your plants "asleep" longer. Do this by planting them in a spot where everything warms up slowly. Because water moderates temperature changes, areas least likely to experience damaging late frosts are those near oceans or large lakes or rivers. You don't want to relocate? Then delay bloom by looking around your yard for a microclimate that is the opposite of the microclimate near that sunny wall—one that keeps a plant cool. Bloom will be delayed on a north-facing slope as well as near the north side of your home, garage, or any other wall. Near that wall, the plant is shaded from low winter sun. Just make sure you plant far enough away from the wall so that summer sun, higher in the sky than winter sun, will fall on it.

Late winter and early spring freezes commonly occur on still nights when the sky is clear. Under such conditions, cold air, being heavier than warm air, hugs the ground and flows downhill, filling up low spots as would water. Also avoid spring frost damage by not planting in low-lying areas, especially if you are growing a low-growing, early-blooming plant such as strawberry. My property is basically flat, but on clear cool nights I can feel the temperature difference in spots even just a few feet lower than the surrounding ground.

Don't forsake the pleasure of growing fruit for lack of a site free from spring frosts. Grapes, blackberries, persimmons, raspberries, jujubes, figs, and a number of other fruit plants bloom long after all chance of frost is past. (And grapes blossom on secondary buds if their primary buds get zapped by frost.) Other fruits, such as gooseberries, cornelian cherries, and currants, have blossoms that are resistant to frosts. And you can easily drape a blanket over a strawberry bed if frost is predicted on a night when the plants are in bloom.

MINIMIZING WINTER COLD DAMAGE

Microclimate influences winter cold also. Because cold winter winds sweep across the tops of hills, the ideal location for fruit plants is right on a slope, rather than at the top or, because of spring frost hazard, the bottom. Make sure that no obstructions, such as walls or dense hedges, stop the flow of cold air down a slope. The microclimate created by the sunny brick wall mentioned earlier, or any masonry wall basking in sunlight, also mitigates winter cold by absorbing the sun's rays and then reradiating heat at night to warm any nearby plants. Plants experience the same effect from proximity to a paved terrace, path, or driveway. Near walls (except on slopes where those walls will pool cold air) or paving is thus a good choice for planting fruits that are borderline winter hardy. Be careful with early bloomers though, because that same warmth will coax earlier growth from these plants.

Fluctuating temperatures can wreak as much havoc on plants as can extremes of temperature. Tree bark is especially susceptible to such fluctuations, which can cause cracking and then infections. Sun beating down on bark on a cold, sunny winter day heats it up, but as soon as the sun drops beneath the horizon later in the day, the temperature of the bark plummets. One way to avoid these temperature swings is to paint the bark white to reflect the sun's heat during the day. Use white latex paint diluted with an equal part of water. An added benefit of this whitewash is that it deters certain boring (as in "makes a hole") insects.

PREVENTING HEAT DAMAGE

On the other hand, if your plants need cooler summer temperatures than your region generally offers, use cooler microclimates such as partly shaded sites (less than full sunlight will sacrifice some yield, but you may be willing to give that up to grow the fruit). You can also try north-facing slopes or near the north sides of walls or buildings.

Pollination Needs

Pollination is the transfer of pollen from the male parts of a flower (the anthers) to the female parts of a flower (the stigmas). Within the flower, pollen from the anthers unites with egg cells in the stigmas to form seeds, and in so doing stimulates the development of the fleshy covering around the seed—the fruit!

Parts of the Flower

MALE FLOWER

Kiwifruit

Petal

Pollen-bearing anthers

FEMALE FLOWER

Persimmon

Stigma to receive pollen

Petal

PERFECT FLOWER

Persimmon

Stigma

Pollen-bearing anther

Petal

Petal

Ovary (where seeds form)

Pollination

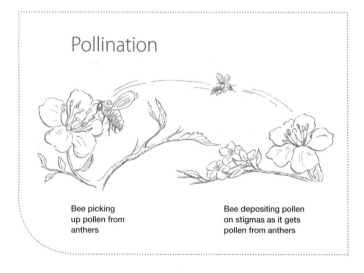

Bee picking up pollen from anthers

Bee depositing pollen on stigmas as it gets pollen from anthers

Pollination can stimulate fruit formation only if the pollen comes from a flower of the same type of fruit. Thus an apple flower can be pollinated by an apple flower but not by a strawberry or pear flower. (There are possible exceptions.)

A flower can be male, female, or both. If a plant has flowers that are either male or female, but both kinds are on each plant, that plant (filbert is an example of this type of plant) is monoecious (Greek for "one house"). A dioecious (Greek for "two houses") plant has only one kind of flower, either male or female, on each plant. Persimmon trees are generally either male or female. Most cultivated fruits have what botanists call perfect flowers; that is, they are monoecious and every flower has both male and female parts so they can provide pollen and form fruit.

SELF-UNFRUITFUL AND SELF-FRUITFUL PLANTS

Not all plants with perfect flowers can set fruit with their own pollen. If they cannot, they are self-unfruitful. Flowers that are self-unfruitful need cross-pollination and will not set fruit unless they receive pollen from a different variety of the same type of plant. Apples need cross-pollination, so a 'McIntosh' tree needs another variety, such as 'Red Delicious', nearby to bear fruit. The 'Red Delicious' will similarly bear a crop using pollen from the 'McIntosh' flowers.

Certain varieties of fruits may have special pollination needs. 'Magness' pear produces poor or little pollen so is incapable of pollinating any other pear. Pears generally need cross-pollination, but not every marriage between two varieties is fruitful. Although 'Bartlett' and 'Seckel' each produce good pollen, an innate incompatibility prevents them from cross-pollinating each other. Hence three different varieties of pears are needed if you want fruit from the 'Magness' pollinator or if you want to grow 'Bartlett' and 'Seckel'. You will find this sort of information listed with the description of a variety in nursery catalogs and in the separate sections for each fruit in Part 2 of this book (starting on p. 68).

The most obvious way to provide a pollenizer, when needed, is to just plant the variety you need. To pollinate effectively, plants should be within 100 feet of each other. Before you choose pollenizers, also make sure that their bloom times overlap with the variety you're trying to pollinate. 'Gravenstein' apple, for example, blossoms very early, so it would be a poor choice to plant with a late-blooming variety of apple, such as 'Rome Beauty'. Generally, there is good overlap of bloom times for different varieties of each kind of fruit.

There are workarounds for planting a pollenizer. Perhaps your neighbor is growing a plant that can sire your plant(s). If not, perhaps you can convince your neighbor to grow such a plant, in which case, if the fruit is perfect-flowered, you'll both reap rewards. Perhaps pollen could be supplied by suitable wild plants nearby. If you know of a suitable pollenizer plant that is not nearby, cut off some flowering branches while the plant is in bloom, then plop their bases into a bucket of water set near your blooming plant. The bouquet's pollen will remain viable long enough to pollinate your plant.

Another alternative to planting a cross-pollenizer is to graft a single branch of a pollenizer plant onto your plant. If the pollenizer also produces good fruit, then you will be able to harvest two different varieties from your single plant.

Not all fruits require cross-pollination to produce a crop. Fruits such as strawberries, raspberries, and most peaches have perfect flowers that are self-fruitful, meaning they can produce fruit with their own pollen, so you can plant just one variety and harvest a full crop.

Self-fruitful and self-unfruitful are two ends of a spectrum, and some plants lie between these two extremes in their pollination needs. In such cases, it pays to provide for cross-pollination, because doing so coaxes partially self-fruitful plants to yield more and bigger fruits.

A few plants set fruit without any pollination whatsoever. Among these plants are certain varieties of persimmon, fig, and mulberry. In such cases, not only can you forego providing a pollenizer branch or plant but the fruits themselves are seedless.

How Seedless Fruits Grow

If it is pollination and subsequent fertilization of the egg cells of a flower that stimulate development of a fruit, how can 'Thompson Seedless' grapes, 'Szukis' persimmons, 'Spencer Seedless' apples, and some other fruits be seedless? There are two ways.

That stimulus of pollination and fertilization might be needed only to get a fruit started, after which the seed aborts, leaving the fruit to continue development. This process, termed *stenospermocarpy*, is responsible for many seedless grapes, including 'Thompson Seedless', 'Jupiter', and 'Mars', and, in some climates, some kinds of pears. Nibble carefully at any one of these fruits and you'll usually come upon some vestigial seeds.

Other types of seedless fruits develop "parthenocarpically" (from *parthenos*, meaning "virgin"); that is, without any stimulation at all from fertilization. Parthenocarpy does sometimes require pollination, though, and can also be induced with plant hormones, as is done when making seedless tomatoes. Persimmons and figs are among the fruits that develop parthenocarpically.

'Canadice' is a seedless, hardy grape.

Choosing a Plant for Its Size

Every fruit plant needs adequate elbow room. A strawberry plant needs its 1 square foot of space and a full-size (standard) apple tree needs its 500 square feet of space, in each case so the leaves of the plant can bathe in sunlight and drying breezes. Such conditions promote good yields and limit disease problems.

The distance you should set your plant away from other plants, buildings, or walls depends on how big your plant(s) will eventually grow. Eventual size is determined by the richness of the soil, pruning, and a plant's inherent vigor. By pruning, you could keep a plant to almost any size. For example, cordon apple trees—just single stems of fruits—can be planted as close as 2 feet to 3 feet apart with appropriate rootstocks and pruning techniques (see p. 27 for instructions).

Except in cases of extreme soil conditions or careful and constant pruning on your part, the inherent vigor of your plant will be the main determinant of its ultimate size. For some types of fruit plants, such as apples and pears, you can choose the eventual size of the plant you

Recommended Spacing between Fruit Plants

This chart gives approximate spacing between fruit plants. Using these measurements, the branch tips of adjacent plants will just touch. Allow only half the distance needed for planting next to a wall or fence. Bush fruits such as blueberry and pomegranate make attractive, edible hedges, in which case you can set plants close enough to make a continuous row.

Fruit	Approximate spacing, in feet
APPLE	
Dwarf	7
Semidwarf	12
Standard	20
APRICOT	15
BLACKBERRY	
Trailing	10
Erect, semi-erect	5
BLUEBERRY	
Highbush	5
Lowbush	2
Rabbiteye	8
CHERRY	
Sweet	25
Tart	10
CURRANT	6
ELDERBERRY	8
FIG	10
GOOSEBERRY	5
GRAPE	8
JOSTABERRY	5

Fruit	Approximate spacing, in feet
JUJUBE	15
JUNEBERRY	
Bushes	6
Trees	15
KIWI	8
MEDLAR	10
MULBERRY	20
NECTARINE	15
PAWPAW	15
PEACH	15
PEAR	
Dwarf	8
Standard	15
PERSIMMON	15
PLUM	10
POMEGRANATE	15
QUINCE	10
RASPBERRY	2
STRAWBERRY	1

Blackberry's forest-green leaves and un-ripe, red fruits harmonize with this red wall and its green, wood trim.

Bright red, jewel-like red currant fruits hang for weeks for your ongoing visual and gustatory pleasure.

The gnarly branches and bright orange fruits of this apricot tree are as pretty as the fruit is tasty.

Luscious Landscaping with Fruit

Look around in spring at fruit trees in bloom. No, not weeping cherries and crabapples, which produce little or no edible fruit. But look at the blossoms on peach trees, sweet cherry trees, and blueberry bushes. They easily rival those of the weeping cherries and crabapples, yet flavorful fruits follow. Even the leaves of fruiting plants have a diversity of colors, sheens, and shapes. The rich, forest green leaves of a black currant bush are a perfect back-drop against which to highlight the white petals of daisies. The glossy green leaves of jujube make a nice contrast to the dull green leaves of juniper. And don't overlook the beauty of some of the fruits themselves: Clusters of red currants dangle from their bushes like sparkling, red jewels; a quince hangs from a branch looking like a muscle-bound, golden apple softened with a downy coat; bright red persimmons decorate bare branches of a tree in winter like Christmas ornaments.

You may want to use fruiting plants in the land-scape in more fanciful ways: trained into geometric shapes known as espaliers, for example. Espaliers require detailed and repeated summer and winter pruning, but reward you with artistic plants that yield prodigious quantities of high-quality fruit.

Plan ahead when incorporating fruiting plants into your landscape. Consider a plant's site requirements. Fruit trees such as mulberry and some persimmons drop ripe fruits, so keep them away from patios, walkways, and driveways to prevent stepping on them and dragging the mess into the house or car. If a particular fruit is going to need any kind of spray, even a natural or organic spray, keep that plant far from patios, decks, and other edible plants such as vegetables.

Finally, consider seasonal interest. A plum tree, for example, is at its best (for viewing, not eat-ing) in spring, when it can provide triple delight, for the fragrance of its blossoms, for limbs laden with showy blossoms, and, a bit later, for its fallen petals that cover the ground with a temporary, delicate, snowlike carpet. Blueberry bushes are attractive year-round, but are most striking in autumn as their leaves turn a crimson color that rivals that of the burning bush euonymous. Just think: With all this, you also get fruit!

Among fruiting plants, you will find those suited to almost every landscape use, whether you need a stand-alone tree as a focal point in your lawn, a vine to clamber over a pergola, a hedge to define your property line, or a groundcover to add visual interest. That fruiting plants lend themselves to such uses should not come as a complete surprise: Some, such as kiwi, were originally introduced as landscape plants, their tasty fruits initially overlooked.

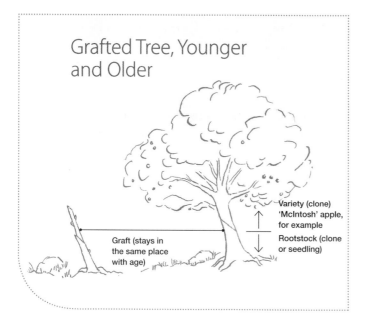

Grafted Tree, Younger and Older

Graft (stays in the same place with age)

Variety (clone) 'McIntosh' apple, for example

Rootstock (clone or seedling)

want from a range of sizes. With tree fruits, a full-size plant is called a "standard." "Dwarf" trees are smaller in varying degrees. Any good nursery that sells dwarf trees should specify just how much different in size the trees are from standards.

DWARF VERSUS STANDARD

A plant might be a dwarf either because it's naturally small or because it's been grafted onto a special dwarfing rootstock. The "rootstock" of a grafted plant provides merely the roots and a short length of trunk upon which is grafted the stem of a desired variety; all growth above the graft, which always remains at the same height, is of the grafted variety. A 'Northblue' blueberry bush is an example of a plant not propagated by grafting; it is naturally small and will never grow to the size of a naturally large 'Bluecrop' blueberry bush. Apple trees are examples of plants propagated by grafting, and a 'McIntosh' apple tree might grow to 25 feet grafted on one rootstock (MM.111), to 15 feet grafted on another rootstock (MM.106), or to only 6 feet grafted on yet another rootstock (M.27).

Fruit size is not affected by plant size. All of the 'McIntosh' fruits will be the same, but the 'Northblue' fruits are different from the 'Bluecrop' fruits. Because of their smaller size, dwarf trees are generally easier to manage than full-size trees. You have less need to climb ladders or climb among the branches because most or all pruning, thinning, and harvesting can be done with both of your feet planted firmly on the ground. Smaller plants are also easier to spray, should this be necessary.

Another advantage of dwarfs is that you can cram more of them into a given area. Instead of seven bushels of fruit from one large 'McIntosh' tree, you could harvest a bushel and a half from each of six dwarf trees occupying the same space as a the single large tree (and each tree could be of a different variety). Not only do you get more variety in apples but, because small trees "harvest" sunlight more efficiently than large trees, you'll also get a greater total yield. Large trees shade themselves, resulting in a lot of the plant's energy going to supporting wood that carries neither leaves nor fruit. Or you could plant a couple of dwarf apple trees, a couple of dwarf peach trees, and a couple of dwarf plum trees in that same space. With smaller trees, you can harvest a greater variety of fruits and spread out the harvest over a longer season. Yet another advantage is that, in many cases, grafted dwarf trees bear their first crops sooner than grafted full-size trees.

With that said, a larger tree might better suit your needs. Perhaps you enjoy putting up a mess of apple-sauce or canned peaches all at once. Generally, large trees tolerate drought, poor fertility, and other undesirable soil conditions better than dwarf trees do. With age, a large tree also develops a majestic quality and provides shade and limbs upon which to climb. And besides, for some types of fruits, such as persimmon and avocado, you have no choice in tree size.

Rootstock Names

Rootstocks for grafted fruit trees are constantly under development for creating plants of certain sizes and adaptation to site conditions (such as dry soils, alkaline soils), pest pressures (like fire blight disease), and winter cold. Much of the early work on rootstocks was done with apples in the early 20th century at the East Malling Research Station in England. Those rootstocks were subsequently given "M" designations followed by a number. Other rootstock developers have used their own designations or used existing species or variety names.

Choosing a Plant for Its Productivity

Part of the skill in raising fruit is to produce enough of it, in steady supply, over a long season. You will want your plants to yield enough to satisfy your needs but not so much that the excess is left rotting on the plant or on the ground. (Neighbors and friends can help you out of the latter dilemma.) A selection of plants that bear fruit over a long season lets you spread out the harvest and preserve the bounty at a more leisurely pace and extends the season during which you can enjoy fresh fruit. That is how I am able to eat fresh blueberries from the middle of June well into September—the season opens with pickings from my 'Duke' bushes and closes with a harvest from my 'Elliot' variety.

Approximate Yields

This chart, which shows the approximate yield for mature plants of each type of fruit, will help you plan what and how much to grow. Numbers will vary from year to year due to climate, variety, weather, pests, and previous years' crops. Want another good reason to plant a variety of fruits? No matter what the conditions are in any given season, it will be a good year for something!

Fruit	Yield at maturity (pounds)
APPLE	
Dwarf	60
Standard	300
APRICOT	150
BLACKBERRY	3
BLUEBERRY	
Highbush	7
Lowbush	1
Rabbiteye	15
CHERRY	
Sweet	300
Tart	100
CURRANT	8
ELDERBERRY	10
FIG	30
GOOSEBERRY	8
GRAPE	15
JOSTABERRY	8

Fruit	Yield at maturity (pounds)
JUJUBE	100
JUNEBERRY	20
KIWI	150
MEDLAR	50
MULBERRY	300
NECTARINE	100
PAWPAW	50
PEACH	150
PEAR	
Dwarf	60
Standard	300
PERSIMMON	200
PLUM	75
POMEGRANATE	100
QUINCE	50
RASPBERRY	3
STRAWBERRY	2

CHAPTER 2

Planting and Growing

Fruit plants aren't the kinds of plants that you merely drop into holes, turn your back on, and come back to later to reap your rewards. Actually, you can almost do that with a few kinds of fruit plants. But you wouldn't totally turn your back on any plant, fruiting or otherwise, from which you wanted best performance.

With attention to planting, feeding, and watering, you'll get the most out of your fruit plants in terms of plant health, yield, and flavor. Mother Nature didn't mean for fruits to taste as good as you can make them taste. She's most interested in seed dispersal, and many animals are happy to help out with that in exchange for some small, puckery fruits. We want better fruits. Extra care is especially important if naturally grown fruits are your goal. This care is part of what makes fruit growing so rewarding: watching plants respond to your attentiveness and then tasting the fruits of your labor.

Soil

Don't call it dirt. *Soil* is a more fitting term for this substance that holds your fruit plants upright, packs them full of nutrients and water, and provides a nurturing environment to their roots. Soil is a mixed bag of components: minerals, air, water, and organic matter. Organic matter is the part of the soil that includes a host of living microorganisms, earthworms, and other creatures as well as the remains of dead plants and animals in various states of decomposition.

About half the volume of an ideal soil is made up of pores, into which seep air and water, and the remaining half is mostly minerals. Organic matter makes up only a small but very significant percentage of the soil volume. It's an important component of the healthy community of soil organisms, called the soil food web, because it nurtures beneficial microorganisms that aid in plant health and protecting roots from pests. Organic matter is what put the "organic" in "organic gardening."

Raised planting mounds are one solution for a soil that is insufficiently well-drained.

AIR AND WATER IN THE SOIL

Fruit plants—most cultivated plants, for that matter—need a soil that offers roots both air and water. Water can be applied, but not air, so your first concern is that water drains sufficiently well through the soil to also leave space for air.

If where you are going to plant is home to a healthy lawn or most other cultivated plants, it will also probably be a nice home for fruit plants. Cattails, purple

Drainage can be assessed by measuring the rate at which the water level drops in a bottomless and topless can pressed into a hole in the soil.

loosestrife, buttercup, cardinal flower, and other water-loving plants signal a soil that remains too wet and hence has too little air. If you're a more quantitative sort, measure drainage in summer by removing the top and the bottom from a straight-sided coffee can and digging a hole into which you sink the can with its bottom edge pressed firmly into the soil at the bottom of the hole. Fill the can with water and let it drain. Fill it again, and measure how long it takes for the water level to drop. Anything slower than 1 inch per hour indicates a drainage problem.

An excessively wet soil could be the result of a high water table, which is the level below which all soil pores are continuously saturated with water. Dig a hole and if water stays at a certain level, that's the depth of the water table. That level might change some during the course of the year, depending on seasonal rainfall. Sometimes a soil has what's called a perched water table, due to an impenetrable layer within the soil that prevents or drastically slows further downward flow of water.

One option for dealing with a high or a perched water table is to plant elsewhere. Another option is to raise the level of the roots farther above the water level by building up a wide mound of soil on which to plant. Make that mound at least 1 foot high and at least as wide as the eventual spread of the branches. A third option is to lower the water level by directing water away to lower ground via ditches or buried perforated pipes. Your local

Wet Soils: Causes and Cures

DRAINAGE

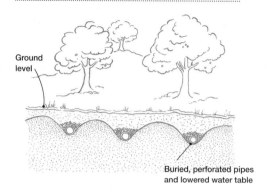

Ground level

Buried, perforated pipes and lowered water table

PARTICLE SIZES AND WATER

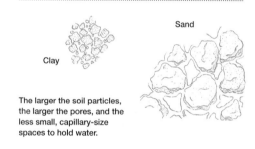

Sand

Clay

The larger the soil particles, the larger the pores, and the less small, capillary-size spaces to hold water.

AGGREGATION, WATER, AND AIR IN SOIL

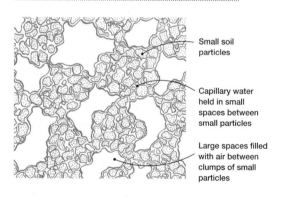

Small soil particles

Capillary water held in small spaces between small particles

Large spaces filled with air between clumps of small particles

USDA-NRCS office can help you with drainage design and implementation. Visit http://offices.sc.egov.usda.gov/locator/app?agency=nrcs to find an office near you.

An excessively wet soil could also be the result of a soil that is rich in clay. Clay particles are very small (less than 0.002mm by one definition), so the pores between the particles are also very small, capillary size, which lets them slurp up and cling tenaciously to water even against the pull of gravity.

Deal with a goopy, clay soil by promoting aggregation of the small clay particles into larger units between which will be commensurately larger spaces, too large for capillary action; gravity, then, pulls water down and out of those large pores. Don't dig, walk, or drive on a clay soil when it is wet because the pressure destroys aggregation. Wait until the soil is just moist enough to crumble easily in your hand. Time and the roots of growing plants promote aggregation. Cover crops are plants—rye grain, oats, sudan grass, and clover are examples—grown specifically to speed aggregation and improve a soil.

Cover Crops and Fruits

Cover crops are plants grown to improve a soil. They do so by increasing levels of organic matter, by suppressing weeds, and by promoting aggregation of soil particles as their roots gently shift particles around, exude glues, and create channels as they live and then die in the ground. Cover crops help nourish plants by latching onto nutrients that might wash out of the soil, unlocking nutrients within soil minerals, and gathering nitrogen from the air to put it into a form plants can use. The plants most commonly used for cover crops are grasses, for their extensive root systems (a total root length of 385 miles has been measured beneath a single rye plant!), and legumes, for their ability to garner atmospheric nitrogen for plants.

Despite all the potential advantages of cover crops, they could also compete with your fruit plants for water and nutrients. So the time to plant cover crops for your fruits is before you set your fruit plants in the ground or at the end of the season when fruit plants' needs for water and nutrients decline. You can also plant cover crops during the growing season beneath mature fruit plants that can tolerate or benefit from the competition. In the latter case, lawn-grass fulfills much of the same function as a cover crop.

Annual additions of organic materials, such as leaves and wood chips, have given my soil a crystalline-like structure with a variety of pore sizes.

Organic Materials for the Soil

Keep your eyes and ears open and you'll probably come up with other local sources of organic materials, but here are a few choices to get you started:

- Compost
- Grass clippings
- Hay
- Leaves
- Pine needles
- Seaweed
- Sawdust
- Straw
- Wood chips
- Brewery waste
- Hulls of peanuts, buckwheat, rice, and cocoa beans

One of the best ways to promote aggregation can be summed up in two words: *organic matter*. Where quick effect is needed, dig an abundance of some organic material into the ground over as large an area as the eventual spread of the roots. Among my favorite materials for this purpose are wood chips, sawdust, and wood shavings; they are abundantly available, long-lasting, and often free for the hauling. Mix a 6-inch depth of any of these materials into the top 6 inches to 12 inches of soil. Also add 20 pounds of limestone for every 100 square feet to counteract acidity, and 30 pounds of a nitrogen fertilizer (having about 10 percent nitrogen, such as soybean meal) to counteract the temporary tie-up of nitrogen by microorganisms. Sprinkle these amounts of limestone and fertilizer on top of the soil every year for the next couple of years; more if growth seems poor, less if growth is overly vigorous.

High concentrations of sodium in a soil, such as naturally occur in some soils of the western United States, chemically prevent clay particles from aggregating. Gypsum, which is calcium sulfate, a naturally occurring mineral, overcomes the effect of sodium by displacing it with calcium. Application rates range from 40 pounds to 175 pounds per 1,000 square feet, depending on the concentration of sodium in the soil. Abundant water, from rainfall or irrigation, is then needed to wash that calcium into the soil and get it to work.

So much for aeration. Plant roots also need water, which, as mentioned above, can be applied. For truly natural, sustainable growing, though, you'll want to make best use of any water that falls on the soil, and the way to do this can be summed up in the same two words that promote better drainage in clay soils:

organic matter. Sandy soils are typically dry because the relatively large sand particles (0.05mm to 2mm by one definition) house between them relatively large pores with little capillary action to hold water. Mixed into a sandy soil, the spongy nature of organic matter enables a soil to absorb water and retain it for the plant to use. Even easier, and equally beneficial, is just to lay the organic materials on top of the ground as mulch. There, they will slow evaporation from the surface, and their decomposition products, naturally working their way down into the ground, will aid in water retention.

Mulches are likewise beneficial for optimizing water use in clay soils. Raindrops pounding on the surface of clay soil can seal the surface, so the water skitters away and erosion results. Mulches soften the impact of raindrops so water can percolate down through the surface.

TESTING FOR AND ALTERING PH

Fruit plants cannot use nutrients in the soil, even if in abundance, unless the soil's pH (acidity) is in the correct range. This range, with some exceptions, is pretty much the same as for other garden plants: 6.0 to 7.5. So if other garden plants are thriving where you want to grow

Soil Types

Rarely is a soil all clay or all sand. Silt particles have a size range between that of clay and sand, and most soils are composed of a mixture of sand, silt, and clay particles. You can estimate the particle-size mix of your soil by feeling it. Squeeze a handful when it is dry and see how well it holds together. Then moisten it and try to press it out between your thumb and forefinger to make a "rib-bon." Rub the wet soil between your fingers: How does it feel?

Soils are named according to how much each of the size-particle ranges expresses itself, so a soil might be called a "sandy clay" or "silty clay." For plants, the ideal is a soil with a range in pore sizes.

Such a soil is called a loam, giving rise to further names, such as "sandy loam," "loamy sand," and "silty clay loam."

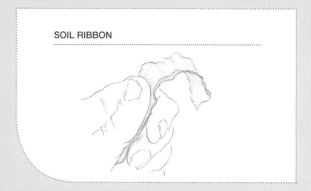

SOIL RIBBON

	Dry	Wet
SAND	Completely falls apart	No ribbon, gritty
SILT	Crumbles into various sizes	Short ribbon, silky feel
CLAY	Hard to crumble	Long ribbon, sticky

fruits, go ahead and plant. Otherwise, test your soil's pH before planting and periodically thereafter.

You can test your soil's acidity with a purchased kit or by sending a sample to a testing laboratory. (Find a soil testing lab by searching the Web for "soil testing.") With test results in hand, make needed adjustments. If the soil needs to be more acidic (lower pH), add pelletized sulfur, a kind of sulfur that is cheaper and less dusty than sulfur used as a fungicide. If the soil needs to be less acidic (higher pH), add ground limestone. Both sulfur and limestone are raw materials mined from natural deposits. The amount of material needed to change the acidity will depend on how much of a change is needed and how much clay is in the soil. To lower a soil one pH unit requires 1 pound to 2½ pounds of sulfur per 100 square feet. To raise the soil one pH unit requires 3 pounds to 10 pounds of limestone for that same 100 square feet. The lower values apply to soils at the sandier end of the spectrum and the higher values apply to more clayey soils.

FEEDING

With pH in order, consider feeding. Why feed at all, you may wonder? After all, who feeds forests and meadows? Fruit trees need feeding because a certain amount of nutrients inevitably are washed through or off a soil, given off as gas, or—in the case of fruit plants—removed with the fruits you harvest. Lost nutrients need to be replaced.

The key to feeding plants can, in general, be summed up in those same two words used for optimizing water and aeration in the soil: organic matter. During decomposition, either on or in the ground, straw, leaves, and other organic materials feed soil organisms, which, in turn, feed your plants as well as release other substances that make it easier for plants to imbibe nutrients already in the soil. With decomposition, these materials in large part disappear, so they need to be regularly replenished. This is as it should be. Nature replenishes natural soils with leaves that drop from trees and old roots that die and break down, rather than by spreading a bag of fertilizer.

Compost

Compost is the semistable, humuslike product of decomposition of primarily organic (living and once living) materials under controlled conditions. It is the Cadillac® of plant foods, actually more than just a food because of its beneficial effects on a soil's biological, physical, and nutritive properties.

Any pile of organic material will eventually become compost, but containing it in a bin is optimal. The bin keeps a pile of raw organic materials from looking like a garbage pile, holds in heat and moisture for sustained microbial activity, and restricts scavengers.

Composting organisms need food, air, and water. The foods needed in greatest quantities are carbon-rich foods and nitrogen-rich foods. Carbon-rich foods are represented by old, dead plant material, such as autumn leaves, hay, straw, sawdust, wood shavings, and wood chips. Nitrogen-rich foods are represented by young, succulent, green plant materials, such as kitchen waste, spent vegetable plants, and grass clippings, and by manures and seed meals (soybean meal, for example).

Composting microbes need more carbon-rich than nitrogen-rich foods. So balance additions of materials rich in one food with additions of the other. Also mix materials of different textures, so that the growing pile is neither too aerated nor too compacted. Water occasionally if the pile is dry. An occasional sprinkling of soil on the pile, while not absolutely necessary, bulks up the final product and absorbs gases.

Some art and some science is involved in making good compost. Still, if you fill the bin with organic materials, the end product will, sooner or later, become compost. The material is ready when it has the earthy smell of a forest floor, it no longer heats up, and the original ingredients are pretty much unrecognizable.

An annual mulch of wood chips or other organic material provides nutrients as well as other benefits to fruit plants.

Using organic matter wisely is not rocket science (although its detailed study is on par with that science). All you need are muscles and a pitchfork. Spread a 3-inch layer of any organic material on top of the ground each year to within a couple of inches of trunks. You can spread the mulch as wide as the spread of the branches, but even a much smaller ring of mulch will at least keep lawn mowers far enough away so that they don't accidentally hit and injure the plant. Organic matter is bulky, and it is the bulk that feeds and nurtures the soil food web. Consider bulky organic matter akin to bulk in the human diet. Both are important components despite their relatively low concentrations of raw nutrients. With the help of rain and soil organisms, the materials and their broken-down products will filter their way into the ground, the same way that soils are enriched and improved in natural settings. Rot is good!

One advantage of feeding plants naturally, rather than with chemical fertilizers, is that plants are offered a smorgasbord of nutrients, rather than just a few. That's because natural feeding is based on organic materials that themselves have a spectrum of nutrients that are released as bacteria, fungi, and other soil organisms break them down. What's more, these soil organisms respond to temperature and moisture, as do plants, so nutrients are made available in sync with plant needs.

Depending on how raw or rotted the organic matter is that you add to the soil, as well as its composition and the soil's native fertility, you may also need to add some concentrated fertilizer, such as soybean meal. As a plant

Essential Nutrients

Like you, me, and every other living creature, plants need food: about 17 essential elements, in the case of plants. Only 3 of them, carbon, hydrogen, and oxygen, come from air and water; the rest come from the soil. Primary macronutrients, which are needed in greatest amounts, are nitrogen, phosphorus, and potassium. Needed in lesser amounts are the secondary macronutrients: sulfur, calcium, magnesium. The remaining elements—boron, chlorine, copper, iron, manganese, molybdenum, nickel, and zinc—are needed in only trace amounts and are called micronutrients. (Sodium, cobalt, vanadium, and silicon are also sometimes listed as micronutrients, and nickel sometimes is not.)

Each nutrient element is important for optimum plant health, no matter what quantity is needed. And more is not better; these elements can be toxic to plants if too much is available.

These grape leaves, yellowing with their veins remaining green, show distinctive, early symptoms of iron deficiency.

grows older and as reserves of organic matter build up in the soil, such fertilizers generally become unnecessary.

Monitor fertility to make sure your plants are neither underfed nor overfed by occasionally testing the nutrient levels in your soil, which is best done at a soil testing laboratory, and by keeping an eye on leaf color and how much new shoot growth occurs each year. Keep in mind the old saying: "The best fertilizer is the gardener's shadow." Be careful about pinning the cause of too much or too little growth on soil fertility: Growth reflects not only how much organic matter and fertilizer you added to the soil but also how you prune, how big a crop the plant is carrying, how you water, and the vagaries of the season. Looking at a plant's leaves is useful because specific nutrient deficiencies often yield telltale visual symptoms. Again, be careful: Diseases, insects, or waterlogged soil also cause changes in leaf color. For information on typical symptoms of some important nutrient deficiencies, where they most likely occur, and quick, natural cures, see the chart on the facing page.

When symptoms of nutrient deficiencies are seen, and if they truly implicate a specific nutrient deficiency, the lacking nutrients can be purchased and applied or, in the case of emergencies, even sprayed on a plant. For soil applications, sprinkle needed materials over the soil as far as the spread of a plant's branches.

If you pay attention to soil aeration and water, and regularly enrich the ground with an abundance of organic matter, you're unlikely to ever see any of these symptoms. With plenty of organic matter, the most commonly seen deficiency—and that would be in a young plant where the soil may not yet be up to snuff—would be nitrogen. Soybean meal, applied in late winter at the rate of 1 pound per 100 square feet, should take care of that problem. Plants also need minuscule amounts of a number of other nutrients—micronutrients—of which organic matter provides a smorgasbord. Just to make sure, I sprinkle powdered kelp, which is rich in micronutrients, around my plants every few years.

SOIL SAMPLING AND TESTING

The bottleneck in the accuracy of any soil test is the actual sampling. Only a small sample is used for the test, so make that sample truly represent the entire area being tested. For even a modest, quarter-acre yard, 1 cup of soil—the amount used for the test—represents only 0.002 percent of the top 6 inches of ground, the home to most feeder roots! That area must have relatively uniform conditions as far as elevation, wetness, prior fertilization, and vegetation, or else needs to be

Nutrient Deficiency Symptoms

Symptom	Possible deficiency	Soil type	Natural remedy
Poor growth and yellowing of oldest leaves	Nitrogen	Sandy	Soybean meal or other nitrogen-rich fertilizer, manure, or compost
Yellowing, then browning of leaf margins	Potassium	Sandy	Wood ashes, greensand, compost or seaweed
Yellowing of new leaves, veins green	Iron	Alkaline (pH greater than 7) and cold, wet soils	Organic matter or manures
Death of growing tips	Calcium	Acidic or saline (high-sodium) soils	Limestone or gypsum
Leaves dwarfed and close together or light in color	Zinc	Alkaline soils where excessive phosphorus fertilizer is used or cold, wet soils; sandy soils; or soils where topsoil has been removed	Manure
Yellowing of old leaves begins at edge, veins green	Magnesium	Acidic soils and sandy soils or where too much calcitic limestone (high calcium) used	Dolomitic limestone (high magnesium) or Epsom salts

divided into more than one sampling area, each with relatively uniform conditions and tested separately. To even out small differences from one spot to another, even over relatively uniform soil, take a half dozen samples from random spots within a test area, avoiding abnormal zones, such as a place where you previously had a compost pile and near boundaries.

At each spot where you are going to take a sample, remove any manure, compost, or plant residues lying on the surface of the soil. Dig a hole 6 inches deep and use a trowel to slice a uniformly thick sample of soil from one of its sides. Make sure to make a full cut from the top to the bottom of the hole to ensure that you have equal volumes of soil along the entire sampling depth. Alternatively, push a purchased or homemade soil sampling tube 6 inches into the ground to retrieve a sample.

As you gather samples from each test area, put them together into a clean bucket. Thoroughly mix the samples to average out differences between them, discarding large stones and other debris as you mix. Then scoop out about 1 cup of this mix for testing. Before you pack up your sample, spread it out on a clean baking sheet to air dry for a day. Avoid contaminating the sample by touching it excessively with your hands or with dirty utensils.

Follow the instructions supplied by the testing laboratory about packing the soil. If you are testing more than one area, label the samples from each area. Equally important is to supply the laboratory with all the information you know about past fertilization history as well as what you intend to grow in the soil you're testing. Indicate whether you wish to have any special tests performed on the soil, such as for micronutrients or toxic elements (like lead).

Finally, keep in mind that a soil test determines fertility and acidity but does not address such plant problems as waterlogging or insufficient sunlight. A watchful eye on plant growth and leaf color is a necessary adjunct to soil testing.

TOP: Potted nursery plants can be planted anytime the soil is not frozen.

BOTTOM: Bare-root plants such as these establish well if the stems are kept dormant until planting and if their roots are kept moist.

When to Plant

Warmer weather beckoning in spring may trigger in you a primal urge to plant, but don't discount planting in other, perhaps less inspirational, seasons. Fruit plants are usually sold either potted or bare-root. The advantage of potted plants is that they can be planted anytime of the year that the ground is not frozen and, if of good quality, suffer no setback in transplanting. Bare-root plants are usually available in greatest variety but can be planted only while they are dormant and leafless. I opt for variety.

That primal urge to plant in spring notwithstanding, autumn is, in many ways, a better season in which to plant fruits. In autumn, the soil is usually moist and crumbly—just right for digging holes—rather than soaking wet (as it often is in spring), or bone dry. Spring's warm weather is also going to cry out the need for pruning, readying the vegetable garden, mowing the lawn, biking, hiking, and countless other outdoor jobs and pleasures. Planting fruits in autumn leaves you with one less thing to do in the flurry of spring activities.

Even fruit plants themselves benefit from autumn planting. Soil temperatures cool slowly in autumn, allowing some root growth even on leafless plants. And if you plant in autumn, when spring finally does arrive the plant is already in place, watered (from winter rain and snow), and ready to grow. Having the plant already in place is especially important with plants such as gooseberries, which leaf out very early in spring. In autumn there's also no danger of shoots growing before plants are in the ground, because temperate-climate plants, at least, must experience winter cold before new shoot growth can again begin; roots grow whenever temperatures are sufficiently warm, typically above about 40°F. There are only a few fruit plants that don't take kindly to bare-root planting in autumn: peach, plum, apricot, cherry, persimmon, and pawpaw.

When you receive plants from a nursery, make sure their roots, or the soil or packing material around their roots, is moist. If you can't get a bare-root plant into the ground right away in late winter or early spring, keep the plant cool to hold back growth. After you check that the roots are moist, wrap those of small plants, such as strawberries or raspberries, in a plastic bag and store them in your refrigerator until you are ready to plant. Hold roots of larger trees, shrubs, and vines until you are ready for them by temporarily planting them in shallow holes in a shady spot to delay or slow down shoot growth. Kept dormant and their roots moist, plants can be held like this for a month or more.

How to Plant

Just before you're ready to plant, soak the roots of bare-root plants in water for a few hours. After soaking them, trim roots back, shortening any lanky ones to about the length of the other ones, and cutting back any that are diseased or frayed to healthy sections of the root. While you plant, keep all roots in water or covered with moist burlap to prevent them from drying out. Give potted plants a thorough watering before setting in the ground.

Don't dig if the soil is very wet or very dry. Digging under either condition is frustrating, and digging wet soil can ruin its pore structure. Soil is ready for digging when it easily crumbles as you gently squeeze it in your hand. If you are planting in a lawn, use a flat-bladed shovel to skim off the top inch of grass and soil at least 2 feet across the area where you are going to plant. (Add the sod to your compost pile or use it to patch other areas of your lawn.)

There's no need for major excavation when digging a planting hole. A width two or three times the spread of a plant's roots and a depth just deep enough for the plant to sit in the ground at the same depth as it did in the nursery (indicated by the old soil line for bare-root plants) is sufficient. The hole should be shaped like a shallow bowl, tapering gradually to full depth in the center to promote proper root growth.

An ideal time to mix any soil amendments into the soil is while digging the hole, otherwise they would work only slowly down from the surface to your plant's roots. If the soil's pH needs adjustment, this is the time to raise it with limestone or lower it with sulfur. Phosphorus is a nutrient that moves slowly down through the soil, so if a soil test indicates a need for phosphorus fertilizer, mix that in with the soil as well. Avoid the temptation to fluff up the soil in the planting hole with copious amounts of compost, peat moss, or other organic materials. If you make soil in the hole fluffy and loose and the surrounding soil is dense, roots will have little inclination to ever leave the planting hole and they may eventually strangle the plant.

When planting a tree grafted on a dwarfing rootstock, be sure to keep the graft (the point along the trunk where the shoot of your desired variety of fruit is joined to a rootstock) above ground, or the upper portion of the graft might grow its own roots and override the dwarfing effect of the rootstock. To identify a graft, look for a crink or a swelling in the stem or a change in the bark.

For bare-root planting, splay out roots in the planting hole and backfill the soil in small portions. As you backfill, avoid air pockets by packing the soil in among

TOP: Cut back frayed or damaged roots cleanly before planting bare-root plants.

BOTTOM: The graft union of a dwarfed tree needs to be above ground level or the dwarfing effect will be lost.

the roots with your fingers or a stick and by occasionally bouncing the plant slightly to settle the soil. For potted plants, just loosen the outside of the root ball before backfilling. For larger trees, vines, or shrubs, when the hole is filled, form a dike of soil 2 inches to 3 inches tall and thick and in a ring as wide as the planting hole, to act as a catch basin for water at the base of the plant.

Your goal is to get roots growing out into surrounding soil as quickly as possible. And when roots get there, soil needs must be met. If lime, sulfur, or phosphorus fertilizer is called for, sprinkle it on top of the ground beyond the planting hole, at a width as far as roots can be expected to spread. These materials will work their way down into the soil by the time roots grow into this area.

Cover the bare soil at the planting hole with a 2-inch to 3-inch depth of compost, straw, leaves, or other organic material such as mulch. Leave a few inches around the stems free of mulch to discourage crown rot and rodents feeding there. Mulch is especially important following autumn planting in regions where winters are cold. It keeps the soil warm as long as possible for root growth and prevents new plants not yet firmly anchored

Cross-Section of Plant in Finished Planting Hole

Berm of soil to form catch basin to hold water

Fluffy organic mulch spread up to a few inches away from trunk

Shallow, wide planting hole, as deep as roots and two or three times their spread

Planting a Fruit Tree

1. Begin by stripping off the thin layer of sod in a circle as wide as the planting hole.

2. Dig the planting hole, tapering down from the surface at the edge to full depth in the middle.

3. Adjust the depth, if needed, so the ground line on the trunk will be at the same level after planting as it was in the nursery.

in the ground from heaving during the ground's alternate freezing and thawing periods.

Now is the time to put stakes into the ground for newly planted trees or vines needing permanent or temporary support. Drive a metal post or a sturdy, rot-resistant wooden post into the ground a few inches away from the trunk, on the side from which the strongest winds blow. Fasten the trunk to the stake with soft rope or old bicycle inner tubes, first tying the material tightly around the stake, then loosely around the plant. (See p. 38 for any pruning that may be necessary immediately after planting.)

Finally, water the plant to get it off to a good start and settle the soil. Slowly sprinkle or pour water over the surface of the planting hole at a rate of about 2 gallons per square-foot area of the top of the planting hole.

Don't turn your back on the plant for the season. Your careful planting will be for nought unless you diligently weed and water during the plant's first and most critical year in the ground.

Watering

A plant needs water to keep cool, to pump minerals up to its leaves, and to make carbohydrates for its structure and energy reserves. A plant may be able to survive on rainfall alone. Or, depending on the plant, soil, and climate, a plant may need your help in the form of irrigation. Bite into a juicy peach and you get a gut level appreciation for fruit plants' water needs. Most fruits are made up of more than 80 percent water.

Before you even touch your hose spigot, much can be done to help plants make the best use of natural rainfall and irrigation. First, add organic matter in and on the soil. As mentioned on p. 22, organic matter promotes efficient water use by facilitating water movement into a soil, helping a soil hold water, slowing the evaporation of water, and snuffing out weeds, which compete

4. Backfill soil into the planting hole, working it in among the roots with your fingers or a stick.

5. Finally, spread organic mulch over the surface of the hole and water thoroughly.

Staking, if necessary, needs to be sufficiently loose and low so that the trunk can move, which helps make it thick and strong.

Buying a Quality Fruit Plant

Starting with a good plant is the first step to eventually sinking your teeth into that spicy, crisp apple or soft, honey-sweet fig. You'll find that good plant at a good nursery, which could be around the corner or a thousand miles from your home. Adaptability of the plant to your climate and site conditions depends on the kind of fruit and the variety, not where the plant is grown or sold. Most fruit plants are clones, so a 'Berkeley' blueberry bush from New Jersey is genetically identical to and similarly adapted to any site as a 'Berkeley' blueberry bush from Washington State, or anywhere else. This assumes that the plant you buy is correctly labeled as to variety. I once purchased a 'Stanley' plum, which is an oval, powdery blue fruit, from a well-known, large nursery, but when the tree finally bore eight years later the round, red fruits were obviously not 'Stanley'. I declined a replacement.

In the case of grafted tree fruits, a good nursery will also specify the name of the rootstock upon which the tree is grafted. By itself, the word *dwarf* tells you little about your prospective plant. An apple tree might be sold as a dwarf whether grafted on an M.26 rootstock or an M.27 rootstock; the former tree, though, will mature at about 12 feet high, and the latter at about 6 feet, although both are dwarf when compared with a full-size tree 20 feet tall or more. Various dwarfing rootstocks dwarf a plant in varying degrees and differ in their adaptability.

Bigger is not necessarily better for a new plant from a nursery. Bigger plants have to grow proportionately more roots before they can establish themselves in their new homes, so they require more care, which mostly means more watering. Research has shown that, after a few years, plants that start off smaller often outgrow their initially larger counterparts. Between 4 feet and 5 feet tall is the limit for a good height on a bare-root plant. If a plant in a container is taller than three to four times the height of its container, its roots are probably too cramped with age.

New roots that have grown to the edge of the pot without starting to encircle the root ball are one sign of a quality potted nursery plant.

If you have the luxury of seeing in person the nursery plant you want to buy, inspect its branches for signs of disease or abuse. Take a look at the roots, too. For a potted plant, if you can slide the root ball out of the pot, look for plump white or tan roots growing just to the edge of the root ball, not circling around and around the outside.

Be aware that some local nurseries purchase bare-root plants and pot them up for sale as container plants. Nothing wrong with that, as long as the bare-root plant was good quality to begin with and was planted in a timely manner, without having its roots cut back to fit into the container.

for water. Second, remove weeds in the vicinity of the plant. Finally, contour the surface of the ground with low mounds to catch and hold water around your fruit plants (see the drawing on p. 28).

HOW MUCH WATER?

Water needs vary based on soil type, climate, season, and the particular plant. Sandy soils need the most frequent watering. Low humidity, wind, and heat all increase the amount of water a plant needs. Lush-growing plants use the highest amounts of water. Peak water needs begin when temperatures become steadily warm in spring and continue until growth slows in late summer and autumn.

A reliable way to tell whether any plant needs water is to dig a hole and feel the soil for moisture. An alternative method, one that avoids pocking your soil with test holes, is to use an inexpensive electronic soil probe.

If your fruit plant tells you it is dry by wilting, water it immediately. Once wilting proceeds beyond a certain point, the plant will not recover.

Large plants use more water than small plants, but large trees commonly send their roots deep into the soil, so except in dry climates they can fend for themselves once established. Berries and most dwarf trees, however, have shallow roots and may or may not need supplemental watering throughout their lives, depending on the amount of natural rainfall they receive. Newly planted trees, shrubs, and vines are a completely different story. They are not yet self-sufficient and won't get off to a rousing start without regular watering during their first season in the ground. If your new plant is large, such care is needed for 2 years or more, because roots need to grow in proportion to the size of the plant before the plant can be on its own.

Except in dry summer regions, in very dry summers, or with initially large plants, watering is necessary for only the first year. As a rough guide, a fruit plant needs to drink in a 1-inch depth of water per week during the growing season. A rain gauge, or any straight-sided container and a ruler, can tell you if 1 inch of rain has fallen. If rainfall amounts are insufficient, water your plants to make up the difference. An inch depth of water is equivalent to about a $\frac{1}{2}$ gallon of water per square foot. To estimate the gallons (rather than the depth) of water a plant needs, estimate the square footage covered by its roots—which is approximately the same as the spread of its crown—and apply half as many gallons of water each week. For example, a young plant with a branch spread of 2 feet might be assumed to have a

TOP: A rain gauge tells how much rain actually fell, which is often different from how much seemed to have fallen.

BOTTOM: The probe of this electronic moisture meter makes it easy to periodically assess moisture a few inches deep in the soil, where it counts.

similar root spread, or about 4 square feet. Thus 2 gallons of water each week should keep this plant happily free from thirst.

There are three exceptions to this "1 inch per week" (or "$\frac{1}{2}$ gallon per square foot") rule. The first exception is for fruit plants in containers. Because of the restricted volume of soil their roots have to explore, such plants

Plant Propagation

Plants are propagated either by sowing seeds or by cloning. Cloning is an ancient practice that uses a piece of a plant to make a whole new plant. These plants are genetically identical to each other and to the plant from which they came. Pretty much any fruit plant that has a variety name, as in 'Bosc' pear or 'Stanley' plum, is propagated by some method of cloning. Here are some ways that fruit plants are cloned:

- **Micropropagation** (for example, strawberries): Also known as tissue culture, micropropagation creates whole new plants starting with just a few cells from the tip of the mother plant. Transferred to a Petri dish a special cocktail of nutrients and hormones, those few cells are induced to multiply, differentiate into roots and stems, and then whole, new plants. Micropropagation generates a lot of new plants in a relatively short time.
- **Stem cuttings** (for example, grapes): Short pieces of stem plunged into moist soil grow roots and new shoots.
- **Root cuttings** (for example, blackberries): Short pieces of roots covered with soil grow shoots and new roots.
- **Suckers** (for example, red raspberries): Shoots that originate below ground are called suckers.
- **Layering** (for example, gooseberry): Branches bent down and held against moist soil eventually develop roots where they touch the soil; new shoots grow beyond the bend. When you sever the new roots and shoots from the mother plant, you end up with whole new plants.
- **Runners** (for example, strawberries): Specialized stems that grow along the ground and form new plants along their length or at their tips.
- **Grafting** (for example, apples): A branch of a named variety, when grafted on a suitable rootstock, which provides roots, becomes a whole new plant. Any growth above the graft union is genetically that of the named variety.

In contrast to cloning, propagation by seed results in plants that are genetically different from each other and from their parent plant. In the case of a few fruits—alpine strawberries, mangoes, and papayas, for example—offspring are the same or only slightly different from the parent. With most fruits, the differences between parent and offspring are dramatic, so most varieties are propagated by some method of cloning.

Because plants propagated from seed are different from their parents, these seedlings are used to develop new varieties of a fruit. A seedling that is superior to the parent will be given a name, and then will be propagated by cloning. 'Bartlett' (origin about 1765), 'McIntosh' (origin in 1811), and 'Concord' (origin in 1849) are examples of variety names (sometimes called cultivar names) given to worthy pear, apple, and grape seedlings that have since been multiplied by grafting (apple and pear) or cuttings (grape). Such seedlings may have been deliberately sown or discovered by chance in a garden, in an orchard, or in the wild.

Besides being of predictable quality, a cloned fruit plant also bears its first crop sooner than would a seedling. A seedling apple tree might not yield any fruit for a decade or more, but a grafted apple tree might bear a few fruits two seasons after you set it into the ground. And even after all those years, you are taking a chance with what the fruit from a seedling apple tree will taste like. On average, only 1 out of 10,000 apple seedlings bears fruits that taste as good as, or better than, the parent plant.

Propagation of Fruit Plants

MICROPROPAGATION

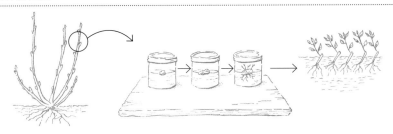

STEM CUTTINGS

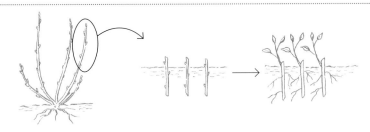

ROOT CUTTINGS

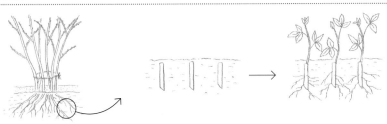

SUCKERS

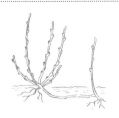

TIP LAYERS

RUNNERS

GRAFTING

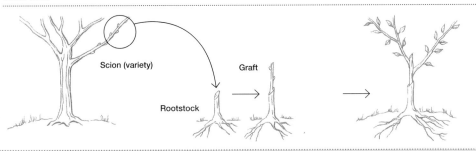

Scion (variety)

Graft

Rootstock

may need water every day—perhaps even twice a day—during their peak of growth in summer. Regularly check the soil for dryness. If the soil is dry, apply water until it flows out of the drainage holes in the bottom of the container.

The second exception is for large, new trees with deep root balls. Multiply ½ gallon of water by the depth, in feet, of the root ball. For example, a plant with a 2-foot-deep root ball needs 1 gallon per square-foot spread of its roots. The third exception is watering in autumn. Plants need less water as days grow shorter and cooler.

WATERING METHODS

There are three ways to water a plant: flooding, sprinkling, or drip irrigation. For greatest efficiency when flooding the ground around a group of plants or a single plant, create a catch basin for your plants (p. 28) and don't let the water flow so fast that it washes away surface soil or mulch. Flooding is not a particularly efficient way to water, and has the potential to erode the soil and the inconvenience of having to move the hose.

Sprinkling is an easy way to water, especially if you have sprinklers set up at permanent locations. Disadvantages of sprinkling are that wetting a plant's leaves makes them more prone to disease and the diffused spray also waters and promotes growth of weeds between your fruit plants. The ideal time to sprinkle is in the morning, early enough so airborne droplets are not blown by wind or evaporated in hot sun, yet late enough so the leaves dry quickly after you turn off the sprinkler.

Drip irrigation is the most convenient and efficient way to water, typically saving about 50 percent of the water that would be used for sprinkling (which, in turn, saves about 25 percent of water over flooding). Because it is easily automated, drip irrigation is almost mandatory for watering fruit plants in containers.

No matter what method of watering you use, water regularly—one to two times weekly with sprinklers or by flooding or daily with drip irrigation—whenever rainfall is insufficient. Besides promoting good growth, regular watering helps prevent nearly ripe fruit from cracking, a particular problem among fruits such as prune plums, 'Winesap' apples, and pomegranates. On the other hand, don't be overzealous with your watering. Overwatering wastes water and suffocates roots, which is as harmful to a fruit plant as underwatering.

TOP: Water from an emitter plugged into a ¼-inch tube that, in turn, is plugged into a ½-inch main line keeps this young blueberry plant watered.

BOTTOM: An inexpensive timer automates my drip system, turning it on and off automatically through the growing season.

Drip Irrigation

Drip, drip, drip went the leaky spigot. And the plants beneath the spigot loved it. Decades ago, an agricultural scientist in rain-parched Israel noticed the luxuriant growth of weeds beneath a leaky spigot, and decided to try this system—deliberately—on crop plants. So-called drip, or trickle, irrigation is the most efficient method of watering because it slowly and frequently replaces the water removed from the soil by plants. The soil does not cycle between periods of excessive wetness and dryness, as it does with both flooding and sprinkling. Drip irrigation also pinpoints water applications, so none is wasted on paths or on weeds growing between your fruit plants, and the leaves of drip-irrigated plants are not wetted, which decreases the chance of disease.

The bare bones of a drip irrigation system consists of a header and emitters. A header is a tube, usually ½-inch or ¾-inch black plastic pipe, that brings water from the hose spigot to various points in your yard. Emitters plug into the header and bring water to individual plants or a bed. Emitters typically drip ½ gallon to 1 gallon of water per hour, with 30 minutes a day of dripping typically quenching plants' thirst. Depending on the size of the plant, one or more emitters may be needed to supply a plant with the amount of water it needs within that 30-minute period. For a continuous row of plants, such as strawberries or hedgerow raspberries, emitters spaced close together create a continuous wetting front (the spread of water in the soil below each emitter). Lines with emitters preinstalled at 6-inch, 12-inch, or 18-inch spacings are available for such purposes.

The emitters themselves are technological marvels. In the early days of drip irrigation, emitters were plagued with problems of clogging and water output that varied with water pressure and the distance of an emitter from the water source. Such problems have been solved with today's self-cleaning, pressure-compensating drip emitters. Microsprinklers are emitters that are miniature sprinklers, spreading out the water near ground level over small areas. Caution is needed with microsprinklers because repeatedly wetting the base of a plant could lead to rot or other pest problems.

Drip irrigation is as friendly to gardeners as it is to plants. A system is inexpensive and works on low water pressure. Best of all, a drip system is easily automated. I turn mine on in April and off in October, and hardly give watering a second thought in the time in between. The only time I shut my system off during those months is during a period of several rainy days. Not that drip irrigation is foolproof. No dramatic columns of water spurt into the air to tell you everything is working, and no rivers of water stream over the ground, so periodically check your drip system to make sure everything is dripping when and as it should be.

In addition to the header and emitters, a few components are needed before water gets into the header. A typical drip irrigation system consists of the following components, beginning at your hose spigot:

- **Anti-siphon valve:** Prevents water from siphoning back into the water supply in case of a drop in water pressure.
- **Automatic timer (or a solenoid valve wired to a timer):** A timer is not absolutely necessary, but automating your system is a lot easier than manually turning the water on and off each time you need to irrigate the plants.
- **Pressure regulator:** Decreases the pressure in the line to about 10 pounds per square inch (psi) and evens out variations in incoming water pressure.
- **A 150- to 200-mesh filter:** Screens out particles in the water. (Yes, the emitters are self-cleaning, but why push that feature to its limit?)

None of the aforementioned components can stand up to subfreezing temperatures. However, the header pipe and emitters can remain outdoors year-round, even in cold climates.

CHAPTER 3

Pruning

The reasons to prune any fruit plant vary, depending on the kind of plant and whether it is young or old. To produce good yields of tasty fruits on manageable plants, most fruit plants need at least annual pruning. Pruning is a key element in growing fruit naturally, because in pruning you remove diseased portions of a plant, preventing further disease spread, and open branches up to light and drying breezes, which limits diseases in the first place. Certain insect pests are also kept at bay with correct pruning.

With a few exceptions, prune your plant while it is dormant during winter and early spring. Deciduous fruit plants will be leafless and growth on evergreen fruit plants will be slowed down. For plants that are borderline cold hardy or are prone to infections at wounds (peaches, for example), the closer to bloom time you prune, the better. That timing also lets you see and remove any branches that aren't awakening because of damage from winter cold.

Tools of the Trade

The tool you need for pruning depends on the thickness of the stem you intend to cut. Your thumbnail is all you need to pinch out the succulent, growing tip of a blackberry cane or any young shoot in summer. Two fingers are all you need to strip young leaves off a growing shoot for developing wide-angled side branches. Your hand is all you need to rip off upright, vigorous shoots known as watersprouts.

Moving on to unattached (to you) tools, hand pruning shears cut stems up to about ½ inch in diameter. This is a good tool to purchase if you're going to own but a single pruning tool. A long-handled lopper will cut through stems 1 inch to 2 inches in diameter, depending on the design of the lopper. For thicker limbs, use a pruning saw. The teeth of these saws—different from saws used in woodworking—are designed so they do not get clogged by wet sawdust. A pole pruner, which has a pruning saw and/or a lopper at its end, or a long-reach lopper or shears lets you prune stems out of arms' reach.

Types of Pruning Cuts

When you prune a stem, you have the option of either shortening it or removing it completely. Although any pruning of branches limits total plant growth to some degree, the difference in cuts is important for its effect on a plant. Pruning wounds a plant, so the ideal cut is made in such a way that healing is rapid and complete. Because clean cuts heal best, keep all pruning tools sharp. You may feel the need to spread pruning paint or some other balm over open cuts, especially large ones. Suppress that need. The paint or balm may make you feel better about wounding your plant, but the plant heals better without any coating.

HEADING CUTS

Shortening a stem makes what is called a heading cut. This type of cut coaxes buds to grow, becoming branches, along the remaining portion of the stem. The more vigorous the stem and the more of the stem that is cut off, the fewer branches develop and the more vigorously each one grows. Heading cuts are useful where you want branching to occur or where you want to locally stimulate growth where it was weak.

When making a heading cut on a young stem, prune just beyond and sloping away from a bud. Cut too close

TOP: Hand pruning shears, a lopper, and one size of saw should take care of all your pruning needs.

BOTTOM: A pruning cut just above and sloping away from a bud (center) promotes rapid healing with minimal chance for infections. A cut too far from a bud (left) leaves a stub that dies back, as does a cut too close to a bud (right) because the bud dries out.

to a bud and it will dry out and die. Cut too far from a bud and a stub will remain, which will die and become a possible entrance for disease.

THINNING CUTS

In contrast to a heading cut, a thinning cut entails the complete removal of a stem. Usually, no localized regrowth results following thinning, making this type of cut useful when you want to open up a dense portion of a plant to light and air. Thinning cuts are also useful when you want to keep a plant from growing too large.

When making a thinning cut, remove the stem or limb just back to the collar of bark near its origin. If a limb is large, don't try to lop it off in one fell swoop or the falling limb will tear down a strip of bark in its descent. Instead, cut back the limb so that it is only

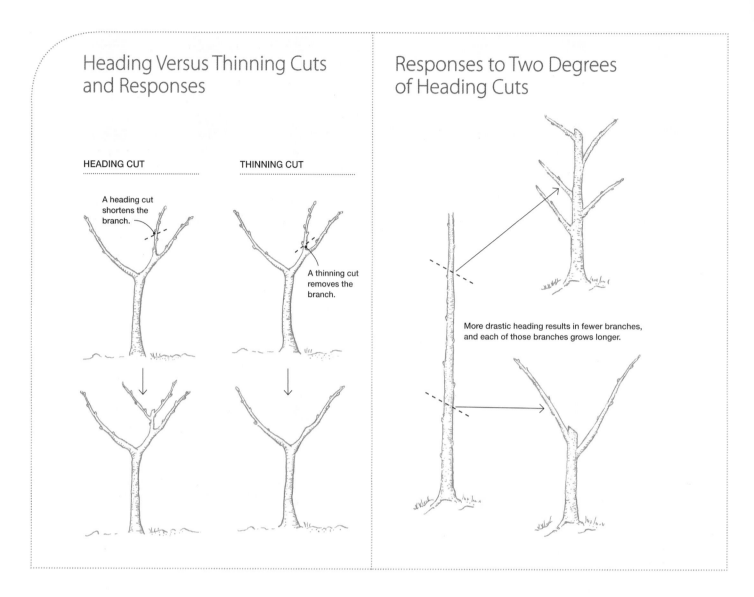

Heading Versus Thinning Cuts and Responses

HEADING CUT

A heading cut shortens the branch.

THINNING CUT

A thinning cut removes the branch.

Responses to Two Degrees of Heading Cuts

More drastic heading results in fewer branches, and each of those branches grows longer.

---

about 1 foot long, beginning with an undercut before you saw the limb off from above. With the bulk of the limb removed, support the remaining portion with your hand as you saw it off to its collar, the fold of bark at the base of the limb.

Pruning Fruit Trees

Pruning a fruit tree involves a certain amount of art, art that takes into account your objectives in pruning and the expected plant responses that, in turn, take into account the kind of fruit and the specific plant with which you're dealing. Don't be disappointed if your fruit tree doesn't conform to the idealized trees described here. In real life, trees don't read books and don't faithfully follow our rules. Given a reasonable pruning job, your tree should, nonetheless, be reasonably beautiful and productive. And a number of fruit trees require little or no pruning, or, at least, art.

PRUNING AND TRAINING A YOUNG FRUIT TREE

The goal in pruning and training your young tree is to direct its growth so that it matures with a set of sturdy and well-placed limbs that, even as it grows old, will be bathed in sunlight and drying breezes and capable of supporting heavy loads of fruit. Use your pruning tools with restraint, because pruning a young tree any more than is absolutely necessary will unduly delay the time of your first harvest.

Begin pruning your tree just as soon as you set it in the ground. If the plant is just a single, unbranched stem, called a whip, shorten that stem to about 30 inches

TOP: Remove a side branch by cutting it back to the swollen collar at its base.

BOTTOM: With collar intact, the finished pruning cut is soon closed off with healthy, new bark.

above ground level. This heading cut stimulates branch growth, and some of those branches will become the main limbs of your tree. Branches that sprout closest to the cut will mostly grow upright and are undesirable because they are poorly anchored and become congested, blocking the interior of the grown tree from ample light and air. When new shoot growth is 6 inches to 8 inches long, cut away all or all but one of those upright new shoots (depending on the eventual tree form you desire, described on p. 40). Alternatively, and especially if too few side branches have sprouted lower down along the developing trunk, do not remove the branches just below your heading cut, but manually and carefully spread all but one them downward and hold them in place by inserting clothespins or toothpicks between them and the trunk-to-be.

Yet another way to promote well-positioned and wide-angled branching is to strip off young leaves from the growing tip of the developing trunk, repeating the process one or two more times at one- to two-week intervals.

As branches develop, carefully select those worth saving and cut away all others. The origin of any branch remains at the same height throughout a tree's life. Too low a side branch will have you cursing as you mow the lawn around the tree and may end up resting its weight of fruit right on the ground, so remove any branch originating lower than 2 feet above the ground. For best harvesting of sunlight and strong attachment, a young side branch should grow outward rather than skyward. A spiral arrangement of side branches allows each of them to enjoy a good supply of nutrients and water. Side branches grow thicker as they mature and become major limbs, so they need adequate elbow room to

Pruning a Young Whip

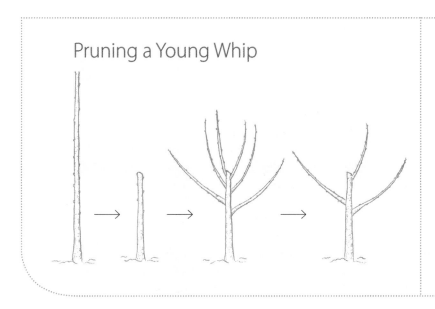

Selecting Scaffold Limbs

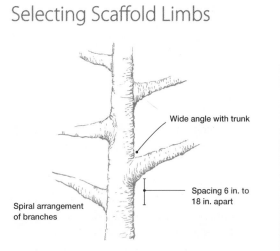

Wide angle with trunk

Spacing 6 in. to 18 in. apart

Spiral arrangement of branches

Feathered Tree before and after Pruning

On a feathered tree, remove branches that are crowded, too low, or damaged. Shorten weak branches for more vigorous regrowth.

develop well. To sum up the ideal in side branch selection: Eliminate low branches and save those that grow outward and originate in a spiral at least 6 inches apart from each other up the trunk.

The ideal side branch knows its place and doesn't compete with the developing trunk. As such, it should be thinner and less upright growing than the stem being preened to become the trunk. If a side branch starts vying to become "top dog," bend it downward with weights or strings to slow its growth. Bending branches downward is useful for developing good form and promotes early fruiting for such fruits as apple and pear. Don't get overly enthusiastic with bending. Too much can result in a runt that is overloaded with fruit, so don't bend too many branches too early in your tree's life.

Rather than arriving with just one upright stem, your new nursery tree might already have branches. Select three or four healthy and well-positioned branches to keep as permanent limbs and cut away all others. Induce vigorous, spreading growth from the branches that you save by shortening each to a few inches long.

As your young tree develops, begin training it to one of three forms: central leader, open center, or modified central leader (see the sidebar at right). If you are going to train your tree to a central-leader or modified-central-leader form, allow the topmost bud to grow upright as a continuation of the developing trunk, called the leader. For an open-center tree, allow three or four branches to grow outward and upward and become main branches, then cut the developing trunk back to

just above the topmost branch so that it does not continue beyond this point.

Pruning continues in subsequent years of training your young tree. For a central-leader tree, treat the leader just as you did the young whip. Shorten it by about one third each year to stimulate branching. Select branches just as you did the first season, removing all others. When the trunk on a modified-central-leader tree is about 8 feet high, shorten it to a weak side branch to discontinue extension of the leader. For the open-center tree, head back the three or four side branches growing off the trunk to get them to branch further. Thin out any stems originating close to the trunk on these side branches.

The only other pruning required on a young tree is the removal of suckers, which are vigorous shoots originating at or near ground level, and watersprouts, which are vigorous upright shoots that develop along branches. Suckers originate from the rootstock of grafted trees. Left to grow, they compete for growth, bear undesirable fruits, and ruin the form of the tree. Watersprouts

Tree Forms

For sturdy limbs bathed in light and air, fruit trees are most commonly trained to one of three forms: central leader, open center, or modified central leader. The central-leader tree is shaped like a Christmas tree, with an upright leader off which grow permanent, major limbs that progressively get shorter toward the top of the tree. The open-center tree has a short trunk capped with three to five permanent major limbs growing outward and upward, giving the tree the shape of an ice cream cone. The modified central leader is a combination of the other two forms. When the trunk of a tree being trained to a central leader reaches a height of about 8 feet, cut it back to a weak branch. This stops further upward growth, and the remaining limbs spread upward and outward.

Fruit trees differ in their natural growth habits. Train a tree to follow its natural inclination.

Pruning a Young Tree to Open-Center Form

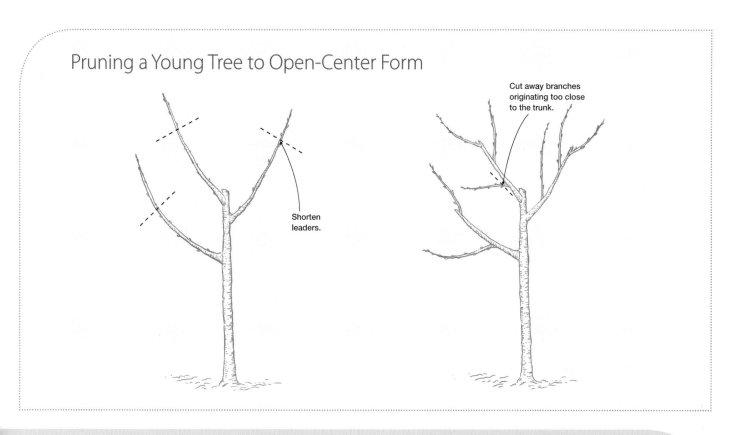

Cut away branches originating too close to the trunk.

Shorten leaders.

Three Forms for Fruit Trees

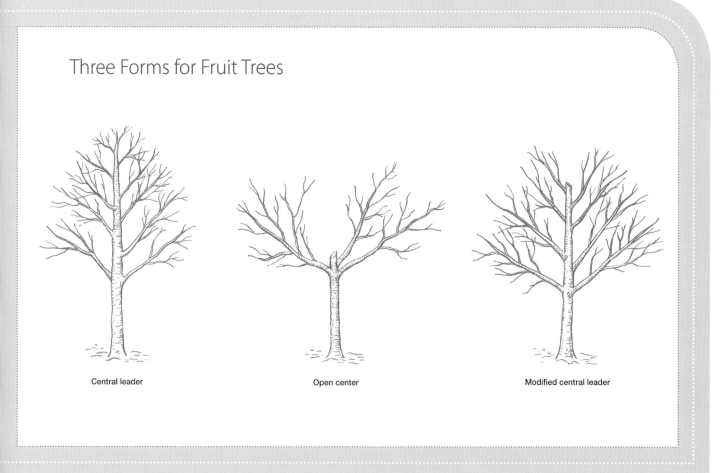

Central leader

Open center

Modified central leader

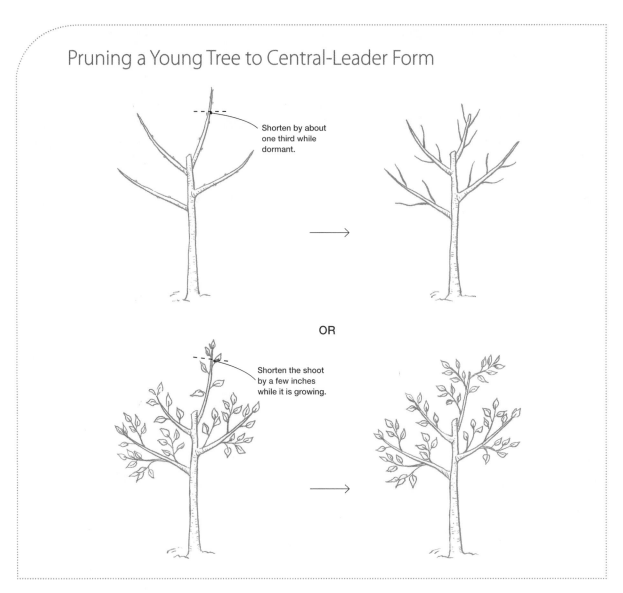

Pruning a Young Tree to Central-Leader Form

Shorten by about one third while dormant.

OR

Shorten the shoot by a few inches while it is growing.

The easiest and most effective way to remove watersprouts, if they are young, is to grab them in your hand and yank them down and off.

behave similarly, and also shade the tree. Cut them away or, even better, yank them off while they're young and green, as soon as you notice them.

PRUNING A MATURE, FRUIT-BEARING TREE

In the case of a mature tree—one that has reached its full size and is bearing regular crops—use your pruning tools to keep the tree healthy, productive, and within bounds. Prune in late winter or early spring.

First, look over your tree for any diseased branches. Dark, sunken areas or little black or red specks on the bark are evidence of disease. Cut any diseased branches back at least 6 inches into healthy wood. Also cut away any dead or broken branches, both of which can provide entry for disease. Early in the season you will be able to

ABOVE: Mature apple trees, such as the tree shown here, tend to be overly vigorous in their upper portions; watersprouts are not very fruitful and shade lower portions of the tree.

RIGHT: Pruning has balanced stem growth on this mature apple tree to leave mostly horizontal, fruitful shoots.

Pruning a Mature Tree

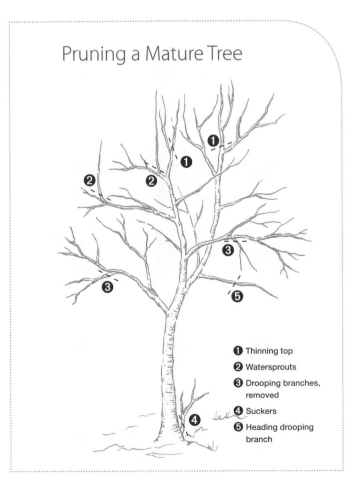

1. Thinning top
2. Watersprouts
3. Drooping branches, removed
4. Suckers
5. Heading drooping branch

recognize dead branches because their buds remain lifeless while those on healthy branches are swelling.

Next, make thinning cuts where necessary. With age, it is common for limbs high in a tree to overgrow lower ones. Counteract this tendency—which makes a fruit tree grow too tall and shade itself—by thinning some of the upper limbs. Shade within a tree decreases productivity and, along with poor air circulation, increases risk of disease. Wherever growth is too dense, use thinning cuts to open up space within the tree. Also cut away watersprouts, suckers, and broken or crossing branches.

Any mature tree will also have a certain amount of twiggy, nonproductive stems. Thin some of them out and head some back where you want to force remaining buds into vigorous growth.

Finally, most fruit trees require some heading cuts to stimulate growth of young wood to replace decrepit, old wood. The amount of stimulation needed varies with the fruit-bearing habit of the tree. Peaches, for example, bear fruit only on wood that is one year old, so new growth is needed each year on which to bear the following year's crop. Apples and pears, on the other hand, need less pruning because they bear fruit on old wood.

When you prune a mature fruit tree, you will unavoidably be cutting off some branches with fruit buds. Don't bemoan the loss of fruit buds—and hence potential fruits—as you prune your tree. That's another benefit of pruning the mature tree. In removing some fruits before they form, your tree can channel more energy into the fruits that remain, making them bigger and better tasting.

PRUNING AN OLD, NEGLECTED TREE

The problem with an old, neglected tree is that it has grown too tall and too dense. The tree shades itself so much that its fruits, if there are any, are born only high up and on the outside edge of the leafy canopy. An old, neglected tree also is commonly overburdened with dead and diseased wood.

Begin whipping an old, neglected tree back into shape by lowering it, using your pruning saw to cut major limbs right back to their origins. Do not do this in one season, or else once-shaded bark will sunscald. Depending on the severity of pruning needed, you may have to spread these major cuts out over three or four years. Also cut away any dead or diseased wood.

Vigorous watersprouts will grow from large pruning cuts. Cut away most of these, but save a few to shade the bark and to grow as replacement limbs for those you removed during renovation. Select new limbs and branches similarly as you would for a young tree (see "Pruning and Training a Young Fruit Tree" on p. 38).

Pruning a Neglected Fruit Tree

1. Prune the neglected tree when it is dormant and over the course of 3 to 4 years.

2. This tree has multiple leaders and is too tall.

3. Preliminary cuts shorten the leaders so further cuts are easier to make.

Thinning Fruit

To get through that critical period just after bloom when late frosts could snuff out developing fruits, most fruit trees have evolved to set more fruits than they can ripen. Once danger of frost is well past, a month or so after bloom, a tree breathes a figurative sigh of relief and naturally sheds those excess fruits. Because this shedding occurs in June in much of the country it is called "June drop" and is no cause for alarm.

A tree just wants to ripen its fruits; we humans, however, want the tree to give us the biggest and best-tasting fruits possible. To harvest such fruits, further fruit thinning, or removal of fruits, is needed. Fruit thinning is also a way to reduce a crop that otherwise might be heavy enough to break off a limb and a way to prevent *alternate bearing*, a tendency of some fruit trees to alternate years of bearing very large and small crops. Fruit thinning even helps keep some pests in check.

For maximum benefit to remaining fruits and to next year's crop, thin fruits as soon as they set, right after bloom. For insurance, though, leave some extra, and thin again after June drop. When you thin fruits, selectively remove those that are smallest or injured by insects or disease. Proper spacing of those that remain on the plant varies by type of fruit, and is spelled out for each fruit in Part 2. Fortunately, there is no benefit to thinning small tree fruits (such as cherries) or bush fruits (such as blueberries) beyond bud removal that occurs as you annually prune these plants. What a tedious job thinning individual blueberry fruits would be!

4. Leaders have been cut back to their origins, lowering the tree and letting more light in among remaining branches.

5. Subsequent cuts, this first year of pruning, thin out or shorten smaller branches to prevent rubbing and get rid of dead wood.

6. This renovated tree is on its way to becoming more productive and healthier, with more and better fruit within reach.

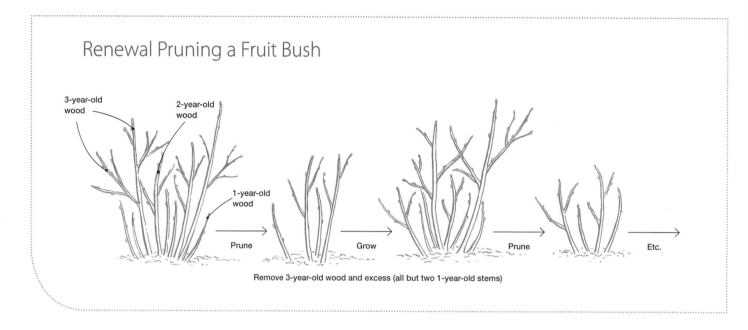

Renewal Pruning a Fruit Bush

3-year-old wood

2-year-old wood

1-year-old wood

Prune

Grow

Prune

Etc.

Remove 3-year-old wood and excess (all but two 1-year-old stems)

Pruning Fruit Bushes

Bushes, in contrast to trees, are bushy; that is, they don't develop single, long-lived trunks. Instead, they annually grow vigorous new stems, called suckers, at or near ground level, and older stems eventually grow decrepit. The distinction between a tree and a bush is not always clear cut. Fig, pomegranate, and quince, for example, can wear either guise. And some definitely bushy plants, such as gooseberry and currant, can be forced into becoming trees—small trees, but with single trunks, trees nonetheless.

Pruning of a newly planted fruit bush is not critical. On bushes such as raspberries, which sucker profusely, cut back all the stems to within 1 inch or so of ground level to force growth of new suckers. For bushes such as blueberries, which make only a few suckers, do nothing, or if the plant seems top heavy, thin out some stems.

Once mature, bushes are generally pruned by renewal, which involves cutting older stems right down to the ground or to vigorous, young shoots originating near ground level, and thinning out new suckers. Annually removing the oldest wood keeps invigorating the bush. Thinning out suckers makes sure that each one that remains has plenty of room to bask in light and air as it ages. The bush is annually renewed, never growing old—above ground, at least.

How much old wood and how many suckers to leave or prune away depends on the particular type of bush fruit: The longer older wood remains fruitful, the longer it can stay. The more suckers a bush grows, the more of them that need to be thinned out. Black currants represent one extreme, suckering profusely and fruiting mostly on wood that grew the previous season. The way to prune a black currant bush, then, is to thin out all but a half dozen of the 1-year-old stems for fruit the upcoming season, then to remove, or shorten to a vigorous 1-year-old branch, any older wood.

Blueberry is a an example of the other extreme in bush fruits, suckering only moderately and bearing fruit on stems that are even 6 years old. Such bushes need less pruning than those that sucker profusely. Most of what you need to do with these bushes is to cut away a couple of the oldest stems and, if excessive, remove the suckers.

Pruning Fruit Vines

A fruiting vine has one or two trunks off which will grow temporary fruiting arms or a trunk off which grow long permanent arms, called cordons, which in turn give rise to the temporary fruiting arms. To stimulate vigorous growth of the trunk-to-be, cut back your new vine at planting to a single robust shoot, and shorten it to two or three healthy buds. The following late winter or early spring, select one or two robust stems as future trunks, removing all others. From then on, training and pruning varies with the kind of fruit and is discussed in Part 2.

Forms for Vines

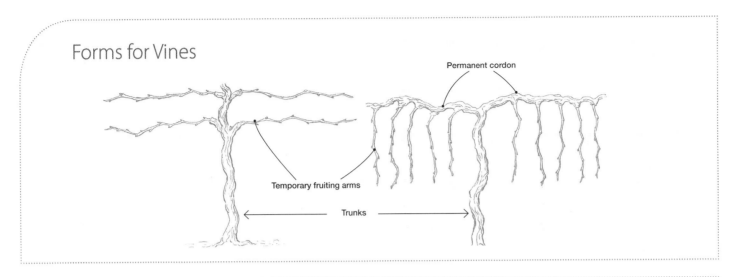

Permanent cordon

Temporary fruiting arms

Trunks

Vine Training

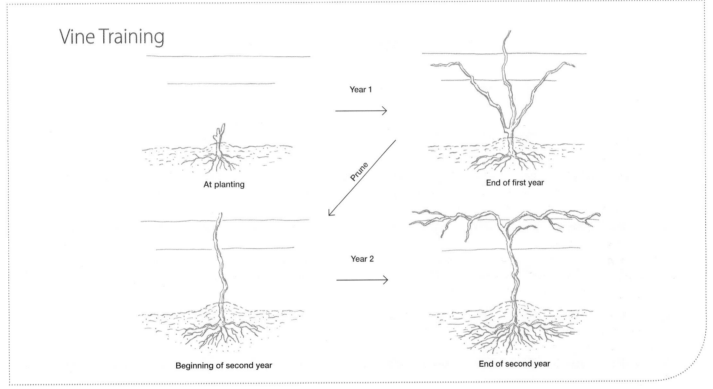

At planting

Year 1

Prune

End of first year

Beginning of second year

Year 2

End of second year

Special Growing Techniques

A few tricks of the trade can make fruit growing more rewarding. For all of the fun and interest growing fruit has to offer, we are, of course, after the fruit itself. Some of these techniques help shorten the time between planting and that first bite. Container growing is a technique that lets you bring fruit growing indoors and expand your fruit palette.

BRINGING FRUIT TREES INTO BEARING

In any fruit tree, a balance exists between shoot growth and fruiting, with more of one being offset by less of the other. Because they haven't yet borne fruit, young fruit trees commonly make very vigorous shoot growth. Although a certain amount of shoot growth is desirable to get the tree to fill its allotted space, shoot growth sometimes persists at the expense of fruiting. Fruit bushes rarely have a problem settling down into a bearing habit. Delayed bearing is also less common on trees with dwarfing rootstocks, which can have the opposite problem of bearing too much too soon and ending up

TOP: Weights hold down small branches to promote good tree form and early fruiting.

BOTTOM: Strings are another way to hold down branches for good tree form and to quell vigorous growth in favor of fruitful growth.

stunted. Still, where a tree seems reluctant to begin fruiting, various techniques can remedy the situation, slowing growth and getting the plant into a "bearing habit."

The first technique to coax a tree into bearing—branch bending—should be started early in a tree's life. Because upright shoots are inherently more vigorous than horizontal shoots, merely bending branches downward slows them down and induces fruit buds to form. Bring the branches down to near horizontal with weights, with string secured to the trunk or to stakes in the ground, or with notched wooden branch spreaders. If you want some additional growth on a branch, do not bring it all the way down to the horizontal but leave it upward at a slight angle. And do not arch the branch as you bend it down, or a vigorous shoot will grow from the high point in the arch.

A second technique to hasten fruiting is bark ringing. Sometime from when the petals fall until a month after blossoming, cut out a thin ring of bark from around the trunk. Make two parallel cuts about ¼ inch apart around the trunk, then peel away the strip of bark. Don't use this technique on stone fruits (peach, apricot, cherry, nectarine, and plum), which are too easily infected at wounds.

In any one year, use one—not both—of these techniques on a fruit tree. At the same time, consider what else, besides youth, might be making your tree overly vigorous. Are you overfertilizing? Are you pruning too drastically? Don't bend down branches or cut into the bark of weakened trees. Such trees need to be invigorated before they can begin fruiting and may even be killed by bark ringing.

FRUIT PLANTS IN CONTAINERS

For centuries, gardeners have enjoyed the beauty, the intimacy, and the gustatory rewards of growing fruit trees in containers. A whole wing at the French palace of Versailles was devoted to potted orange trees. Orange trees are not cold hardy at Versailles, so the plants spent winters indoors in their "orangerie."

Containers are a way you can also grow fruit not normally hardy in your area. Many tropical and subtropical fruit plants, such as figs, pomegranates, guavas, and, of course, citrus, are ideal container-growing candidates in northern areas. Cold-hardy plants such as apricots, apples, and cherries also are suitable container subjects and can be moved to shelter in spring if frost threatens their blossoms. An ornamental fruiting plant in an equally ornamental pot might be just the plant to decorate a sunny terrace balcony or roof deck if you live in an apartment or don't have a yard. Do you want to impress dinner guests? Bring fruit to the table right on the (small) tree!

Just about any fruit plant can be grown in a container, but best suited are those that are dwarf and lack taproots. The plants may be naturally dwarf or made so by being grafted onto dwarfing rootstock. Most fruit plants do not have taproots, notable exceptions being persimmon and pawpaw.

Any standard potting mix is suitable for fruit plants (use a very acidic mix for blueberries, though), as is any container, as long as it has drainage holes. I use a homemade potting mix, the same as I use for other potted plants and seedlings, consisting of equal parts soil, compost, peat, and perlite, with some soybean meal added. Except for strawberries, which you can grow even in 6-inch pots, use a pot at least 1½ feet wide and deep. Fertilize as you would any other potted plant, slackening toward the end of summer to allow the plant to toughen up for winter.

Repot your plant each year into a larger size pot as it grows. Once the plant gets as big as you would like it to, which may be determined by how large a pot you can move around and the size of your doorways, continue to repot it every year or two, right back into the same pot in which it is growing. To make space for new root growth, root-prune when you repot by tipping the plant out of its pot and slicing off roots around the edge of the root ball. Then put the plant back into its pot and pack new potting soil into the space between the root ball and

This potted 'Meiwa' kumquat tree, a subtropical plant, bears every winter while looking out the window at snow and frigid temperatures.

My Potted Mini-Orchards

I once had a mini-orchard in pots. (I was a graduate student, knowing that, once degree was in hand, I'd move—with orchard in tow, of course.) Midsummer watering needs of my mini-orchard wouldn't let me leave my home in summer for more than six hours at a shot. At my present home, where I've lived for almost 30 years, I have fewer potted fruits and have untethered myself from them with automatic watering via a drip irrigation system. I cluster my potted fruits in a couple of areas and direct water to each plant with a length of ¼-inch tubing terminating in a ½-gallon-per-hour emitter. With a well-drained potting mix (from extra perlite), plants are not harmed by once- or even twice-a-day watering, with enough water to run out the bottom of the pot. The dripping season begins when plants begin growing strongly in spring and continues until they slow down in early fall. I water by hand later in fall, when plants' water needs are low.

the edge of the pot. To compensate for each year's loss of roots during repotting, prune the branches more than you would for a plant growing in the ground.

Fruit plants in containers have two special needs: attention to water in summer and a suitable home in winter. Roots in pots cannot explore as much soil for water and nutrients as can roots in the ground, so in midsummer heat a potted fruit might need watering every day. If you are going away for a day or two, temporarily move the plant into partial shade.

Even winter-hardy, temperate-zone fruits need extra protection in winter when grown in pots, because their roots, having evolved in the ground, where winter temperatures do not plunge as much as air temperatures, can't endure as much cold as the stems. Ground temperatures never get as cold as air temperatures. The most obvious solution is to give roots the same protection they get in nature by plunging them, pots and all, into holes in the ground. Or protect plants left sitting on top of the ground by piling a loose type of insulating mulch, such as wood chips or leaves, around and up to the rim of pots. A third alternative is to move the plants somewhere not frigid, but cold, such as an unheated garage, shed, or basement. One place definitely not suitable for cold-hardy plants in winter is inside your home; these plants must experience a certain amount of chilling hours (see p. 7) before they will resume growth in spring.

Once protected for the winter, deciduous potted plants need little further care. One thorough watering may be all the plants need until they resume growth again in spring. Because the plants are leafless in winter, they do not need light.

Tropical and subtropical plants can't tolerate very cold temperatures so should spend winter indoors. Those that retain their leaves in winter also need bright light, such as from an unobstructed south-facing window. The warmer the indoor temperature, the more light a plant requires. Keep in mind that subtropical fruits, such as oranges, enjoy cool rather than warm indoor temperatures in winter.

Evergreen fruits can experience some shock when moving indoors. The transition from cool, moist autumn

Repotting a Houseplant

1. It's late spring, and this potted kumquat needs room for new root growth without moving to a larger pot.

2. Tipped on its side, the root ball slides out of the pot easily.

3. Using a sharp garden knife, slice a couple inches of roots and soil from all around the outside of the root ball.

weather to warm, dry indoor conditions makes leaves yellow and drop—not good for an evergreen, although they will recover, albeit weakened. Avoid this problem by moving the plant indoors before outdoor temperatures have cooled too much, while your windows are still open, before your furnace or wood stove has kicked on, and while temperature and humidity indoors are not drastically different from outdoors. Otherwise, move the plants indoors to a very cool, brightly sunlit room.

Evergreen fruits similarly need acclimatization when temperatures become suitably warm and it's time for them to go back to the great outdoors. Start the plant out in a partially shaded, well-sheltered area away from the wind and cold, such as in a protected corner of your house, for a couple of weeks. After that period, the plant should be ready to face and enjoy the good growing conditions offered. Be ready to whisk the plant temporarily to shelter or indoors if cold weather threatens.

Deciduous plants wintering in the protection of a cool basement or unheated garage sometimes begin growing before being moved outdoors. When the plant is moved outdoors, the growth that began in relatively low light is very susceptible to getting burned by bright sunlight and the slightest frost, so acclimate the plant as described for evergreens.

Avoid burning new growth on these plants in the first place by holding back growth for as long as possible. Keep the plant as cold as possible without damaging it, and slightly thirsty. Then move the plant outdoors as early as possible in late winter or early spring, although not, of course, so early that cold can damage the plant. The more dormant the plant, the more cold it will tolerate. If bitter cold threatens, temporarily move the plant back to a protected location.

Because they need winter quarters, watering, root pruning, and fertilizing, fruits growing in containers obviously require more effort than that required for growing them in the ground. But working closely with the plants and watching them respond can be a reward in and of itself—along with reaping delectable fruits.

4. Back in the same pot, there's now room to pack new potting soil around the roots.

5. With a stick and your fingers, pack the potting soil into the space to make sure there remain no empty pockets without soil.

6. Pruning back stems balances out root loss, keeps the top of the plant from growing too large, and stimulates new growth for flowering and fruiting.

CHAPTER 4

Pests and Diseases

Don't put off the pleasures of growing fruit because you're intimidated by the threat of pests and diseases. True, all sorts of creatures, may consider your fruits as tasty as you do and may vie for them. However, if you start with clean, healthy plants; sited well; and kept healthy with correct pruning, watering, and feeding, you can avoid many, perhaps all, pest problems. Much also depends on where you live and what you choose to grow, although many fruits, such as blueberries and raspberries, can be free of pest problems just about everywhere.

Attitude is an important component in dealing with pests and diseases in home-grown fruit. You're not growing fruit to sell, so your fruit can tolerate a certain amount of damage, especially if it's only cosmetic. In the dark, bite into an apple scarred from plum curculio and the fruit's taste and texture will be indistinguishable from that of an unscarred fruit. My philosophy when growing fruits is not to look too, too closely at the plant and fruit. A little leaf damage does no harm to a plant; in fact, photo-synthesis in undamaged portions of the leaf compensates for the loss. If I start to panic about some pest damage, I take a calming breath and then stop to appreciate just how bountiful my harvests are in spite of damage. For many pests and diseases, eradication isn't feasible; rather, it's learning the dances that keep them at acceptable levels.

This is not to recommend sticking your head in the sand when it comes to fruit pests and diseases. Apple maggot tunneling renders a whole apple fruit inedible. A rabbit gnawing on the bark of a young tree can kill it. Brown rot, under the right conditions (right for the fungus, wrong for us) can cause an entire crop of juicy, ripe plums to morph into fuzzy, gray, plum-shaped masses. On the flip side, it can be interesting to study the complex interaction of a pest or disease, a host plant, and the environment, and especially so when such study results in good-tasting fruits. Most important is to keep a close eye on your plants, not only to watch for pests and diseases but also to observe how the plant is growing in response to your ministrations in pruning, feeding, and watering. Your close attention will increase your personal satisfaction in growing fruits, as well as bring in the bounty.

The Culprits

The rogue's gallery of pests and diseases includes, but is not limited to, birds, mammals, insects, arachnids, mollusks, fungi, bacteria, nematodes, and viruses. The first step in getting the upper hand on any problem is identifying its cause. Then get to know a little something about the culprit before taking any action.

LARGER ANIMAL PESTS

The larger pests, including deer, rabbits, squirrels, and various kinds of mice, are most familiar, if only because they are easiest to see. They will feed pretty much any time of year, selecting from fruits, roots, shoots, and bark according to what is available and their needs.

SMALLER ANIMAL PESTS

Smaller animal pests include insects, mollusks, and arachnids, all visible to the naked eye but not always obvious unless your eyes are in the right place at the

TOP: Don't let the innocent look fool you; rabbits can be devastating—often deadly—to fruit plants as they feast on the bark.

BOTTOM: Rabbits have gnawed the bark off the lower branches of this apple tree.

right time or you're looking very closely. You don't need to become an expert on these creatures to harvest fruit from your yard, but it is helpful to know a few things about them. For instance, how they eat. Insects either chew or suck. A pesticide that coats the outside of a plant and must be ingested will not kill a sucking insect because the insect inserts its thin feeding tube down inside plant tissues. Insects breathe through holes (spiracles) in their bodies, and some powdery materials can clog these holes. Mollusk pests are slugs and snails, which mostly feed at night but leave telltale silvery trails evident the next morning. Arachnids are spiders, and pest arachnids include some species of mites that thrive best in dry, dusty conditions.

DISEASES

Diseases are caused by fungi, bacteria, viruses, nematodes (wormlike creatures that are the only animals in this group), and some other very small creatures that mostly are invisible to the naked eye. For an infectious disease to occur it needs a susceptible host plant, a source of inoculum, such as fungal spores, and a favorable environment in which to fester. Low light and high moisture or humidity produce ideal conditions for most fungal and bacterial diseases to grow and spread.

The fact that all three conditions—a susceptible host, an inoculum source, and a suitable environment—are absolutely necessary for diseases to occur opens the door to many ways of limiting or avoiding them.

Take note that we also have many friends among these organisms. Many are downright beneficial to plant growth. For instance, mycorrhizal fungi form a symbiosis with the roots of most plants. Their trailing ends of fine, fungal threads, infecting roots at one end, ramify extensively throughout the soil to act like effective extensions of the roots. Many bacteria, fungi, nematodes, and viruses are beneficial, such as the predatory nematodes that kill fungi by puncturing their cells and sucking out the juices.

Natural Pest and Disease Control

Once you have identified and learned something about a pest or disease problem, you're ready to take action, if necessary. As mentioned at the beginning of the chapter, action is often not needed. Plants can tolerate a certain amount of damage. If some sort of control is warranted, choose from the array of natural approaches listed below.

RESISTANT PLANTS

Your first line of defense against any plant problems is to choose plants that are resistant to potential pests and diseases. That choice might be the kind of fruit or the variety of fruit that you grow. Not all pests and diseases are everywhere; choose kinds or varieties of fruits resistant to those pests and diseases most likely to thrive in your region. The nice thing about this approach is that once the plant is in the ground you're done worrying about the pest or disease. Well, sort of, because resistance is not usually an all or nothing proposition, but one of degrees. In a wet season, for instance, you might have to take further action to limit, say, apple scab disease on an apple variety that is resistant, but not immune, to scab. Plant resistance is more important in avoiding disease problems than in avoiding insect or other animal problems. Insects and other animals are generally not that finicky about what they eat or attack.

CULTURAL CONTROLS

The *culture* in "cultural controls" refers to *cultivation*, as in growing. You do what you can to optimize growing conditions so your plant can stand up to—or, at least, recover from—a pest or disease. Site selection, including the use of microclimates, is one cultural control available. Soil care, such as maintaining high levels of organic matter, helps roots fend off diseases and generally makes plants healthier. Pay attention to plant nutrition. Prune to let air and light in among the branches. In other words, give your plants the best possible growing conditions they can have.

CLEANLINESS

Yes, cleaning up your plants—and the ground beneath them—plays a role in dealing with pests and diseases, a significant role in some cases. Start cleaning at the very start, right when you plant. If a pest or disease typically arrives on infected or infested nursery stock, buy from a nursery that ensures its stock to be free of such problems. After that, do your own cleaning. Apple scab disease, for example, spends the winter in old leaves beneath apple trees. Raking up, burying beneath mulch, or hastening decomposition of those fallen leaves (by shredding leave as you mow or sprinkling on some nitrogen fertilizer) decreases the amount of disease spores that can potentially waft up into the tree with the following spring's warm, wet weather. This makes a good case for cleaning up old, rotten fruits as well as diseased leaves and branches.

PHYSICAL CONTROLS

Pests and diseases sometimes can be dealt with *mano a mano*. A physical control might be a barrier, such as a rabbit-proof fence, or a spray that irritates insects and makes them opt to go elsewhere, or a bag that protects a fruit from intruders. A simple and very satisfying physical control is to merely pluck offending insects off of a plant and drop them into a can of soapy water. The soap makes everything too slippery for the insect to just go for a swim and then fly or crawl away.

The red color of this fake apple, coated with sticky Tangle-Trap®, fools Ms. apple maggot into laying eggs on it rather than on my apples, which are not nearly as red.

Trapping, whether the prisoner is an insect or a furry predator, is another physical control. Fruit is an obvious bait to use for a trap. Pheromones, another kind of bait, are sex attractants that draw male insects seeking mates; purchased traps baited with pheromones round up males so females don't get to lay fertile eggs. It's nasty, but effective.

REPELLENTS

Repellents, which are effective mostly against animals, work on what a pest sees, smells, tastes, or hears or perhaps on multiple senses at a time. The effectiveness of any repellent depends on the hunger of the animals and how much food is available elsewhere. One benefit of biodiversity—defined as a wide variety of flora and fauna, which you can create near your fruit plants by incorporating flowers and herbs among your plantings—is that certain pests might be deterred, or at least fooled, by the panoply of sensory inputs.

Repellents are quite effective against furry animals. For furry pests, such as deer and rabbits, repellents are mostly based on animal products (for vegetarian animals) and/or hot pepper, whose natural hotness comes from capsaicin. For example, rabbits, which are vegetarians, won't gnaw through bark, no matter how tasty, if it's coated with some concoction that includes egg whites. (I guess that makes rabbits vegans.) Hot pepper sprays, homemade or commercial formulations, prevent feeding by rabbits, squirrels, deer, and other furry animals, but not birds. Research has not shown hot pepper to be effective against insect or disease pests.

Besides animals, you also might pass up a hot peppered apple, which is why the sprays are recommended for use only on nonfruiting plants or in the dormant season. These repellents need to be reapplied as they dissipate or wash off, although some last a month or more. They are most effective if applied before any feeding occurs and when used in rotation with other repellents so that animals don't habituate to any one product.

BIOLOGICAL CONTROL

For biological control we press into service certain plants, animals, and diseases to control pestiferous animals and disease-causing organisms. Insects get sick: *Bacillus thuringiensis*, a bacterium sold under such friendlier-sounding names as Thuricide® and DiPel®, infects and kills lepidopterous caterpillars, which are the caterpillar stage of butterflies and moths, such as codling moth (the "worm" in the apple). My chickens and ducks provide attractive and effective biological control of any unfortunate insects or slugs lurking beneath my fruit trees. Beneficial insects eat or parasitize insect pests.

For some pests, you can purchase an appropriate biological control. But don't discount widespread, naturally occurring and introduced diseases, predators, and parasites of these pests. Mites have their mite-y predators (predatory mites), *Trichogramma* wasps help check populations of codling moth, and milky spore disease kills Japanese beetle grubs. As Jonathan Swift wrote in 1733:

> So, naturalists observe, a flea
> Hath smaller fleas that on him prey;
> And these have smaller still to bite 'em;
> And so proceed ad infinitum.

Biological Controls for Common Fruit Garden Pests

Pest Group	Potentially Useful Biological Controls
Aphids	Lady beetles (*Coccinella septempunctata*, *Adalia bipunctata*, and others), green lacewings, aphid predator midge, pirate bugs, big-eyed bug, predatory plant bug, aphid parasites, *Beauveria bassiana*
Mealybugs	Mealybug destroyer (*Cryptolaemus montrouzieri*), green lacewings, mealybug parasites (*Leptomastix dactylopii*, *L. abnormis*)
Armored scales	Scale predators (scale picnic beetle, *Cybocephalus ipponicus*), green lacewings (*Chrysoperla* spp.), armored scale parasite
Soft scales	Scale predators (scale picnic beetle, *Cybocephalus ipponicus*), green lacewings (*Chrysoperla* spp.), soft scale parasite
Spider mites	Spider mite destroyer (*Stethorus*), spider mite predator midge, six-spotted thrips (*Scolothrips sexmaculatus*), predatory mites, pirate bugs
Caterpillars	Green lacewings, pirate bugs, predatory plant bug, spined soldier bug, trichogramma wasps, caterpillar parasites, *Bacillus thuringiensis* var. *kurstaki*, insect viruses

Many annual and perennial flowers help nourish predatory insects that contribute to the well-being of this fruitful pear tree.

Applying generous amounts of compost and other organic materials to the soil feeds beneficial organisms, helping to limit many pest and disease problems, especially those below ground.

Many predatory insects feed on nectar at some point in their lives, so grow some nectar plants for them. Small, wide-opening flowers are among the best nectar producers and include such tasty or fetching plants as cilantro, dill, coneflower, coreopsis, alyssum, goldenrod, cosmos, and sunflower.

Birds, of course, feed on many insect pests, providing yet another reason for birdbaths, birdhouses, and shelter for birds. All of which, again, makes a good case for promoting biodiversity in your yard. Plus it looks pretty.

NATURAL PESTICIDES AND FUNGICIDES

To me, spraying or dusting a pesticide or fungicide—even a natural one—is the least fun and least interesting way to deal with a pest or disease problem. As evidenced by the aforementioned slew of other options, spraying or dusting is often unnecessary. Still, it's good to have sprays and dusts in your quiver of options. When using any spray or dust, choosing the correct material and applying it at the right time are most important for effectiveness. Although dusts do not have to be diluted and mixed up, they have, for me, the overshadowing disadvantage of drifting off target, so I suggest spraying a material if this option exists.

The ideal pesticide or fungicide is nontoxic to humans, pets, nontarget insects, and any other creatures except for the targeted pest or disease. That spray may be something as benign as a forcible stream of water to knock aphids off of leaves or periodic spritzes of water to offset the hot, dry conditions in which mite pests thrive. Misuse of any pesticide or fungicide, sometimes even correct use, can lead to new pest problems or cause some damage to a plant. For example, spraying clay can lead to buildup of pest mites; copper fungicides sometimes cause leaf russeting. Balance the benefits against the risks of using any pesticide or fungicide, and minimize risks with careful use. Using a pesticide in any manner not explicitly spelled out on its label, whether it's timing of the application or the target pest, not only may prove ineffective but can also do you harm—and is illegal!

Here is a list of some pesticides that are low in toxicity, environmentally friendly, inexpensive, and readily available for use in the home garden:

- *Bacillus thuringiensis* var. *kurstaki* (DiPel, Thuricide, etc.): This bacterium (known as Btk) controls the hungry caterpillar stage of lepidopterous insects but is harmless to just about everything else. The caterpillars, which include apple codling moth and Oriental fruit moth, have to eat this stuff for it to work, whereupon the insect stops feeding and then dies. Btk is most effective against small, recently hatched caterpillars and may be limited in efficacy if the insect doesn't eat enough.
- **Bicarbonates**, including sodium bicarbonate (baking soda), ammonium bicarbonate, and potassium bicarbonate (Kaligreen®, Remedy®, Greencure®, etc.): Bicarbonates are effective against some fungal diseases, such as powdery mildew, gray mold, black rot, and grape phomopsis. Start application at first sign of disease. For best protection, repeat at 1-week to 2-week intervals until conditions are no longer favorable for disease development. Bicarbonates are usually more effective if combined with a surfactant such as soap or oil (see below).
- **Clay** (Surround™ WP Crop Protectant, a formulation of kaolin clay): Surround controls a number of insects. Where summer sunlight is very intense,

Applying and maintaining a dusty coating of clay naturally avoids many pests and diseases that attack fruits.

it also protects against sunscald. Apply Surround to dry leaves and let it dry. The coating gives trees a very pretty, silvery look. Reapply after rainfall to maintain a dusty surface.
- **Copper compounds** (Bordeaux mix, Kocide®, etc.): Copper compounds control both fungal and bacterial diseases, including fire blight, peach leaf curl, black knot, cherry leaf spot, bacterial leaf spot, and bacterial canker. These compounds also are resistant to being washed off by rain. Bordeaux mix is a copper formulation that has been used for more than 100 years, but newer formulations are easier to dissolve in water, less likely to clog sprayers, and somewhat more effective with less damage to plants. As a protectant, copper formulations work best if in place before infection occurs. Don't use copper with abandon because it can accumulate in the soil to the point of damaging earthworms and other soil microorganisms. Use copper when no alternatives exist.
- **Horticultural oil** (Stylet-Oil®, Sunspray®, etc.): Specially formulated horticultural oils smother insect pests and can eradicate some fungal diseases after plants have been infected. Plants can be damaged by oil sprays; avoid damage by spraying when the air is dry and temperatures are between 40°F and 90°F, and do not spray water-stressed (dehydrated) plants. Stylet-Oil is the most highly refined horticultural oil and, therefore, the least likely to

damage plants. Do not apply oils within two weeks of spraying sulfur. Oils generally are most effective against small, immobile, or slow-moving, soft-bodied insects (such as aphids, scales, leafhopper nymphs, whiteflies), and mites.

- **Neem:** Neem in various forms is made from extracts of the seeds of the neem tree (*Azadirachta indica*). Three forms are available: azadirachtin (Agroneem®, AZA-Direct®, AzaMax®, Azatrol®, Ecosense®, Neemix®, Safer® Brand 3-in-1 Garden Spray), one of the active ingredients in the extracts; neem oil products (Trilogy®, Triact®, Green Light® Neem Concentrate, NimBioSys™), which is the oil pressed from the seed with at least some of the components separated from it; and neem oil soap products (Organica® K⁺ Neem™), which are soaps made from the neem oil and potassium salts of fatty acids.

    Generally, the least purified neem oil products, such as NymBioSis, are the most effective; the effect of purified oils is essentially the same as other oils, mentioned earlier. Neem controls a wide variety of insects and some mites and snails as a repellent, as a feeding deterrent, by contact and ingestion, and by upsetting molting (which prevents insects from becoming adults). It also has some fungicidal activity, and its pesticidal and fungicidal effects can spread within a plant when it is absorbed either into roots or, more efficiently, into leaves. Neem products are most effective if used on immature insects before pest levels get too high and, because neem's effectiveness dissipates relatively quickly, with repeated applications.

    Maintain effectiveness of neem oil products by keeping them cool. Because cooled neem oils become thick as butter, warm up just what is needed for each use, mixing the material vigorously with warm water (and an emulsifier, such as soap, in the case of neem oils) to the dilution specified on the label. I consider the jury to still be out on the usefulness of neem products for fruit pests and diseases.

- **Soap** (including commercially formulated insecticidal soaps such as Safer Brand Insect Killing Soap and M-Pede®): Soaps control fungal diseases as well as, by direct contact, soft-bodied insects such as

Signal Words

All pesticides have what's known as a "signal word" on their labels, a word denoting the material's toxicity to humans by ingestion, inhalation, or contact with the eyes or skin. The signal word *caution* indicates that the material is slightly toxic or relatively nontoxic, *warning* indicates moderately toxic, and *danger* indicates highly toxic. A mere smidgen of a material marked *danger* might kill you. Don't be fooled into believing that just because a pesticide is natural it's safer: Nicotine sulfate is a natural extract of tobacco whose signal word is *danger*; the more malignant-sounding synthetic pesticide malathion is much less toxic, with the signal word *caution.* Always read the labels on pesticides and take the recommended precautions against breathing sprays or dusts or getting them in your eyes, when applying even benign materials.

The signal word, in this case *caution*, gives you a quick idea of the potential hazard of using any pesticide, natural or otherwise.

How to Spray

The easiest and safest way to apply any spray material is with a 2-gallon or 3-gallon hand-pump sprayer such as you find at any hardware store, garden center, or big discount store. If a 2-gallon or 3-gallon sprayer isn't big enough for your needs, use a backpack sprayer, whose 4 gallons of spray are discharged as you pump the attached handle with your left hand. Sprays, although they usually need to be mixed, are more likely to end up on their targets than are dusts. Try to mix up only enough material for what you need, and don't save excess. Thoroughly clean any sprayer (three rinses) after each use, being aware, depending on the material, of how to dispose of the rinse water. When you do spray, get enough material on

Hand-pump sprayers of various sizes are useful when a natural spray is needed for backyard fruit.

the plant so it just starts to drip off. An inch of rainfall will wash off enough of most pesticides to render them ineffective, so reapplication becomes necessary.

Diluting Pesticides

How much powder or granules to use

VOLUME OF LIQUID (GALLONS)	100	25	5	1
AMOUNT OF POWDER TO USE	4 oz.	1 oz.	3/16 oz.	1/2 tsp.
	8 oz.	2 oz.	3/8 oz.	1 tsp.
	1 lb.	4 oz.	7/8 oz.	2 tsp.
	2 lb.	8 oz.	1 3/4 oz.	4 tsp.
	3 lb.	12 oz.	2 3/8 oz.	2 Tbs.
	4 lb.	1 lb.	3 1/4 oz.	2 2/3 Tbs.

How much liquid to use

VOLUME OF LIQUID (GALLONS)	100	25	5	1
AMOUNT OF LIQUID TO USE	1 gal.	2 pt.	6 1/2 oz.	1 1/4 oz.
	4 pt.	1 pt.	3 1/4 oz.	3/8 oz.
	2 pt.	1/2 pt.	1 9/16 oz.	3/16 oz.
	1 1/2 pt.	6 oz.	1 1/4 oz.	1/4 oz.
	1 pt.	4 oz.	7/8 oz.	3/16 oz.
	8 oz.	2 oz.	7/16 oz.	1/2 tsp.
	4 oz.	1 oz.	1/4 oz.	1/4 tsp.

Dilution of liquid products to various concentrations

DILUTION RATE (GALLONS)	1	3	5
1 in 100	2 2/3 Tbs.	1/2 cup	3/4 cup + 1 2/3 Tbs.
1 in 200	4 tsp.	1/4 cup	6 1/2 Tbs.
1 in 800	1 tsp.	1 Tbs.	1 2/3 Tbs.
1 in 1,000	3/4 tsp.	2 1/2 tsp.	1 1/3 Tbs.

aphids and mealybugs. Soaps are generally not very effective against chewing insects. Soaps can damage plants, especially if they are water stressed. They are most effective under conditions that are favorable for slow drying, such as early morning or early evening, and on overcast days. Once dried on the plant, soaps become ineffective against insects.

- **Spinosad** (Entrust®): Spinosad is a fermentation product produced by a soil-dwelling microbe, specifically an actinomycete (named *Saccharopolyspora spinosa*). It is somewhat effective against some caterpillars and other insects.

- **Sulfur:** Used as a fungicide for more than 2,000 years, sulfur controls a number of fruit diseases, such as powdery mildews and scab. It can damage plants, though, and might do so if used within 2 weeks of spraying oil or if temperatures after spraying rise above 90°F. Sulfur is a protectant, so it must be applied to plant surfaces before disease spores arrive. Sulfur also is a miticide. It can be applied as a spray or a dust.

Controls for Common Pests and Diseases

A few pests, listed below, are general feeders that attack many varieties of plants, including fruit plants. Controls for less common pests and diseases are discussed in Part 2 under the fruit heading for which they apply.

DEER

Deer can jump either high or wide, so they are stopped only with one 8-foot- to 10-foot-tall fence or two 4-foot-tall fences spaced 5 feet apart. A cylinder of fencing 6 feet tall or more around an individual plant can also serve as a deer barrier, but it is a disincentive for you to weed, mulch, prune, or otherwise care for the jailed plant. For large areas or whole properties, black plastic deer fencing is both unobtrusive and relatively inexpensive.

Among repellents, mesh bags filled with human hair or bars of deodorant soap hung in trees are somewhat effective, as are sprays based on potions containing eggs and/or hot pepper (see the sidebar on p. 55). The aroma of Milorganite® and other composts based on biological waste materials is also repulsive to deer's sensibilities. Deerchaser™ is a convenient, battery-operated electronic repellent that uses low-level sound and light and activates only when deer enter the protected area. Dogs, if outdoors, awake, and in the vicinity of deer, are also good repellents.

Hunting is an option if legal and if you or others are so inclined.

RABBITS

A fence 2 feet tall keeps rabbits at bay unless snow lifts them higher than the fencing. When enclosing a large area rather than individual plants, bend the bottom 6 inches to 12 inches of fencing at a 90-degree angle and face it outward from the enclosed area to keep rabbits from burrowing underneath.

The previously mentioned sprays for deer, based on egg and/or hot pepper, are also effective repellents against rabbits. Fortunately, rabbits and deer feed mostly on dormant fruit plants, so you won't end up with fruits that taste like rotten eggs or hot pepper. Looking at a chewed stem tells you whether the culprit was a rabbit or a deer. Rabbits make clean cuts, whereas deer leave frayed stems. Also, except in very large amounts of snow, rabbits don't feed 6 feet up in the plant!

Outdoor dogs and cats, if sufficiently enthusiastic, can keep rabbit populations low. Trapping, using nuts, alfalfa pellets, or—of course—fruit, such as apple slices, as bait, is also effective. As with deer, hunting is an option where it's legal and you are so inclined.

Just attach a battery-powered Deerchaser to a pole, wall, or tree trunk to protect the nearby area from deer.

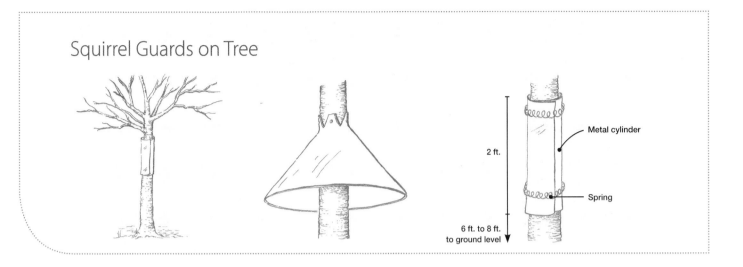

Squirrel Guards on Tree

Metal cylinder

2 ft.

Spring

6 ft. to 8 ft.
to ground level

SQUIRRELS

Squirrels are wily creatures and thus present the most formidable threat to the fruits themselves. These pests will climb over any sort of fencing to feast on both green and fresh fruits. Hot pepper sprays would repel them, but you don't want to be spicing up your fruits during the growing season.

Keep squirrels off sufficiently isolated fruit trees by training branches so that none droop or originate lower than 6 feet to 8 feet from ground level, and then fasten either a 2-foot cylinder or an inverted cone of sheet metal wrapped around the trunk 6 feet to 8 feet above ground. Attach the cylinder with a few wire bands held together with springs so the trunk is free to expand with age.

I have found that squirrels avoid running in high grass, probably because they cannot run fast in this terrain, something they are especially keen on being able to do when dogs are present. They have totally avoided fruit plants in my once-a-year mowed meadow except when given access to a mowed "highway." Keep vegetation low around the plant itself to avoid competition of meadow or grass plants for water and nutrients.

Hunting and trapping are also effective, although squirrels are not easy to trap.

VOLES

Voles, also known as meadow mice or field mice, will feed on bark at ground level in winter, injuring or killing plants. Some sort of commercial tree guard (plastic spirals, plastic mesh, etc.) or a 2-foot-tall cylinder of ¼-inch hardware cloth at the base of a tree foils voles in winter. Repellents painted or sprayed on the bark might be effective, as well as rough gravel placed in a small ring at the base of the plant. Mulch is good for

plants but also provides a nice home for voles. Ideally, replenish mulch in late fall, after voles have found their winter quarters, and keep it a few inches away from tree trunks. Voles also enjoy the shelter from predators of the same high grass or meadow that, as noted earlier, keeps squirrels at bay. I mow low in fall, after fruits are harvested and squirrels are no longer a threat. In a more suburban setting, mowed lawn provides unfriendly habitat for voles.

Effective additions to the arsenal against voles are cats, and, to a lesser extent, dogs.

BIRDS

Fencing does nothing against birds—unless the fenced area is also covered on top. And a fenced cage is just what I recommend for groups of fruit bushes, either erected temporarily while fruit is ripe or with only the top added during ripening. Either way, access (for you) is more pleasant than crawling under a bird net draped over individual plants. My blueberry cage encloses a 25-foot by 30-foot area with permanent fencing on the sides, held up by posts, with rebar from post to post. I drape a net over the top from June to September, during which time we conveniently enter through a rustic locust gate, covered with netting, to pick quarts and quarts of fresh blueberries.

A net can be thrown over individual trees, if not too large, as fruit is ripening.

APHIDS

Aphids are small, soft-bodied insects that may be green, yellow, brown, red, or black and typically congregate at the tips of stems and undersides of leaves. After inserting its hypodermic-needle-like stylet into a plant, an aphid sucks plant sap, stunting the plant and causing curling, yellowing, and distortion of leaves. While feeding, aphids secrete sweet, sticky honeydew onto the plant, and this honeydew is later invaded by a fungus. The fungus is not destructive except that, if extensive enough, its black color can weaken the plant by blocking light. Aphids also damage plants by acting as carriers for certain plant viruses.

A number of options exist for controlling aphids. One is to do nothing, because aphid populations often naturally plummet as fast as they soar. A change in environmental condition could cause this waning, as can aphids' many natural enemies, which include ladybugs, parasitic wasps, and fungal diseases. However, aphids also have a natural ally—ants. Ants herd and protect aphids and eat their honeydew. One way, then, to control aphids is to control their ant "farmers" by preventing them from getting up into the plant. A band of masking tape wrapped around a tree trunk and then coated with sticky Tangle-Trap, an insect-trapping adhesive, stops ant traffic from extending above the band, as long as no alternate routes allow their travel.

Aphids are delicate creatures. For a light infestation, I'll quickly run my fingers under infested leaves and along infested stems, crushing the critters. When this is not practical, a strong blast of water is often enough to knock them off a plant. For stronger medicine, use insecticidal soap or oil sprays, or purchase predatory insects and release them around the infested plants. Be careful when using insecticides, as they may disrupt natural controls of aphid populations.

SCALE INSECTS

Like aphids, scale insects are sucking insects, with the same effects on plants as aphids. Unlike aphids, scale insects settle under a protective covering as they feed. The "soft scales" nestle on stems and leaves and have a waxy, sometimes cottony, covering that can be of various colors. "Armored scales" appear to be brown bumps, or look like miniature oyster shells, on stems and leaves. The brown bumps sometimes can be mistaken for part of the plant itself.

In addition to being subject to predators, naturally occurring or purchased, scales can also be controlled by rubbing them off with your fingers or a coarse cloth, or with a cotton swab dipped in alcohol. For larger infestations, oil sprays applied while plants are dormant are preventative and summer oil sprays are curative. Sprays of insecticidal soap or neem are effective only during

the mobile crawler stage, after youngsters hatch and are moving to their feeding area on the plant and are not yet protected by their covering. As with aphids, controlling ant movement also helps control scale insects, and too ready use of pesticides can knock out their natural controls.

JAPANESE BEETLES

Copper-colored Japanese beetles emerge in summer to feast on a number of different plants, the telltale signs of their arrival being not only the beetles themselves but also the lacework remains of plant leaves. Among fruit plants, Japanese beetles are especially fond of grapes and raspberries.

The first line of defense is to pluck or knock beetles off of plants in the early morning, while they are still sluggish, and drop them into a jar of soapy water. This morning ritual is important and effective for small infestations because the mere presence of Japanese beetles draws more of their clan. If beetles are more numerous than are easily removable by hand, spray Surround or neem to provide deterrence, again beginning early, before populations get out of hand. Traps are available for Japanese beetles, but they are a two-edged sword, also attracting beetles to your yard, sometimes more than are trapped. Traps work best if placed far from plants or if used on a communitywide basis. Traps have been effective for me when beetles have not been too numerous, and supplied plenty of dead beetles for poultry feed.

After 4 to 6 weeks of feeding, beetles begin to die off, and eggs that have been laid all summer hatch into grubs that spend winter in the soil and will emerge the following summer. Favored egg-laying habitats are moist, grassy areas—perhaps you want to rethink that well-watered, lush lawn. Milky spore disease (a natural bacterial pest of the beetles) and parasitic nematodes are two commercially available controls that target the grub stage. Neither will, of course, stop beetles that hatch from grubs in your neighbors' lawns from flying over to feed at your yard, so, as with trapping, milky spore and nematodes work best on a communitywide basis. Especially in colder regions, milky spore is of limited efficacy, not usually carrying over year after year from a one-time application.

MITES

Mites are arachnids, like spiders, and are very small, barely visible to the naked eye. Evidence of mite damage is bronzing of leaves and, if you look closely, fine web-

bing and the mites themselves, usually on the undersides of leaves. These pests are most prevalent under hot, dry, dusty conditions and when pesticides have killed too many of their predators. Regular, forceful, thorough sprays with water often offer adequate control, as do sprays of stronger materials such as oil, insecticidal soap, or sulfur. Water-stressed plants are most susceptible to mites and most likely to be damaged by the stronger sprays. Predatory mites and other natural controls can be purchased.

POWDERY MILDEW

Powdery mildew is a fungal disease whose name describes it: patches of white powder on leaves, shoots, flowers, and/or fruits. That whiteness comes from white fungal threads covering plant surfaces, if you look through a magnifying glass, from chains of white spores. (With downy mildew, another fungal disease, spores grow on branched stalks that look like little trees.) A few different fungi cause powdery mildew, so don't worry that powdery mildew that shows up every year on your lilac bush (caused by *Microsphaera penicullata*) will spread to your gooseberries, which have their own powdery mildew fungi (caused by *Sphaerotheca morsuvae*). The first line of defense against powdery mildew is to plant varieties resistant to the disease. Good air circulation and avoidance of excessive nitrogen fertilizer also help keep the disease in check. And then there are sprays, the most simple of which is water! Although the fungus thrives in humidity, a forceful spray of water washes spores off the plant and the spores drown in water. Sprays of oil, soap, or bicarbonates are also effective.

Final Thoughts

I hope I have sufficiently emphasized that pest problems, first, can often be avoided and, second, when they occur, can be dealt with in all sorts of ways.

Plant naturally pest-resistant fruits. Learn to tolerate a certain amount of damage and fruit loss. If you need to spray, read and follow directions on the label. The extra spraying or other effort needed for maximum yields of 100-percent blemish-free fruits is a lot more than needed for, say, very good yields and 90-percent blemish-free fruits, so is not justified in a home setting. Being able to set your own standards is one of the luxuries of growing your own fruit.

TOP: Scale insects, looking like nothing more than bumps on the bark, are sucking plant sap and weakening this apricot tree.

BOTTOM: Japanese beetles are not picky eaters, feasting on hundreds of kinds of plants, including some fruit plants. Fortunately, they're subject to natural controls and environmental conditions.

CHAPTER 5

Harvesting and Storage

Just as you wouldn't bother to cut a wilted, browning, old rose blossom to put into a vase, you wouldn't—or shouldn't—harvest fruits except in their prime. After all, one reason you're growing fruits is so that you can savor them at their luscious best.

The moment of harvest, especially the first harvest, is an exciting one. Perhaps I am overly sensitive to this moment because as a child we planted a pear tree that seemingly grew for years and finally bore one, prominently placed fruit—which turned out to taste insipid because my little sister plucked it from the branch prematurely! Planning and caring for fruit plants is an enjoyable experience in so many ways—but let's face it, the gustatory rewards trump everything else. Timing is the key to rounding out that experience.

Harvesting Fruit

With few exceptions, harvest fruits when they are fully ripe. Most fruits do not improve in flavor if they are picked underripe and left to "ripen," as many people believe, on a kitchen counter. Softening occurs, perhaps even some sweetening, but such softening and sweetening are more akin to early stages of rotting than to ripening. Aromas and flavor constituents will be flat.

The most obvious way to tell if a fruit is ripe is by its color. Ripe strawberries are red, ripe apricots are orange, and ripe blueberries are blue. Don't even consider picking a fruit until it is fully colored. With some fruits, this color change is subtle; then it's the background color we're interested in. Red apples and peaches do not necessarily turn red when ripe, because direct light is needed for this color change. Watch for the background color to change from grass green to very light green or creamy yellow. Naturally green or yellow apples will turn pale or golden when truly ripe and flavorful. On the other hand, ripe blueberries, cherries, grapes, and plums color up whether or not they're exposed to direct light.

Usually, a fully ripe fruit also softens a bit and separates readily from the plant. In the evolutionary scheme of things, a fruit is merely a vehicle for spreading seeds, and a mature fruit with fully developed seeds falls easily from the plant. Check out those seeds. An apple whose seeds are not yet dark brown was not ripe for picking; you knew that, of course, because the apple tasted underripe. And taste is an obvious, albeit belated, way to assess ripeness.

Waiting for ripe fruit to fall is not always a practical way to harvest fruits, and with some fruits, falling might occur when they are past their prime for eating. Pick most tree fruits by cupping them in the palm of your hand, then giving a slight twist around, then up. If the fruit is ripe, it will part easily from the plant. Other ripe fruits—blueberries and raspberries, for example—drop when tickled. Still others, such as citrus and pomegranate, need to be clipped or given a sharp tug.

There are some exceptions to this rule to wait until fruits are fully ripe before harvesting them. For cooking into jams and pies, fruits hold together better and provide a welcome, tangy flavor if picked slightly underripe. Fruits that you intend to store keep better if harvested before they are fully ripe. Some fruits, such as apples, kiwifruits, and persimmons, can actually ripen during storage. Late apples such as 'Idared' and 'Newtown Pippin' improve in flavor during their storage period.

Timely harvest lets you experience naturally home-grown fruit at their luscious best.

European pears and avocados are two fruits that *must* be picked underripe to ripen off of the plants. Left on the tree until fully ripe, a European pear will be brown and mushy inside. (Pick Asian pears when they are fully ripe, though.) Avocados that ripen on the tree develop off flavors. Harvest these fruits when they are sufficiently mature, then ripen them off the plants. The time to harvest these and other fruits is discussed in Part 2 in each fruit section.

Full-size apple trees, shown in this early 20th-century photo, are robust and long-lived but don't yield as much per land area as do dwarf trees—and they require tall ladders for picking.

Storing Your Bounty

Once your fruit plants mature, you will undoubtedly begin to harvest more fruits than you can eat at one sitting. Your way out of this pleasant dilemma is to give fruit away, preserve it, or store it fresh. You can preserve your surplus by drying, canning, or freezing it and by making jams and jellies.

Fresh fruits are a real treat any time of the year, and with careful attention to kinds and varieties of fruits, as well as storage conditions, you could eat fresh fruit almost year-round. Fresh fruits store best when kept at high humidity. Most tropical fruits store best at slightly cool temperatures; most other fruits store best at temperatures just above freezing. Cool or cold temperatures slow ripening of slightly underripe fruits, aging of fully ripe fruits, and growth of decay-causing microorganisms. High humidity, as well as cool or cold temperatures, slow water loss from fruits and prevent shriveling. A perforated plastic bag or a plastic storage container with its lid slightly ajar maintains close to the optimum 90-percent humidity for fruits stored in the refrigerator. In fall and winter you may find other areas around your home—a garage, an unheated foyer or room, or a basement—that provide the right storage temperatures for your fruits if you run out of refrigerator space.

Remove fruit from cool or cold storage before you are ready to eat it. A pear or kiwifruit that was picked underripe for storage needs to finish ripening at room temperature. Even cool- or cold-stored fruit that is already ripe should be allowed to reach room temperature before you eat it, so that you can appreciate its full flavor.

Storing an Abundance of Fruit

I harvest fruits that ripen in cool fall weather into homemade plywood boxes that start out sitting in the covered porch outside the north side of my house. As outdoor temperatures turn colder and colder, I move the boxes to my unheated garage, then the unheated mudroom, and, finally, to my minimally heated basement, each location providing successively greater protection from outdoor cold.

A few years ago, I insulated a small trailer and installed a cooling system that combines an air-conditioner with a nifty little invention, a Kool-Bot™ (www.storeitcold. com), that fools the air-conditioner into cooling the air down to 32°F or any other temperature at which I set it. This cooler allows me to easily store fruits that ripen in the still warm temperatures of late summer and early fall.

Average Length of Storage, Per Fruit

Fruit	Days of storage possible, under good conditions	Fruit	Days of storage possible, under good conditions
Apple	90–140	Medlar	60
Apricot	7–14	Mulberry	2–3
Avocado	a few months, right on the tree	Nectarine	14–28
Blackberry	2–3	Papaya	7–14
Blueberry	14	Pawpaw	90
Cherry (sour)	3–7	Peach	14–28
Cherry (sweet)	14–21	Pear	60–210
Citrus	a few weeks, right on the tree	Persimmon (American)	4
Currant	7–14	Persimmon (Kaki)	90–120
Elderberry	7–14	Pineapple guava	7
Fig	7–10	Plum	14–28
Gooseberry	14–28	Pomegranate	180
Grape (American)	15–56	Quince	60–90
Grape (vinifera)	90–180	Raspberry	2–3
Jujube	365	Seaberry	4
Juneberry	2–3	Shipova	14
Kiwifruit	50–270	Strawberry	5–7
Mango	21		

Harvesting a Pear

1. Harvest a pear by first cupping it in the palm of your hand.

2. Lift up and twist at the same time.

3. If the fruit is ready to be picked, it will separate easily where the fruit stalk meets the branch.

The Fruits

Apple

Malus domestic

GROWTH HABIT
Depending on rootstock, a tree that matures
at 6 feet to 25 feet tall

POLLINATION NEEDS
Perfect flowers, but requires cross-pollination

LIGHT REQUIREMENT
Full sunlight

CLIMATE
USDA Hardiness Zones 3–9; AHS Heat Zones 8–1;
heat and cold tolerance depend on variety

REGIONS
Pest control usually needed east of the Rocky
Mountains

Most people consider apples when they first think of growing fruit. And with good reason: The fruit is well known and can be grown almost everywhere. Apple trees do need some winter cold for their annual rest and some varieties can tolerate bitter cold, so with choice of appropriate variety, apples can be grown from Hardiness Zones 3 to 9. Rootstocks and varieties offer a range in tree sizes, from plants that never grow taller than 6 feet to those that eventually tower to 40 feet.

Not to dissuade you from growing apples, but they are among the most difficult fruits to grow. The required annual pruning is a bit trickier than that for most other fruits. And especially east of the Rocky Mountains, apples have significant pest problems. In those parts, without attention to pest control, you'll usually get few or no apples worth eating, although the tree itself will grow well. But you probably don't want to grow apple trees just for their wood!

Still, if you approach apple growing realistically and do what's needed, you have the opportunity to eat some mighty fine fruit. Timely harvest and choosing the best varieties from among the thousands give my (and your) apples flavor far superior to any apples that you can buy at the supermarket. I almost gave up on growing apples a few years ago, mostly because of pest problems. But I put a little more effort into my apple growing, and the quality of the apples I pick makes that effort more than worth it. Apples are traditionally associated with autumn, but if you are a real fan of apples you can grow varieties that ripen in summer as well as those late apples that store well until spring.

With an appropriate rootstock, an apple tree can be grown in a pot on a deck.

Growing

The size of your property should not keep you from planting apples, because a dwarf tree—which produces full-size fruits—can grow in as little as 4 square feet of space or less. Still, choose the site with care.

No matter what size or variety of apples you plant, all do best growing in full sunlight. Apples bloom fairly early in spring, so choose a site or a microclimate that is not prone to late spring frosts. A few varieties, including 'Jonagold', 'Mutsu', Gravenstein', 'Winesap', and 'Baldwin', are pollen-sterile so cannot pollinate other varieties. If you grow one of these varieties, arrange for three different varieties (two besides a pollen-sterile variety) for pollination. All three varieties will yield fruit.

Apple trees tolerate a wide variety of soils, but prefer one that is not waterlogged, especially during the growing season. The soil should be moderately fertile and slightly acidic. If you prune, fertilize, and water correctly, shoots on a young tree should grow about 3 feet in a season, while those on a mature tree should grow about 18 inches. Pay special attention to the soil for dwarf trees; most dwarfing rootstocks need the best soil conditions in terms of fertility and water.

Pruning

Right after you plant an apple tree, begin training it to a central-leader, modified-central-leader, or open-center form. Any of these forms is suitable for apple, although upright varieties such as 'Red Delicious' are inclined to grow as central-leader trees, whereas spreading varieties such as 'Golden Delicious' naturally tend to grow as open-center trees.

TOP: This old apple branch is overburdened with fruiting spurs.

BOTTOM: Thinning out and shortening excess spurs rejuvenates them and gives them more room, resulting in better fruit.

PRUNING A YOUNG APPLE TREE

Be careful about pruning apple trees when they are young. Too much pruning, especially of standard trees (that is, trees grown on seedling or other rootstocks that eventually become large trees), stimulates vigorous growth instead of fruiting. Dwarf trees, on the other hand, and especially with certain rootstocks, such as M.27 and Bud.9, tend to fruit at too young an age at the expense of growing; they get stunted. Prevent stunting by pruning more severely to stimulate shoot growth, and/or—even better—by gritting your teeth and pulling off some young fruits so that the tree can channel energy into growing shoots.

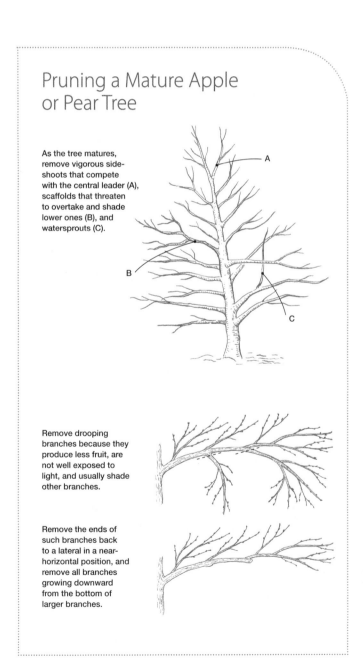

Pruning a Mature Apple or Pear Tree

As the tree matures, remove vigorous side-shoots that compete with the central leader (A), scaffolds that threaten to overtake and shade lower ones (B), and watersprouts (C).

Remove drooping branches because they produce less fruit, are not well exposed to light, and usually shade other branches.

Remove the ends of such branches back to a lateral in a near-horizontal position, and remove all branches growing downward from the bottom of larger branches.

PRUNING A MATURE APPLE TREE

Once a tree reaches full size and fruits regularly, prune annually to keep the tree open and to stimulate some new growth to replace very old wood that is no longer fruitful. Prune your mature, bearing tree by thinning out visually vigorous stems, which mostly originate higher in the tree. Also head back (see p. 37) weak stems, which usually arise lower in the tree. The goal then is to leave your tree with mostly horizontal and slightly upward-growing stems after you finish pruning.

Eventually, fruiting spurs become overcrowded and decrepit, at which point you need to invigorate them and give them more room by thinning some out and shortening some others. When a whole limb of fruiting spurs declines with age, cut it back to make room for a younger replacement.

A few apple varieties—'Cortland', 'Rome', 'Granny Smith', and 'Idared', for example—bear fruits at the end of willowy stems about 6 inches long, rather than on spurs. Avoid shortening too many stems on mature trees of these varieties or you will end up cutting off too much of your potential crop. Leave stems of moderate length and encourage compactness and branching by shortening very long stems instead.

Pruning spurs and branches removes fruit buds and hence potential fruits—but usually not enough. Left to itself, an apple tree will overbear in most years. Each flower bud opens to five flowers, only one of which should be allowed to develop into a fruit. And even then, where flower buds are close together, thin fruits further so that they are 5 inches apart. If all this fruit thinning seems excessive, keep in mind that only 5 percent of flowers normally need to set fruit to yield a full crop of high-quality apples.

Pests and Diseases

A few major insects and diseases attack apples, and one or more of these require your control efforts in all areas, except perhaps parts of the western United States and Canada. One option to control many of the pests is to bag individual fruits, a seemingly daunting task until you consider that, once bagged, there's nothing further to do except pick and eat the apples, and that each bag can potentially yield a perfect apple. (*Potentially* because, depending on pest, locations, and types of bags, bagging does not always spell success.) Use small paper bags, special bags sold for bagging apples, or mesh bags repurposed (disposable nylon ankle socks, for example). Any bag that excludes light will also keep an apple from turning red, although not affect flavor. If you like your apples red, open any light-excluding bags a couple of weeks before harvest to let the sun shine in and redden the fruits. If you enjoy or don't mind pale apples, light doesn't matter.

APPLE SCAB

Worldwide, the most serious disease of apples is apple scab, producing corky, brown…well, scabs on the fruits

Thin out apples to leave the largest and most pest-free fruits spaced no closer than 5 inches apart.

Only a small percentage of apple blossoms normally need to set fruit for a full crop.

and leaves. The disease overwinters on old infected leaves on the ground, and these leaves provide spores to infect new growth each spring. Subsequent infections continue from that newly infected growth, spreading scab throughout the growing season whenever warm, wet weather prevails. Your first line of defense against scab is to plant a scab-resistant variety such as 'Liberty', 'Redfree', or 'Chehalis'. Your second line of defense is sanitation. Clean up or bury fallen leaves beneath mulch in autumn. Also, prune for quick drying of leaves and fruit. Scab is also controlled with sulfur- or copper-containing fungicides beginning early in the season.

CEDAR-APPLE RUST DISEASE

Cedar-apple rust disease produces orange spots on leaves and fruits. Because cedar-apple rust needs both cedar and apple trees to complete its life cycle, the disease is especially prevalent in humid regions where wild cedars (*Juniperus* spp.) abound, such as much of the eastern United States and Canada. Susceptible cedars, wild and cultivated, include *Juniperus chinensis, J. pinchotii, J. silicicola, J. utahensis,* and many varieties of *J. communis, J. virginiana,* and *J. scopulorum.* Disease spores travel for miles in the air, so removal of cedar trees may not be a practical means of disease control. Instead, prune for good air circulation and plant resistant varieties such as 'McIntosh' and 'Liberty', or else spray. Copper or sulfur fungicides give reasonable controls and Surround offers suppression, but all must be applied early, as leaf buds are opening and before you see any infections. Infections occur only early in the season, and there is no further spread of new infections from old infections.

FIRE BLIGHT

Fire blight sometimes attacks apples, leaving branches and leaves looking as if they had been singed by fire. Blackened leaves remain attached to branches, and tips of new shoots curl over like shepherds' crooks. Again, one control is to plant resistant varieties. Also, don't prune or fertilize heavily, because the resulting very succulent growth is especially susceptible to fire blight

TOP LEFT: Brown spots on leaves are symptoms of apple scab disease.

CENTER LEFT: Apple scab also attacks fruits, resulting in brown, corky lesions.

BOTTOM LEFT: Cedar-apple rust disease is shown here on cedar trees, one of the two hosts (apple being the other) that the disease needs to complete its life cycle.

attack. If fire blight shows up, control it with diligent pruning. Cut away infected branches as soon as you notice them, and keep checking for new infections. Cut 6 inches into healthy wood and sterilize pruning shears by dipping them in, or wiping them with, alcohol, Listerine®, Lysol®, or Pine-Sol® between cuts. In winter, look for dark sunken cankers where the bacteria are resting, and prune infected branches 6 inches back into healthy wood.

SUMMER DISEASES

Pruning also helps control so-called summer diseases, such as black rot, bitter rot, and white rot, all of which cause soft, rotten areas on fruits. Look over branches as you prune in winter, keeping an eye out for, and pruning away, stems that have dark, sunken cankers of disease. Don't leave prunings beneath your trees because they might provide inoculum for these and other diseases. Old rotten or dried apples left on the tree also could harbor disease for the following year's infections. Copper sprays, beginning midsummer, also offer control.

POWDERY MILDEW

Powdery mildew disease puts a white coating on leaves and russets the fruits. Control powdery mildew by pruning away dormant buds in winter that show white fungal growth; by planting resistant varieties; or by spraying summer oil, soap, bicarbonate, or sulfur.

CODLING MOTH, PLUM CURCULIO, AND APPLE MAGGOT

Three prominent insects that may ruin your fruits are codling moth, plum curculio, and apple maggot. If you bite into an apple and find a large, white "worm" (not a half a worm, you hope), that is the codling moth larva. You also may notice one large hole on the outside of the fruit, where the larva entered. Plum curculio, present east of the Rockies, leaves a crescent-shaped scar and causes fruits to fall. If a fruit does not fall, it is perfectly edible, with only a superficial half-moon blemish. Apple maggot, also found mostly east of the Rocky Mountains, is a small maggot that tunnels throughout the fruit, dimpling the outside and leaving brown trails within. Usually, it renders the fruit inedible.

Consider alternative measures to augment or replace spraying for insect pests. Codling moth larvae prefer to enter fruits that touch each other, so thin fruits religiously to decrease damage. Pheromone traps that attract

TOP: Dimpling is a sign that apple maggots are tunneling inside the fruits, ruining them.

BOTTOM: Plum curculio insects mar fruits with characteristic crescent-shaped scars (or half-circle scars on ripe fruit).

male moths leave no one around to fertilize females; traps are most effective with isolated trees and should be hung high in the branches. Codling moth has multiple generations, with larvae resting in the ground or beneath bark flakes on trees. Give them something better to rest beneath: a band of corrugated cardboard wrapped around the trunk 18 inches or more above ground level. And then, before they awaken, remove the bands and burn them (heh, heh). Some people swear by scented traps made by hanging jars containing a mix of 1 cup of cider vinegar, $\frac{1}{3}$ cup of cider molasses, and 1 teaspoon ammonia, all diluted to 1½ quarts with water. If all this doesn't make enough trouble for the codling moth, give them a virus, codling moth granulosis virus, sprayed on as Cyd-X® or Virosoft® CP4.

Apples for Special Purposes

- **Apples for warm regions (low-chill varieties):** 'Anna', 'Beverly Hills', 'Ein Sheimer', 'Winter Banana'.
- **Apples with especially good flavor:** 'Ashmead's Kernel', 'Chestnut Crabapple', 'Cornish Gilliflower', 'Cox's Orange Pippin', 'Esopus Spitzenberg', 'Fireside', 'Gala', 'GoldRush', 'Hudson's Golden Gem', 'Idared', 'Jonagold', 'Kidd's Orange', 'Macoun', 'Melrose', 'Mutsu' ('Crispin'), 'Newtown Pippin' ('Albemarle Pippin'), 'Pitmaston Pineapple'.
- **Apples for cooking:** 'Cortland', 'Gravenstein', 'Rhode Island Greening'.
- **Apples that are especially disease resistant:** 'Chehalis', 'Enterprise', 'Liberty', 'Pixie Crunch', 'Redfree', 'Sundance', 'William's Pride'.
- **Apples for very cold climates:** 'Centennial', 'Haralson', 'Honeycrisp', 'Wealthy'.
- **Apples for cider:** 'Grimes Golden', 'Harrison Cider Apple', 'Roxbury Russet', 'Virginia Crab', 'Winesap' (Ciders made with these apples are not ordinary ciders, which taste like nothing more than sugar water. The recommendations and suggestions come from Tom Burford, orchardist, nurseryman, apple consultant, and author of *Apples: A Catalog of International Varieties*).

Lee's Picks

'Liberty', 'Macoun', 'Hudson's Golden Gem', 'Jonagold', 'Esopus Spitzenberg', 'Chestnut Crabapple', 'Newtown Pippin'

Hard 'Red Delicious' apples hung on wires and coated with Tangle-Trap are very effective baited traps for apple maggots.

The old-fashioned way to deal with curculios was to jar the tree early in the morning by hitting limbs with a padded mallet and catch the dislodged curculios for disposal on a sheet spread on the ground while they played dead. Use padding on the mallet to avoid damaging the bark. Jar the tree daily for the 6-week curculio season. Letting chickens run beneath trees has similar benefits.

Once codling moth and plum curculio exit stage left, apple maggots enter stage right. You can effectively trap this pest on fake apples—red spheres, coated with sticky Tangle-Trap, hung in the trees. Hang one trap per dwarf tree or four to eight per large tree, at eye level and a couple of feet within the canopy and not obscured by leaves. Even better and more apple-like for traps are the rock-hard 'Red Delicious' apples I buy at the supermarkets. With a wire run through them and a coating of Tangle-Trap they last more than a month, at which point I buy more of these very effective "apple traps" for apple maggot. No need to clean these traps at the end of the season; I just throw them in the compost pile.

Codling moth and plum curculio are most active early in the season and can be kept at bay by spraying Surround on multiple occasions before that time. It's the dustiness of Surround that bothers Ms. Curculio, so get a thick layer of the material on before she appears. Spray three applications before the trees even bloom and re-apply every 7 to 10 days. Whenever there is more than $\frac{1}{2}$ inch of rainfall, spray again, no matter how many days have passed. Sprayed trees look dusty white, very Mediterranean, and attractive. Curculios are gone about 6 weeks after bloom, as is the first generation of codling moth, so those early sprays might be enough. Entrust is another spray that will control codling moth and apple maggot, but not curculio.

'Pitmaston Pineapple' is an old British variety with a pineapple-y flavor.

'Wealthy' is a cold-hardy apple that tastes best eaten very soon after harvest.

Selection of Plants and Varieties

For a plant that has been enjoyed for thousands of years, it is no wonder that there are thousands of different apple varieties. There are not only numerous varieties but also many rootstocks from which to choose.

Choose a variety that suits your taste preferences and then choose a rootstock suitable for your site. Semi-dwarfing rootstocks such as MM.106 and M.26 produce trees that grow only about 15 feet tall and wide, so are suitable where space is limited. Where space is even more cramped, or for growing in pots, plant a tree grafted onto fully dwarfing rootstock, such as M.27, P.22, or G.65. M.27 and P.22 produce trees that mature at only 6 feet tall; G.65 matures at about 8 feet tall. Dwarfing or semi-dwarfing rootstocks also are useful even if you have abundant space but would like to have more trees, each a different variety.

The rootstocks mentioned are only some of those available. Rootstocks also have been selected for their ability to tolerate adverse soil conditions. For instance, MM.111 is adapted to growing in dry soils; M.7 is tolerant of fire blight and adapted to a wide variety of soils. Dwarfing rootstocks generally have weak root systems so the trees need staking throughout their life.

Interstem trees, sometimes available, have the benefit of vigorous roots (or some other desired characteristic, such as tolerance to wet soil) and dwarfing. Such trees are created by grafting a stem of a dwarfing rootstock about 1 foot long onto another rootstock, which will provide roots for the tree, and then grafting the desired variety on top of that dwarfing interstem. The interstem piece of a dwarfing rootstock, for reasons not thoroughly elucidated, dwarfs the parts of the tree above it even though the dwarfing rootstock does not have its roots in the ground.

Rootstocks are the usual but not the only way to make dwarf apple trees. Some varieties, such as 'Cascade Delicious' and 'Starkspur Compact Mac', are naturally dwarf and will be so on any rootstock. Spur-type apples, because they grow proportionally more spurs than long shoots compared with standard varieties, tend to make naturally smaller trees. 'Spur Red Delicious' is one of many spur types; 'Golden Sentinel' is one of a few upright spur types. A spur-type variety on a very dwarfing rootstock ends up as a very small tree, all of which highlights the fact that final tree size reflects the interaction of the variety, the rootstock, and the growing conditions.

Apple Rootstocks and Tree Sizes

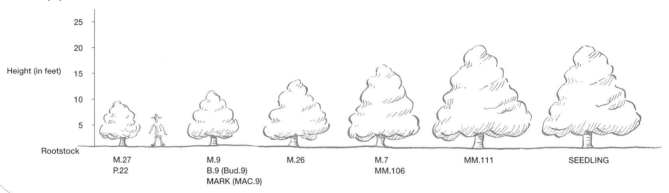

Height (in feet)

25
20
15
10
5

Rootstock

M.27	M.9	M.26	M.7	MM.111	SEEDLING
P.22	B.9 (Bud.9)		MM.106		
	MARK (MAC.9)				

Interstem Tree

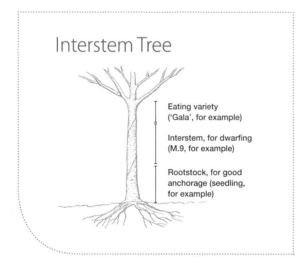

Eating variety
('Gala', for example)

Interstem, for dwarfing
(M.9, for example)

Rootstock, for good
anchorage (seedling,
for example)

'Anna' This early-ripening apple is yellow with a slight blush of redness; stores for a couple of months at cool temperatures, a low-chill variety.

'Ashmead's Kernel' About 200 hundred years ago, Dr. Ashmead of Gloucester, England, found this apple growing in his garden; fruit has a russeted golden brown skin, with a reddish bronze cheek; flesh is aromatic and crisp with excellent flavor; production is erratic; ripens late and keeps well, during which time the flavor changes from very tart to sugary.

'Beverly Hills' The fruits are small to medium size, with a good-quality, tart flesh reminiscent of 'McIntosh' enclosed in a pale yellow skin splashed with red; dislikes hot weather and is moderately well suited to coastal, southern California climate; a low-chill variety.

'Centennial' A sugary, sweet crabapple, juicy with a nutty flavor, and a yellow skin overlaid with scarlet; tends to alternate bearing; very cold hardy; tree is compact; early ripening.

'Chehalis' Large and greenish yellow, this variety is similar to 'Golden Delicious' but crisper and ripens in summer; not resistant to rust disease but does resist the other major diseases.

'Chestnut Crabapple' Yes, this is a crabapple, which means nothing more than a small apple; reddish bronze, striped fruits

with sweet and crunchy, delicious, nutlike flavor; reliably productive; disease resistant; ripens early and keeps well on the tree.

'Cornish Gilliflower' This fruit was discovered in a cottage garden in Cornwall, England, about 200 years ago; an ugly apple, russeted brownish red over an olive base; flavor is supreme, a rich sweetness, with a hint of clove.

'Cortland' Dark red skin and a snow-white flesh that does not discolor when exposed to air; excellent for eating fresh (but not for long after harvest) and for cooking, especially as applesauce; keeps well on the tree but does not keep well after being picked; ripens mid- to late season.

'Ashmead's Kernel' is an old British variety whose flavor turns sugary sweet after some time in storage.

'Cox's Orange Pippin' Sprightly and distinctively flavored fruit has a skin that is orange and red, washed with deep red over a yellow background; susceptible to scab and powdery mildew; yields can be low, the fruit tends to be small, sometimes cracks or gets sunburn, and flavor is inconsistent from year to year; nonetheless, 'Cox's Orange Pippin' remains among the most popular apple varieties in England; ripens mid-season.

'Ein Shemer' This fruit is similar to 'Golden Delicious', with a yellow skin that has a slight blush, and a crisp, sweet-tart flesh; resistant to scab and well suited to hot summer climates; low-chill variety.

'Enterprise' A late-ripening, red apple that is quite tart at harvest but becomes spicy sweet and richly flavored after a few weeks of storage; resistant to fire blight, cedar apple rust, and scab, moderately resistant to powdery mildew; keeps well for many months in storage for good eating through the winter.

'Esopus Spitzenberg' An old American variety that is crisp and juicy with a rich, somewhat tart, excellent flavor; skin is a rich yellow, covered with a mix of bright and dark red; productivity is low and erratic; susceptible to fire blight, scab, and canker; in cold storage, the fruit keeps well until spring; the favorite apple of Thomas Jefferson; ripens mid- to late season.

'Fireside' A large, red fruit with coarse yellow flesh and a chewy skin; excellent for fresh eating throughout winter, with sweet and sour flavor and hints of pear; cold hardy; resistant to cedar apple rust, susceptible to scab and fire blight; ripens midseason.

'Gala' A juicy, sweet apple considered one of the best early apples; skin is a beautiful golden yellow, with a pink-orange blush; bears at a very early age, even on one-year-old wood; needs thinning in order to get good fruit size; in contrast to most other early apples, 'Gala' stores well, until Christmas and beyond.

'GoldRush' The fruits are greenish yellow with a red blush at harvest, turning to deep yellow in storage, sometimes with a fine netlike russet; the pale yellow flesh is very crisp with a complex, spicy flavor that is high in both sugar and acid levels and slow to brown when sliced; best flavor develops after a couple of months of storage; moderately resistant to powdery mildew, scab, and fire blight, susceptible to cedar apple rust; ripens late and keeps well.

'Gravenstein' A large yellow apple with red stripes whose crisp texture and slightly tart, aromatic flavor is excellent when dead ripe; stores poorly, which is fine because 'Gravenstein' also cooks into delicious pies and sauces; tends to alternate bearing; ripens unevenly.

'Grimes Golden' A probable parent of 'Golden Delicious', 'Grimes Golden' has a clear yellow skin sometimes roughened with yellow or russet dots; yellowish flesh is crisp and tender with a spicy sweet flavor; a good all-purpose apple, especially for cider; ripens midseason and keeps fairly well.

'Haralson' Crisp, juicy, sweet-tart flesh within a red and yellow skin; bears fruit at an early age; naturally small tree; somewhat resistant to fire blight and cedar-apple rust; very cold hardy; ripens late and stores well through the winter.

'Harrison Cider Apple' Originating in Essex County, New Jersey, in the early 19th century, 'Harrison' was once grown extensively to be blended with other cider apples or used alone to make an extremely dark, rich cider; skin is yellow with black stippling; rediscovered in 1976, 'Harrison' is scab and rot resistant, bears annual, full crops, and keeps well in storage; also good fresh and has a quince-like flavor.

TOP: 'Cox's Orange Pippin' is difficult to grow but worth it for its delectable, sprightly flavor.

BOTTOM: 'Gala' is an early-ripening apple with rich, sweet flavor.

'Honeycrisp' Don't let this variety hang on the tree past its prime and don't grow it where summers get hot (USDA Hardiness Zone 6 or higher) and you'll get, as the name implies, a sweet, rich, crisp apple; very cold hardy; stores well.

'Hudson's Golden Gem' A beautiful, golden russeted apple whose skin sparkles with gold flecks when hit by sunlight; the flavor matches the beauty, a nutty flavor with rich, honeyed sweetness that hints of pear; resistant to scab and somewhat resistant to other apple diseases; precocious and productive; ripens mid- to late season and keeps well.

'Idared' Bright red skin and pure white, juicy flesh; fruit develops excellent flavor after a period of storage, from about February onward; annually productive and scab resistant; ripens mid- to late season.

'Jonagold' A hybrid of the sprightly 'Jonathan' and the aromatic 'Golden Delicious'; fruits have a "cracking" texture—they are crisp, but when you bite into them, they explode with juice and excellent flavor; fruits are large, yellow with a splash of light scarlet; pollen sterile; precocious; keeps well on the tree; ripens late.

'Kidd's Orange' An offspring of 'Cox's Orange Pippin' and 'Red Delicious' that retains the complex 'Cox' flavor and, thanks to its latter, American parent, is less temperamental and sweeter than its British parent; skin flushed orange-red, with some russet; precocious; not a heavy bearer; resistant to scab and mildew; ripens midseason.

'Liberty' A large, red apple with delicious, sweet-tart flavor and a texture like firm snow; flavor improves after a short time in storage; bears at an early age and is very productive; resistant to fire blight, powdery mildew, cedar apple rust, and scab; grow this variety.

'Macoun' A hybrid of 'McIntosh' and 'Jersey Black' that is similar to 'McIntosh', but smaller and ripens about a month later; flavor is excellent, but fleeting; one day after picking, the fruit will have noticeably less flavor, which is all the more reason to grow it yourself. (I harvest my 'Macoun' apples once or twice a day as they drop to the ground.)

'Melrose' A hybrid of 'Jonathan' and 'Delicious', melding the tartness of the former parent with the sweetness of the latter parent; large fruits; productive; good quality in storage until spring; ripens midseason.

'Mutsu' ('Crispin') A large, round, yellow apple, with a delicate spicy flavor; texture is pleasantly coarse, reminiscent of biting into a snowball; pollen sterile; ripens mid- to late season.

'Newtown Pippin' ('Albemarle Pippin') Red blushed, greenish yellow apple that needs storage to bring out its flavor; do not eat until after New Year's Day; excellent flavor, these apples were shipped from the United States to England in the 18th century; needs long summers with plenty of sunlight; ripens late season.

'Pitmaston Pineapple' A small, russeted apple, admittedly not very pretty but has a crisp flesh with a rich flavor and more than a hint of pineapple; ripens mid- to late season.

'Pixie Crunch' A dark red apple with very crisp, breaking flesh and a slightly tart, spicy, full flavor; resistant to scab and moderately resistant to fire blight; only slightly susceptible to apple maggot; ripens early and keeps well for a couple of months.

TOP: The name of this apple, 'Honeycrisp', says it all.

BOTTOM: Rich, sweet flavor and gold-flecked, yellow skin characterize 'Hudson Golden Gem' apples.

'**William's Pride**' The dark red fruits, crisp and sweet-tart, ripen best in northern gardens; flesh near the skin turns pink and turns soft soon after peak ripeness; resistant to major apple diseases; very cold hardy; ripens early and keeps for a few weeks.

'**Winesap**' A deep red or maroon skin with a yellow background on its shaded side; yellow flesh is sweet, crisp, and aromatic with a vinous flavor; reliably and heavily productive; suitable fresh as well as for cooking and cider making; late ripening; keeps well.

'**Winter Banana**' This beautiful fruit, waxy yellow with a pinkish blush, was once widely used in fruit baskets; flavor is aromatic, and the slightly yellowish flesh does have hint of banana flavor; stores well; precocious; good pollinator; resistant to cedar-apple rust, but susceptible to fire blight; ripens mid- to late season; low-chill variety.

'**Redfree**' A summer apple with medium, glossy red fruits with crisp, juicy flesh that has a mild flavor; resistant to major apple diseases; fruits ripen unevenly and can be stored for up to two months.

'**Rhode Island Greening**' An old American apple that was once widely grown in the Northeast; excellent for cooking, also good fresh or dried; grass-green fruit turns a little yellow as it ripens; reliably productive.

'**Roxbury Russet**' Originating early in the 17th century in Roxbury, Massachusetts, this variety is probably the oldest named variety of apple in America; skin is green with a bronze blush and a bit of russeting; a good all-purpose apple, especially good for cider; stores well; ripens in late September and early October.

'**Sundance**' With a blush of red, this tasty yellow apple is crisp with a spicy, citrus-y flavor; resistant to fire blight, cedar apple rust, and scab, moderately resistant to powdery mildew; ripens mid- to late season and keeps well for a week on your kitchen counter or up to 6 months if refrigerated.

'**Virginia Crab**' A small apple (and small tree) that is a dull red mixed with faint streaks of greenish yellow and has numerous small white spots; flesh is stringy and astringent; makes a very flavorful dry cider, which maintains its quality for a long time and ferments very slowly; ripens midseason.

'**Wealthy**' For best flavor, pick the tart, very juicy fruits when they are fully ripe, then eat them almost immediately; precocious and productive; good pollinator; has a long bloom period; ripens midseason.

TOP LEFT: Good growing, timely harvest, and immediate eating make 'Macoun' among the most delicious of apples.

BOTTOM RIGHT: 'Liberty' is notable for resistance to all four major apple diseases as well as for its good flavor.

Apricot

Prunus Armeniaca var. *Armeniaca*

GROWTH HABIT
Depending on rootstock and variety, a tree maturing at 10 feet to 25 feet tall

POLLINATION NEEDS
Most varieties are self-fruitful

LIGHT REQUIREMENT
Full sunlight

CLIMATE
USDA Hardiness Zones 4–9; AHS Heat Zones 8–2

REGIONS
Pest control usually needed east of the Rocky Mountains; best climates are those with hot, dry summers and steadily cold winters

My friend Levante, from Hungary, where apricots are popular in everything from soup to brandy (*palinka*), just had to have his fresh apricots. True, New York, where Levante lives, does not have the ideal climate, but with a sunny, sloping site not too far from the Hudson River, he planted, and planted, and planted. Apricot's very early blossoms often succumb to late spring frosts, insects and diseases take their toll, and fluctuating winter temperatures weaken or kill trees. Nonetheless, some years Levante is able to gather baskets and baskets of apricots, and these he freely shares, at which time we settle into an almost drunken stupor from a flood of the rich, sweet fruits.

Even if you live where conditions are not ideal for apricots, the tree-ripe fruit is so rich and sweet that you may want to give it a try as long as you can resign yourself to inconsistent crops. Even those years when you do lose a crop, the early, pinkish white blossoms, at least, provide a welcome and beautiful antidote to the exiting stark winter landscape.

Apricots have hybridized and been hybridized with related members of the *Prunus* genus to yield interesting fruits with complex flavors or, at least, names. Apriums are hybrids with plums where more genes have been contributed by apricots. Plumcots and pluots, emphasizing the plum parents, are discussed with plums (p. 186). Can you guess the mixed parentage of a "peacotum?"

And there's even more interesting and tasty goings on beneath that fuzzy orange skin. You perhaps have cracked open an apricot pit and noticed its resemblance to an almond. Apricots and almonds are related and, in fact, some apricots, such as 'Harcot' and 'Moorpark', bear sweet, edible, almond-like nuts. The bitter pits of other varieties of apricots and bitter almonds release deadly cyanide when eaten. (Luckily you'd probably break your teeth trying to eat one before you actually could swallow it!)

Growing

For success with apricots, site the tree with care. Plant in full sunlight and a microclimate without frosts once the blossoms open. Apricots require perfect drainage but are otherwise not finicky about soil. The plants grow well over a relatively wide pH range. With good care, new shoots on an apricot tree should grow 12 inches to 18 inches each year.

Pruning

Prune your apricot annually, preferably just as growth begins in spring, and beginning the year you set your tree in the ground. Train your young tree to either an open-center or modified-central-leader form (pp. 40–41).

Apricot trees bear fruit two ways: on spurs, or laterally on branches. Spur fruits grow on branches 2 years old and older, and branch fruits grow on 1-year-old branches, so trees must be pruned annually to stimulate growth of only a moderate amount of renewal wood each season. Spur buds bear larger fruits, but blossom up to a week earlier than lateral buds. In frost-prone areas, prune heavily for more young growth and hence more laterally borne fruits to yield more reliable harvests, even if the fruits will be smaller. Use heading and thinning cuts to remove old wood that is no longer fruitful and to stimulate new growth for the following season's fruit. Keep the branches open so they all can bathe in light and air.

If you are fortunate enough to have a very heavy set of fruit on your tree, thin the fruits to about 2 inches apart. Otherwise, no thinning is necessary.

Grow It Naturally

- Plant in a microclimate with abundant summer sun, good air circulation, and protection from late spring frosts.

- Make sure soil drainage is perfect.

- Paint trunks or whole trees white in winter to modulate fluctuations in bark temperature and to delay spring bloom.

- In less than perfect growing regions, choose varieties, such as 'Hargrand', 'Harval', and 'Jerseycot', that are disease resistant and can tolerate spring frosts.

Pests and Diseases

Plum curculio is an insect that attacks apricots early in the season east of the Rocky Mountains, leaving a crescent-shaped scar on the fruit. Blemished fruit that remains on the tree is subject to disease, but most of these damaged fruits will fall to the ground. Control "curcs" with early and heavy sprays of Surround, building up several layers before the tree blooms, and then maintaining the dusty layer with repeated sprays every 7 to 10 days. You can also jar the tree in early morning, letting the bugs fall onto a sheet or tarp placed under the branches. Then gather up the fallen buggers and destroy them. If you have chickens, letting them run under apricot trees also offers control. Curculio controls need to be continued for 8 weeks after bloom.

The other important insect pest of apricots, oriental fruit moth, makes a large hole as it enters a fruit or causes branch tips to wilt when it bores into a branch. This pest also has been controlled with Surround, as well as with Entrust or Bt, with *Macrocentrus ancylivorus* parasitoid wasp, and in commercial orchards, with pheromones.

Borers attack apricots, causing individual branches or whole trees to die back. Trees that are growing vigorously and have healthy, undamaged bark are less apt to be attacked. Entrust also controls borers.

On fruits, brown rot disease begins as a circular brown area that eventually envelops the whole fruit, turning it fuzzy and gray. Besides spraying, picking off dried-up fruit mummies, on which the disease overwinters, helps control brown rot, as does planting resistant varieties, such as 'Alfred', 'Goldcot', 'Harcot', 'Hargrand', and 'Harlayne'. Sulfur, copper, bicarbonate, or neem sprays are somewhat effective. Use sulfur or copper sprays with caution because they can damage the plant.

Are there small, round, olive brown to black spots forming on your fruits? If so, that's a symptom of bacterial spot, a disease that thrives in humid weather. Spots may also appear on leaves. Keep this disease in check by pruning the tree so that branches get good air circulation and exposure to sunlight, by maintaining good growing conditions so trees remain vigorous, and by keeping the bark free from injury. Prune while the tree is blossoming so healing is rapid. A number of varieties are resistant to bacterial spot, including 'Harcot', 'Hargrand', 'Harglow', and 'Harval'.

Various bark cankers (sunken, dark lesions) also can weaken or kill an apricot tree. A tree well hardened for winter, with a trunk that is protected from winter sun with a coating of white latex paint, is less apt to develop bark cankers.

These 'Harlayne' apricots, a variety that tolerates cold and some disease, are ready for picking.

Selection of Plants and Varieties

Many varieties of apricot exist, with varying adaptations, so choose varieties suited to your region. Newer varieties are always being bred, especially for disease resistance and quality. In the west, keep an eye out for flavorful new varieties, such as 'Robada', 'Apache', and 'Nicole', which are the result of breeding with apricots from Central Asia. From research in New Jersey comes later-blooming varieties, such as 'Early Blush', 'Sun Gem', 'Orangered', and 'Jerseycot'.

Apricots are generally propagated by being grafted on any of the many peach or plum rootstocks. 'Krymsk 1', a new dwarfing rootstock still under test, seems to be tolerant of cold, drought, and waterlogging, and creates about a half-size tree.

APRICOTS

'Alfred' Medium fruit has a sweet, rich flavor; skin sometimes has a pink blush; resistant to brown rot; productive, cold hardy, and vigorous; adapted to eastern growing conditions and beyond; relatively reliable for an apricot.

'Blenheim' This old English variety is grown commercially in California for drying and canning; pale orange fruits are sweet, aromatic, and very juicy; tree requires 400 hours of chilling, so blooms early; adapted to drier regions with cooler summers.

'Earlicot' Large fruit with very good flavor; adapted to dry regions; needs any other apricot variety as a pollenizer; blooms and ripens early.

'Goldkist' Very good flavor; low-chill variety (300 hours); blooms very early; ripens early.

'Harglow' Fruits are good fresh or cooked, resistant to cracking; tree is compact; blooms relatively late.

'Hargrand' Fruits are very large and orange, with a speckled blush and good flavor; resistant to cracking; productive; cold hardy in winter and in bloom; somewhat resistant to diseases.

'Harlayne' Fruit has a good flavor and texture, medium in size with a red blush on its skin; cold hardy; moderately resistant to diseases.

'Harval' Very good flavor; productive; reliable in less-than-perfect apricot-growing regions because of disease resistance and flowers that are both cold hardy and late to open.

'Jerseycot' Good flavor, in some years reminiscent of melon; reliably productive in many regions; blossoms are cold hardy and relatively late opening; disease resistant.

'Katy' This low-chill variety (500 hours) bears early in the season.

'Manchu' Developed in South Dakota in the 1930s, this fruit is large and yellow and best used for cooking; very cold hardy and productive; one of the so-called Manchurian apricots, others of which are 'Moongold' and 'Sungold'.

'Moorpark' An old English variety now grown commercially in California for fresh eating, canning, and drying; fruits are very large, juicy, and sweet; blossoms open early; ripens over a long period of time.

'Perfection' Fruit is large, only mediocre in quality (despite its name); hardy; early bloom; needs cross-pollination by any other apricot variety.

'Scout' Smooth, mild, sweet fruits are good for fresh eating as well as for making into jam; cold hardy; vigorous.

Stems loaded with apricot fruits are a flavorful welcome near the front door of a home.

'Sugar Pearl' Good flavor comes from parentage nestled in apricot trees of western Asian apricots; hardy; widely adapted; late blossoming; productive.

APRIUMS

'Cot-N-Candy' Large, sweet, and juicy fruits; white flesh resembles apricot but has plum aftertaste; shrubby, self-fruitful, and blossoms very early; needs thinning.

'Flavor Anne' Large, very sweet, orange fruits; requires little chilling; ripens very early.

'Flavor Delight' This is a three to one mix of apricot and plum, partially self-fruitful; requires 200 to 300 chilling hours, so blossoms early; ripens early.

'Honey Rich' Very flavorful fruits and very delicate skin; low chill (400 hours); ripe fruits hang well on the tree.

Avocado

Persea americana

GROWTH HABIT

Depending on rootstock and variety, a tree maturing at 12 feet to 24 feet tall

POLLINATION NEEDS

Partially self-fruitful; better crops with cross-pollination from a variety with a different flower type

LIGHT REQUIREMENT

Full sunlight

CLIMATE

USDA Hardiness Zones 9–11; AHS Heat Zones 8–2

REGIONS

Avocado growing limited by climate, with no regional pest problems; spread of ripening dates varies somewhat with location

Avocado is a tropical plant, well known even to people living in cold climates, where it's commonly grown as a houseplant. The fruit itself is widely known because it's common in markets almost everywhere. These fruits are unique in that they are extremely high in a healthful oil rich in antioxidants and phytochemicals.

Avocados usually are broken down into three horticultural races. Mexican avocados (*P. americana* var. *drymifolia*) are the most cold tolerant, thriving in dry, subtropical climates. They require 7 months to 9 months from bloom to ripening, at which point a dark skin encloses a very rich (that is, high in oil) flesh that sometimes, along with the leaves, has the scent of anise. West Indian avocados (*P. americana* var. *americana*) are the least cold hardy, thriving best in humid, tropical climates and experiencing cold damage at freezing temperatures. The shiny green or reddish fruits take about 7 months to ripen, at which point the flesh is sweeter, milder, and less rich than fruits of the Mexican race. Guatemalan avocados (*P. americana* var. *guatemalensis*) are intermediate in characteristics and ripen after 14 months to 18 months to a moderately rich flesh enclosed within a rough, green skin.

Life, and avocados, are thankfully not so simple: The three races hybridize readily, and many existing varieties are in fact hybrids, the best of which combine parental qualities. Superior plants, usually of chance seedlings, have been noted and then propagated by grafting since pre-Columbian times. The probable origin of avocado was in southern Mexico, but the fruit was cultivated from the Rio Grande to central Peru long before the arrival of Europeans.

In practical terms, for best fruiting grow an A-type and a B-type avocado together or make other arrangements for cross-pollination between these two types. And then don't worry about fruit set. In bloom, an avocado tree is drenched with flowers, thousands of them, over a long period of time. Relatively few need to set fruit to get a full crop.

For the best-quality fruit, plant a named variety or graft a stem from a named variety onto a rootstock you grow from seed. Grafted trees should start bearing within two years to four years. For best growth, plant your tree in full sun in—and this is very important—well-drained soil. Avocado trees grow more cold hardy with age, so if cold is a potential problem, protect young trees by wrapping them for winter.

GROWING AVOCADO IN COLD CLIMATES

As many cold-climate gardeners know, avocados are easy to grow in sunny windows in winter. Fruiting under such conditions is rare because these trees are usually grown from seed. With good growing conditions—outdoors in full sun in the tropics or subtropics—avocado seedlings take 10 or more years before they are old enough to fruit. Windowsills usually can't accommodate a seedling 10 years old, and under cold-climate conditions a seedling needs to grow longer than 10 years before maturing to flowering age. Grafted trees flower not only much sooner but also at a much smaller size. So if you live in a cold climate and want to grow avocados, your best bet is to buy or make a grafted tree: you then increase your chances for a crop, you get the crop earlier, and the plant need not grow to a size that takes over your house.

Growing

Talk of pollination brings us to one of avocado's quirks. If you must know, the flowers are perfect and exhibit protogynous dichogamy with synchronous daily complementarity. Put more simply, the female parts of the flower bloom first, followed by the male parts. Avocado varieties are either "A" blooming type or "B" blooming type. An A-type flower will be functionally female one morning, then functionally male the afternoon of the next day. A B-type flower will be functionally female in the afternoon, then functionally male the next morning. At lower temperatures, opening of both types of flowers is delayed, which might end up reversing the behavior and even lead to self-pollination of flowers.

Grow It Naturally

- Plant in soil with perfect drainage.
- Plant a variety adapted to your climate.
- Mulch.

This avocado tree offers shade and good eating.

Pruning

Avocado trees need little pruning. Head back stems on young trees to promote branching, especially on very upright growing varieties. Prune older trees as needed to keep them in bounds or from growing too tall.

Rejuvenate your tree, if needed, by lopping back major limbs (not below the graft union, though) and selecting a few new sprouts to create a new framework of branches. The previously shaded trunk and stems are apt to sunburn, so paint or spray them with a 50–50 mix of white latex paint and water to reflect the sun's rays. Severely pruned trees will start flowering again within a year or two.

Pests and Diseases

The major pest of avocado is root rot, best avoided by planting in well-drained soil and by proper watering. Use organic mulch beneath the tree—but keep it a few inches away from the trunk—to promote growth of beneficial microorganisms that are antagonistic to root-rot fungi and suppress this disease. Disease-free nursery stock also helps, as do rot-resistant rootstocks, such as 'Uzi', 'Zentmyer', and 'Dusa'.

A few other pests might rear their ugly heads. On fruits, avocado scab starts out as oval, slightly raised, and brown to purplish brown spots. As infected fruits mature, spots coalesce and the centers of these spots become sunken. On leaves, typically those higher up in the tree, scab starts as small spots less than $1/8$ inch in size, especially common on underside veins, and the center of the spots eventually drops out to give a "gunshot-hole" effect. Cool, moist conditions favor scab, and young fruits and leaves are most susceptible. Resistant varieties (Mexican varieties, with their thin skins, are typically susceptible), a good site, and spraying copper, if needed, keeps scab in check.

Harvesting

Another quirk of avocado is that it is among the few fruits that will not ripen on the tree. Start homing in on the harvest date by learning the harvest season for the particular variety you have. After that, keep an eye on size and fruit color. Mature, ready-to-harvest fruits are full size, with dark-colored varieties starting to darken and green varieties turning yellowish. In either case, cutting into a sample fruit should reveal a paper-thin seed coat around the single, large seed. Clip fruits off individually.

No need to be swimming in avocados once ripening begins. Not all fruits mature at the same time, and mature fruits can be left hanging on the tree for a while in good condition. Just how long they can be left hanging depends on temperatures (cooler equals longer) and the particular variety.

Once mature, hold fruits at cool, not cold, temperatures for further storage or begin ripening them indoors, which takes a few days. Ideal temperatures for ripening are between 55°F and 75°F. When the flesh gives slightly as you press the fruit near its stem end, the ripe, buttery, full-flavored flesh is ready for slicing into salads, mashing for guacamole, or scooping out with a spoon and putting right into your mouth. Thick-skinned avocados, such as some Guatemalan varieties, may not reveal to the touch that the flesh below has softened. In that case, check for softening by how easily you can push a toothpick into a fruit near the stem end.

Starting an Avocado from Seed

To do your own grafting, you need an avocado seedling on which to graft. Seedlings are easy to raise if you don't let the seed dry out. Plant it, pointy side up (larger end—or base—facing downward), directly in a container of potting soil, or stick three toothpicks in its side and suspend it (again, pointy side up) above a jar of water, allowing the base to sit in the water. In the latter case, pot it up after roots, which will be entertainingly visible, have made some growth.

Theoretically, you could make guacamole from your indoor avocado if you graft it and it grows in a sun-streamed window. Even better, give your tree a summer vacation outdoors as long as temperatures are warm. A period of slightly cooler-than-usual room temperatures (lower than 68°F) helps to induce bud formation, after which flowers soon follow. Many years ago, I grafted a branch of a named variety onto my windowsill seedling and only a year later the tree was froth-

Avocado pits are easy and interesting to sprout, but don't wait too long to transfer the growing plant to soil.

ing in creamy white blossoms. I never did get fruit, despite my efforts in hand pollination. Grafting two branches, one of an A type and one of a B type, should have done the trick. In fact, fruit production is an iffy proposition at best from a cold-climate potted tree that lives outdoors only seasonally.

Selection of Plants and Varieties

FLOWER TYPE A

'Anaheim' Guatemalan; fruits are glossy green, very large, with fair to good flavor; tree is hardy to 32°F, fairly small, upright, and productive; ripens June to August; especially adapted to California conditions.

'Choquette' West Indian; fruit is large and green with a glossy skin and good flavor; tree is hardy to 26°F, medium size, spreading, and tends to alternate bearing; scab resistant; ripens November to February; especially adapted to Florida conditions.

'Greengold' Guatemalan × Mexican hybrid; green fruits with an excellent, rich, nutty flavor; medium-size tree bears heavily, in some places tending to alternate bearing; ripens February to May; especially adapted to Hawaiian conditions.

'Gwen' Origin unknown; fruits are small and green, with excellent flavor; tree is hardy to 30°F, small, to about 14 feet tall, and productive; grows well in pots; ripens March to November.

'Hass' Guatemalan × Mexican hybrid; fruit is medium with pebbly and purplish skin and excellent flavor; tree is hardy to 26°F; medium size and spreading; tends to alternate bearing;

ripens over a long season beginning in winter; especially adapted to California conditions.

'Holiday' Guatemalan; fruit is medium with dark green, pebbly skin and good flavor; tree is hardy to 30°F; small, up to 12 feet tall; this variety also goes by name 'XX3'.

'Mexicola' Mexican hybrid; small fruit with a thin, black skin and excellent flavor; cold hardy to perhaps 30°F; tree is medium size, spreading, and bears reliably and regularly; ripens August to October; especially adapted to California conditions.

'Pinkerton' Guatemalan × Mexican hybrid; medium fruit has a pebbly, green skin and very good flavor; tree is cold hardy to 30°F; low, spreading, and bears young and heavily; ripens October to January; especially adapted to California weather conditions.

'Reed' Guatemalan; large fruit keeps well on the tree, and the pebbled, green skin encloses flesh with excellent flavor; tree is hardy to 30°F and columnar, so it grows well in tight spaces; ripens May to September; especially adapted to California conditions.

'San Miguel' Unknown hybrid; fruit is small to medium with a thin purple skin and excellent flavor; tree is medium size, spreading; bears moderately and regularly; ripens September to November; especially adapted to Hawaiian conditions.

'Wurtz' ('Little Cado') Guatemalan; small, green fruits with good flavor; tree is dwarf and hardy to 32°F; ripens May to September.

FLOWER TYPE B

'Bacon' Mexican; fruits are smooth, green, and small to medium with fair flavor; tree is hardy to 25°F, spreading, and productive; ripens October to March; especially adapted to California conditions.

'Brogdon' Complex hybrid; fruits are medium with pebbly, purplish skin and excellent flavor; tree is hardy to 22°F, medium size, and upright; ripens July to September; especially adapted to Florida conditions.

'Fuerte' Guatemalan × Mexican hybrid; fruits are medium with good flavor; rough skin has small, raised, yellow dots; tree is hardy to 26°F, spreading, and tall; ripens November to March; especially adapted to California weather conditions.

'Lula' West Indian; fruit has rough, glossy, and pale green skin, and flesh has good flavor; tree is hardy to 28°F, productive, and early bearing; very susceptible to scab; ripens November to January; especially adapted to Florida conditions.

'Reed' avocado fruits are large but the tree is narrow, good where space is limited.

'Nabal' Guatemalan; somewhat self-pollinating; fruits are medium and have nearly smooth, green skins and excellent flavor; tree is hardy to 27°F, tall, and upright; head the stems (see p. 37) when the tree is young to develop good branching; ripens June to October; especially adapted to California conditions.

'Sharwil' Guatemalan × Mexican hybrid; fruit is medium with green skin and a long shelf life; flesh has excellent flavor; tree is low and spreading; ripens January to May; especially adapted to Hawaiian conditions.

'Whitsell' Guatemalan × Mexican hybrid; fruit is medium and has dark green skin and flesh with excellent flavor; tree is hardy to 30°F, very small, and bears heavily in alternate years; ripens March to July.

'Zutano' Guatemalan × Mexican hybrid; small to medium fruit has smooth, green skin and good flavor, but stringy flesh; tree is hardy to 25°F and columnar, so grows well in tight spaces; ripens December to January; especially adapted to California conditions.

Familiar in markets and having rich, delicious flavor, 'Haas' ripens over a long season.

Blackberry

Rubus spp.

GROWTH HABIT
Suckering bush with arching or trailing canes

POLLINATION NEEDS
Self-fruitful

LIGHT REQUIREMENT
Full sunlight

CLIMATE
USDA Hardiness Zones 5–8; AHS Heat Zones 9–2;
heat and cold tolerance depend on variety

REGIONS
No regional limitations within hardiness and
heat zones

'Chester' blackberry makes a decorative and edible companion to this gray cedar wall.

The thornlessness of thornless blackberries is, in my opinion, beauty in and of itself. It's not just that these plants are nonintimidating; the smooth, greenish stems and lush green leaves really are quite ornamental and made more so as a background for the large white blossoms.

Blackberries have perennial roots and biennial canes. Each cane bears fruits in its second season, then dies. (Canes of a few varieties fruit at the end of their first season.) In any growing season, as older canes are fruiting, then dying, new ones are making their first season of growth. Any planting, then, has both 1- and 2-year-old canes, giving you an annual harvest. The plants spread by tip layering; that is, by hopscotching along as arching or trailing canes root at their tips and make whole new plants, which go on to tip layer and make more plants, and so on. Left to their own devices, blackberries grow to become a tangled patch of canes.

You'll taste your first berries the year after you plant, and have a full crop by the third year. Because blackberries eventually pick up viruses and other diseases from wild plants, plan on replanting them in a new location every decade or so. Start each new planting with certified, disease-free plants from a nursery, no matter how kind or appealing is the free offer of plants from your neighbor.

If your fingers are not stained after you've picked blackberries, you're not eating them at their very best. Wait until the berries are fully colored and, with some varieties, turning dull black, then give individual berries a gentle pull. A dead ripe blackberry should drop into your hand with only the slightest coaxing. Eat.

In the wild, blackberries are found growing almost everywhere. Some of these wild plants creep along the ground, whereas others grow upright like small trees. These growth habits have been bred into cultivated blackberries, so you can choose from erect as well as semitrailing and trailing varieties. Varieties also have even been selected or developed that lack those ominous thorns.

Classification by growth habit is convenient. The most cold hardy of the lot are erect varieties. They are also very heat tolerant. Trailing varieties, with lanky, flexible canes, are sometimes called "dewberries." Western trailing blackberries yield large, burgundy to black fruits having distinctive flavors. And then there are semi-erect varieties; they don't tolerate quite as much cold as erect types. Within each of these categories are both thorny and thornless types. Thorny varieties have the edge in flavor, but I, for one, tired of battling thorns and traded in my thorny 'Darrow' for thornless 'Chester'.

Growing

Although wild blackberries often grow along the partially shaded edges of woods, the plants fruit best and are healthiest in full sunlight. Try to select a location as far as possible from wild brambles to avoid the spread of disease to your plants. The soil should be well drained and rich in organic matter.

Spacing, which may be as close as 3 feet apart to more than 6 feet apart, depends on the type of blackberry that you plant and the training system you use. Erect blackberries are self-supporting, but other types are easier to manage if you train them on a trellis. Erect a trellis by sinking two sturdy posts deep into the ground at the ends of your row, then stringing two wires between them, one at 3 feet above the ground and the other at 5 feet above the ground. Tie or weave the canes onto the wires.

Another way to train blackberries is to grow them in hills (as in "stations," not mounds), with a post at each hill to which the fruiting canes are tied. Hills vary from 6 feet to 9 feet each way; the distance, once again, depends on the vigor of the plants.

Pruning Erect and Semierect Blackberries

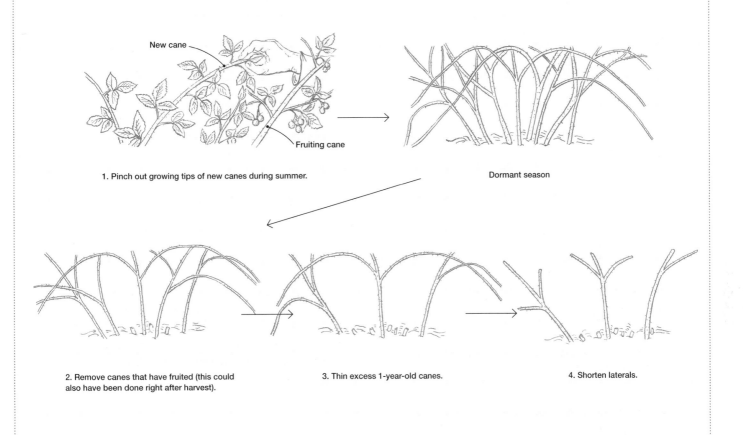

New cane

Fruiting cane

1. Pinch out growing tips of new canes during summer.

Dormant season

2. Remove canes that have fruited (this could also have been done right after harvest).

3. Thin excess 1-year-old canes.

4. Shorten laterals.

Pruning Trailing Blackberries (Dormant Season)

1. Cut away canes that have fruited.

2. Thin new canes to about 10 per plant.

3. Shorten new canes to about 7 ft.

4. Shorten laterals to 12 in. to 18 in.

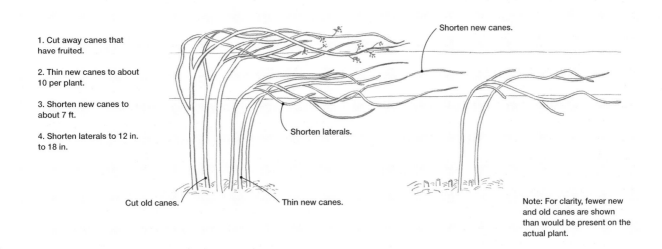

Shorten new canes.

Shorten laterals.

Cut old canes.

Thin new canes.

Note: For clarity, fewer new and old canes are shown than would be present on the actual plant.

Pruning

Blackberries' biennial canes and their aggressive spread make a case for annual pruning. On all but the trailing or trellised semi-erect types, prune twice each year. Do your first pruning in summer, pinching out the tip of each new cane just as it reaches a height of 3 feet. Not all canes reach this height at the same time, so look over your plants every couple of weeks for any that need pinching. Pinching causes the canes to branch and helps keep them upright.

Prune all types of blackberries, even those pruned in summer, in late winter, just before growth begins. First cut away at ground level any cane that bore fruit the previous season—these canes are dead anyway. (You can also prune away these canes in summer, right after they finish fruiting.) Next, thin out new canes, which will fruit this coming season, saving those that are thickest but leaving no more than six per clump. Finally, except on trailing varieties, shorten any lateral branches on the canes you save to about 18 inches, leaving weak canes shorter and vigorous canes longer. Trailing varieties need only old canes removed and new canes thinned.

A convenient way to manage the long canes of trailing types is to let new canes trail on the ground, which they are anyway wont to do, lifting the second-year canes, which will fruit, up to the wire of a trellis. If winter cold is a potential problem, those reclining canes can be left on the ground where they are easily protected for winter with a blanket of straw or leaves. Late the following winter, cut away the old canes that fruited, lift the younger canes up onto the trellis for fruiting, and let new canes that season trail on the ground. And so on year after year—all much more fun if canes are thornless.

Relatively new on the scene are so-called primocane fruiting blackberries. These varieties begin fruiting on new canes toward the end of their first season. The canes can fruit again farther down along the same canes earlier the next season, so they potentially let you harvest at two different times each year. If you are willing to sacrifice the earlier crop (on second-year canes) and make pruning a lot easier, just mow the whole planting to the ground each fall after harvest. Mowing—and disposing of prunings—also lessens problems with diseases or winter damage to canes from cold or animals. This system will work only where summers are long enough to ripen fruits.

Pests and Diseases

Dying canes (except for those naturally dying after they finish fruiting) could be the result of borers, verticillium wilt, or crown gall. Borers are least likely to attack vigorous canes, but, in any case, diligently cut away and destroy canes that have been attacked. Verticillium is a soilborne disease that is best avoided by not planting blackberries where tomatoes, peppers, eggplants, raspberries, or other hosts for the disease have recently grown. Varieties such as 'Logan', 'Marion', and 'Olallie' are resistant to verticillium. Avoid crown gall by starting with disease-free plants, by avoiding injury to the crowns of plants, and, if problems are expected or have been experienced, by sterilizing pruning or digging tools when working with the plants.

Bright orange pustules on the leaves in spring are signs of orange rust disease. Immediately dig up and destroy infected plants. Ignore plants having orange pustules late in the season because this is a different disease, cane and leaf rust, and does little damage.

Purple spots on leaves or canes indicate anthracnose or leaf and cane spot disease. Plants in a well-pruned patch dry off quickly, especially if the site gets full sunlight with good air circulation. Other ways to thwart these diseases include sulfur sprays and planting a resistant variety such as 'Black Satin', 'Cherokee', or 'Arapaho'.

Reddish, twisted flowers that do not develop into fruits are symptoms of double blossom disease, common in the Southeast. Cut all infected canes to the ground right after harvest and destroy them. 'Arapaho,' 'Hull', 'Lavaca', 'Boysen', 'Triple Crown', and 'Navaho' are some varieties resistant to this disease.

Fruits that remain red, hard, and sour have been attacked by redberry mites. A few applications of summer oil every 2 to 3 weeks, beginning when berries are green, will smother the mites.

Selection of Plants and Varieties

Blackberries vary in their adaptation to climate, specifically in cold hardiness, so a specific USDA hardiness zone has been listed among the information for each variety. You may also wish to seek information from nurseries and your local Cooperative Extension office on varieties best suited to your region. Once you have some choices, narrow your selection on the basis of growth habit, thorniness, and, of course, flavor.

THORNY

'Boysen' Trailing; fruits are very large and dark maroon, soft and very juicy, with an excellent, tangy flavor; plants are vigorous and productive; adapted to Pacific Coast and South; late ripening; USDA Hardiness Zone 7.

'Brazos' Erect; fruits taste good and are large; ripen early in the season; disease resistant, very productive, and tolerant of heat and drought; USDA Hardiness Zone 7.

'Cherokee' Erect; medium to large fruits are very tasty; early ripening; disease resistant; USDA Hardiness Zone 6.

'Cheyenne' Erect; large fruits with good flavor; ripen early in the season; productive and moderately disease resistant; USDA Hardiness Zone 6.

'Darrow' Erect; medium fruits have excellent flavor; ripen early and over a long season; productive; among the most cold-hardy varieties; USDA Hardiness Zone 5.

'Lavaca' Trailing; this seedling of 'Boysen' bears maroon fruits that are very large and sweeter than those of its parent; moderate disease resistance; USDA Hardiness Zone 6.

'Marion' Trailing; fruits have excellent flavor, are medium, and ripen midseason; very vigorous and productive; adapted to Pacific Northwest; USDA Hardiness Zones 7–9.

'Olallie' Trailing; fruits are large and sweet; ripen late in season; plant is vigorous and productive; adapted to California, western Oregon, and Gulf Coast; low-chill variety; USDA Hardiness Zone 9.

'Prime-Ark 45' Erect; primocane fruiting; fruits have good flavor, the best of primocane fruiting varieties, although quality declines at temperatures above 85°F; needs long summer to ripen primocane fruits; USDA Hardiness Zone 7.

'Prime-Jan' Erect; primocane fruiting; fruits have good flavor although quality declines at temperatures above 85°F; needs long summer to ripen primocane fruits; USDA Hardiness Zone 7.

'Prime-Jim' Erect; primocane fruiting; fruits have good flavor although quality declines at temperatures above 85°F; needs long summer to ripen primocane fruits; USDA Hardiness Zone 7.

'Doyle Thornless' blackberry decorates this fence with its canes and flowers.

THORNLESS

'Apache' Erect; fruits have good flavor and are very large with small seeds; productive and resistant to orange rust; ripens mid- to late season; USDA Hardiness Zone 6.

'Arapaho' Erect; fruits taste very good, are medium, and have small seeds; ripens midseason (earliest of thornless varieties); USDA Hardiness Zone 6.

'Black Satin' Semi-erect; fruits are large, very tart, and ripen late in the season; resistant to anthracnose; USDA Hardiness Zone 6.

'Chester' Semi-erect; fruits are large and sweet; ripen late in season; productive and widely adapted; most cold hardy of thornless blackberries; USDA Hardiness Zone 5.

'Doyle Thornless' Trailing; fruit is tart but flavorful; high yielding; hardiness questionable, possibly USDA Hardiness Zone 6.

'Hull' Semi-erect; large, sweet fruit has very good flavor and ripens mid- to late season; productive and somewhat disease resistant; widely adapted; less cold hardy than 'Chester'; USDA Hardiness Zone 5.

'Thornless Boysen' Trailing; very similar to 'Boysen' except thornless; USDA Hardiness Zone 7.

'Triple Crown' Semi-erect; fruit is very large with excellent flavor; ripens late season; productive and somewhat disease resistant; widely adapted; less cold hardy than 'Chester'; USDA Hardiness Zone 5.

Blueberry

Lowbush blueberry: *Vaccinium angustifolium*
Highbush blueberry: *V. corymbosum*
Rabbiteye blueberry: *V. asheii*

GROWTH HABIT
Lowbush blueberry: spreading, suckering shrub that grows up to 18 inches tall; highbush blueberry: suckering shrub that grows to 7 feet tall; rabbiteye blueberry: suckering shrub that grows to 15 feet tall

POLLINATION NEEDS
Partially self-fertile so cross-pollination increases yield and size of fruit

LIGHT REQUIREMENT
Full sunlight

CLIMATE
Lowbush blueberry: USDA Hardiness Zones 3–7; AHS Heat Zones 8–1
Highbush blueberry: USDA Hardiness Zones 4–7; AHS Heat Zones 7–1
Rabbiteye blueberry: USDA Hardiness Zones 7–9; AHS Heat Zones 9–2

REGIONS
Can be grown free of pest problems in yards almost everywhere

I contend that anyone who has a patch of sunny ground and doesn't grow blueberries is being foolish. Blueberries are easy to grow and the plants are attractive year-round. Spring brings clusters of dainty, white, bell-shaped flowers. All summer long the leaves stay a healthy, slightly bluish color and then, in autumn, fire up into crimsons and yellows. Winter cold brings a reddish hue to the leafless stems. And with all this, you also get a healthful fruit, richer than most other foods in antioxidants, which protect against inflammation and are thought to be a leading factor in healthful aging.

The best reason to grow blueberries is because they taste so good. By planting a number of different varieties, you can conceivably eat fresh blueberries from the end of June to early September and freeze the surplus. I have 16 bushes that yield about 180 quarts of blueberries each year, half of which goes into the freezer.

Although wild blueberries have been harvested for centuries, this native fruit has been planted and cultivated only since the beginning of the 20th century. Three species of blueberry are grown for their fruits. Most common, and mostly what you see fresh on grocers' shelves, are highbush blueberries (*V. corymbosum*), native to the East Coast and parts of Michigan. There are northern and southern types of highbush blueberries. The southern types are able to awaken after winter with fewer hours of chilling. The Southeast is home to the second species, rabbiteye blueberries (*V. asheii*), whose fruits are smaller, darker, and have tougher skins than highbush blueberries. Rabbiteye plants tolerate hotter weather and drier soils than the other two species. The third species, lowbush blueberries (*V. angustifolium*), grows wild on rocky hillsides in the Northeast. The plants spread underground to form a solid mat of stems, each rising less than 18 inches high. The berries, which turn up on market shelves in cans and are usually destined for pies, are sweet and often pale blue, with a

TOP: Lowbush blueberries bear fruits on low, spreading plants.

BOTTOM: With white, bell-shaped blossoms in spring, a spreading growth habit, and crimson leaves in autumn, a lowbush blueberry is perfect for luscious landscaping.

powdery "bloom." You can also grow lowbush blueberries as ornamental, edible groundcover. I grow them in a bed along the front and side of my home.

Highbush and lowbush blueberries have been hybridized to produce medium-size plants, called "half-highs," which are cold hardy and produce tasty fruits. Half-highs generally do not spread underground like lowbush blueberries.

Grow It Naturally

- Make sure soil is very acidic (pH 4 to 5), well drained, moist, and high in organic matter.
- Fertilize and prune annually.
- Mulch in late autumn.

Growing

Blueberries are easy to grow as long as their rather special needs are met. Sunlight, for one, is extremely important, despite the fact that in the wild they commonly grow in the dappled shade of forests. The plants fruit best in full sunlight as long as the soil has sufficient moisture.

Blueberries are also finicky about their soil needs, which are quite different from those of most other cultivated plants. If you grow rhododendrons or azaleas successfully, you can do the same with blueberries; all of these plants are in the same botanical family and have similar soil requirements. And even if you don't grow rhododendrons or azaleas successfully, you can grow blueberries successfully by following a simple prescription for getting their soil right.

Blueberries thrive in soils that are very acidic, well drained, moist, infertile (yes, you read that right), and high in organic matter. If soil drainage is poor, grow the plants in raised beds or on wide, raised mounds. Test the pH before you plant, and if it's not in the blueberry-friendly range of 4 to 5, add sulfur, a naturally occurring mineral. In sandy soils, add ¾ pound of sulfur per 100 square feet for each pH unit the soil is above 4.5. Use three times this amount of sulfur for heavier soils. Pelletized sulfur, which resembles small, yellow lentils, is easier to spread and cheaper than sulfur powder. Mix sulfur in with the soil in the planting hole when you plant and spread it on top of the soil beyond the planting hole as far as the expected spread of the roots.

Key ingredients to a good start for blueberries are peat moss in the planting hole, sulfur if soil is insufficiently acidic, and mulch.

PLANTING AND WATERING

Now you're ready to plant. Mix a generous bucketful of peat moss with the soil in each hole before planting. Add a 3-inch depth of mulch, made up of wood shavings, pine needles, leaves, or other organic material, to the ground after planting. Do not use compost, as it is too rich in nutrients for blueberries. Water immediately after planting and as often as needed to keep the soil

Pruning a Highbush Blueberry

1. Before pruning, this mature highbush blueberry bush has stems of various ages, some too old for best fruit production.

2. Begin reducing the number of older stems.

3. Continue to remove old wood and also reduce number of youngest shoots.

moist. In fact, keep the soil moist for the first few years after planting. I use drip irrigation (p. 34), but if you water by hand, figure on about 1 gallon to 3 gallons per plant per week, according to plant size.

MAINTENANCE

Annual maintenance includes replenishing the organic mulch, adding sulfur as necessary, fertilizing, and pruning. As the older mulch decomposes, the bottom layer will enrich the soil with organic matter as well as protect the very shallow roots of blueberries from the heat of the summer sun and weed competition. Check the pH of your soil every few years (p. 21). The youngest leaves of the plant starting to yellow (with veins being the last to yellow) is a more direct, if belated, sign that the soil needs sulfur. Fertilize lightly with a fertilizer suitable for acid-loving plants. I use soybean meal at the rate of about 1 pound per 100 square feet, which I apply, along with the mulch and, if needed, sulfur, each autumn after blueberry leaves fall.

If your soil is very alkaline, don't try to acidify it. Instead, dig out a 2-foot-deep by 6-foot-wide hole and replace it with a mixture of equal parts peat moss and either sand or perlite. If your water is alkaline, a fertilizer injector could be used to add vinegar into the water, or you can just compensate for the alkalinity by adding sulfur to the soil annually.

Pruning

After four years, highbush blueberries need annual dormant pruning to keep them productive and prevent them from growing too tall. Flower buds form along stems that grew the previous season, and each bud opens to about a half dozen flowers. The best and biggest berries are borne on stems that grow off of wood that is younger than 6 years old; the bases of such stems are typically about an inch in diameter.

Because blueberries bear fruit on stems that grew the previous year, sufficient new growth is needed for a bountiful harvest. My bushes, which have borne heavily and reliably for more than 2 decades, produce a couple of feet of new growth each year.

4. Cut any drooping stem back to a vigorous side branch.

5. Pruned, this bush has been reduced to a few each of older, younger, and middle-age stems.

Begin pruning highbush blueberries by cutting away the oldest wood (wood that is at least 6 years old or is thicker than 1 inch at its base). Cut it right to ground level or to a low, vigorous, upward-pointing branch. Also cut away any stems that appear diseased or dead or rub up against other stems. Finally, shorten thin and twiggy stems that droop to the ground and thin out growth in the center of the bush. Some varieties bear too heavily. Slightly shorten stems that have many plump fruit buds near their ends so that only about five remain on each stem. Doing all of this results in larger berries, especially for varieties that naturally bear small fruit.

Prune rabbiteye blueberries the same way as described for highbush blueberries, but less severely. Prune lowbush blueberries by clipping or mowing all stems right to the ground every second or third year in winter. The plants do not bear fruits the season after pruning. To maintain a crop of lowbush blueberries year after year, mow a different half of the bed every second year, or a different third of the bed every third year.

Pests and Diseases

Birds are the major pest problem of blueberries, and the only reliable protection against birds is netting. The ideal is a walk-in cage, either temporary or permanent, erected over the entire planted area. Blueberries are pretty plants so consider giving them a pretty cage, and

A blueberry "gazebo," netted top and sides, makes harvesting easy while keeping out birds.

begin by not calling it a cage. A fruit salon? A fruitery? A blueberry gazebo?

Blueberries usually have few or no other pest problems. Occasionally, though, blueberry maggots—small, white wormlike insects—turn up in the fruits. Thorough harvest of all sound and infested fruits helps thwart this pest, as does a thick mulch, renewed yearly. Red spheres coated with sticky Tangle-Trap placed among the bushes just before the first berries ripen also control Ms. Maggot looking for a fruit on which to lay eggs. Hang one trap for every 30 square feet of planting.

Mummy berry is a disease that causes fruits to fall before they ripen, or to turn reddish, then tan, and shrivel into hard mummies on the plant. Picking off all fruits, good and bad, throughout and right to the end of the season, helps control this disease, as does the annual renewal of mulch, which buries infected fruits you miss. 'Bluetta', 'Burlington', 'Darrow', 'Dixie', 'Jersey', and 'Rubel' are resistant to mummy berry.

Brown or gray mold on the fruits or leaves is a sign of botrytis blight, a disease most prevalent in cool, wet weather. Avoid botrytis blight by disposing of dead twigs and rotted fruits, pruning to keep the bush open to the drying effects of air and sun, and being careful not to overstimulate growth with fertilizer.

Every autumn, long after harvest and after leaves and any old or pest-ridden berries have dropped to the ground, I spread soybean meal and a 2-inch to 3-inch blanket of wood shavings, wood chips, pine needles, autumn leaves, or sawdust beneath my 16 blueberry bushes. This mulch should keep pests from emerging each spring to bother my bushes. The bushes have never had any pest problems worth noting.

Harvesting

Blueberries are not at their best until they turn blue and even then are not fully ripe. The berries need to hang for a few more days to achieve full flavor. The way to get only the ripe and blue blueberries off the plant is to tickle the clusters of fruit. Only the ripe ones will drop into your hand. Some varieties need more tickling than others to harvest.

Lowbush blueberries are sometimes harvested with a more brute force method. A blueberry rake, which looks like a large comb attached to the business end of a dustpan, is combed through the plants, plucking off the berries. Once leaves, bits of stem, and green berries are cleaned off, you're left with blue blueberries.

Selection of Plants and Varieties

NORTHERN HIGHBUSH

'Berkeley' Berries are medium large, light blue, and of good quality; vigorous, upright bush with inconsistent productivity; fruit tends to drop if harvest is delayed; ripens midseason.

'Bluechip' Berries are large with excellent flavor; vigorous, upright bush; disease resistant; ripens midseason.

'Bluecrop' Berries are large and very light blue with good flavor; upright, moderately vigorous bush is productive and somewhat drought resistant; berries sometimes drop when ripe; ripens midseason.

'Blueray' Berries are large with very good flavor; upright bush bears consistently; flowers are rosy pink when beginning to open; ripens early midseason.

'Duke' Berries are medium with excellent quality; very productive; one of the earliest northern highbush varieties to ripen.

'Earliblue' Berries are medium to large with good flavor; bush is upright with red canes and early blossoms; ripens early.

'Elliot' Berries have good flavor if you make sure to let them hang long enough; bush is productive and upright; one of the latest ripening northern highbush varieties.

'Jersey' Berries have excellent flavor, even if they are small to medium; bush is upright and has good fall color; ripens over a long period, from mid- to late season.

'Wolcott' Berries are dark blue and of good quality; hang in loose clusters; plants are upright and productive; ripens early and over a short period of time.

SOUTHERN HIGHBUSH

'Cape Fear' Large, very light blue berries have excellent flavor and hang very well on plant (do not let hang too long or off-flavors develop); bush is vigorous and productive; requires 500 to 600 chilling hours.

'Emerald' Large, high-quality berries; vigorous, upright, productive bush; berries are large and have good flavor; ripen midseason; requires 250 chilling hours.

'Millennia' Berries are large and dark blue, with good flavor if not borne too heavily; prune heavily to prevent overbearing, especially with young plants; ripens early.

'Misty' Large, light blue berries with excellent flavor, stores well; bush is tall and upright and tends to overbear and weaken the plant, so prune heavily to remove excess flower buds and flowers from very young plants; ripens early to midseason; requires 200 chilling hours.

'Sharpblue' Berries are medium, dark color, and good quality; productive; ripens early; requires 150 chilling hours.

RABBITEYE

'Beckyblue' Fruits are medium, with good flavor; plant is tall and spreading; needs cross-pollination.

'Climax' Berries large with good flavor; bush is 6 feet to 10 feet tall and productive; ripens late; requires 250 chilling hours.

'Prince' Medium fruits with excellent flavor; upright, productive plants grow to 6 feet tall, blooms early; ripens early along with midseason southern highbush types.

'Tifblue' Berries are large and light blue, with good flavor; bush is vigorous, very productive, and among the more cold hardy rabbiteye varieties; ripens late season; requires 600 chilling hours.

'Woodard' Berries are large, light blue, and very high quality; bush is moderately vigorous; ripens midseason.

LOWBUSH

Although there are a few varieties of lowbush blueberry, mostly only seedlings are available. Even commercial growers rely mostly on wild plants.

'Brunswick' Berries about ½ inch with excellent flavor; plants grow about 1 foot tall, production erratic; berries hidden by foliage; concentrated ripening season.

'Chignecto' Berries have excellent flavor and are held above foliage; bush moderately productive, vigorous plants; ripen over a long period.

'Cumberland' Very good flavor; grow to be 10 inches tall.

HALF-HIGH

'Chippewa' Berries are medium to large and very sweet; bush grows to 3 feet tall and is very hardy; ripens early.

'Friendship' Berries are small and deep blue with a good "wild berry" flavor; bush grows to 4 feet tall; ripens early.

'Northblue' Berries are large and dark blue, slightly tart but with good flavor; bush grows to 2 feet tall, not spreading underground; ripens early to midseason.

'Northsky' Berries are small and sky blue in color, with good flavor; bush grows 10 inches to 20 inches tall.

Cherry

Sweet cherry: *Prunus avium*
Tart cherry: *P. cerasus*
Nanking cherry: *P. tomentosa*
Cornelian cherry: *Cornus mas*

GROWTH HABIT

Sweet and tart cherries: range from small to large trees, depending on variety and rootstock; Nanking cherries: large, rounded shrubs, 8 feet tall and wide; cornelian cherries: small to medium single or multitrunked trees

POLLINATION NEEDS

Sweet cherries: most varieties need cross-pollination, and varieties must be compatible to cross-pollinate; tart cherries: self fruitful; Nanking cherries: require cross-pollination and no varieties are available so plant two or more seedlings; cornelian cherries: partially self-fruitful so bear better with cross-pollination

LIGHT REQUIREMENT

Full sunlight

CLIMATE

Sweet cherry: USDA Hardiness Zones 5–9; AHS Heat Zones 8–1
Tart cherry: USDA Hardiness Zones 3–8; AHS Heat Zones 8–1
Nanking cherry: USDA Hardiness Zones 3–6; AHS Heat Zones 7–1
Cornelian cherry: USDA Hardiness Zones 4–8; AHS Heat Zones 8–4

REGIONS

The best areas for sweet cherries are dryish regions without extremes of summer or winter temperatures; tart cherries and especially Nanking cherries and cornelian cherries are widely adapted

Take your pick: Do you want sweet cherries to pluck right from the tree and eat fresh, or do you want tart cherries for piping hot cherry pie? Perhaps you want to have your pie and eat it, too. Cherries offer a spectrum of flavors, from sweet to tart, and everything in between. For example, duke cherries, although less commonly available from nurseries, are natural hybrids of sweet and tart cherries, combining their qualities. Don't discount tart cherries for fresh eating; some varieties are tasty right off the tree, and you may enjoy tart—even very tart—fresh fruit.

And there are even more cherries to choose from. Nanking cherry, a bush native to the hills of Manchuria, is very cold hardy, very tolerant of drought and heat, and very easy to grow. The plants flower and fruit profusely, so they make great ornamental edibles. The fruits are small but sweet-tart and tasty right off the bush. Cornelian cherry is actually a dogwood relative usually grown as an ornamental for its very early yellow blossoms, red fruits, attractive mottled bark, and pretty form. It reliably pumps out large crops every summer. The fruits are extremely tart and are good, easier-to-grow substitutes for true tart cherries in pies and jams.

Taste is not the only difference among these cherries. Sweet cherry is the most difficult to grow because it prefers winters that are not too cold, springs free of late frosts, and summers that are not too hot. And one other thing, please: no rain as fruits begin to ripen. All other types of cherries are much more cosmopolitan and grow and fruit well over a wide range of growing conditions.

In addition to considering whether you want to grow sweet and/or tart cherries, consider the eventual size of the tree. Although sweet cherries do grow into large trees, dwarf rootstocks are becoming available and some varieties, such as 'Compact Stella' sweet cherry and 'Northstar' tart cherry, are naturally dwarf. The standard rootstocks for cherry trees, some of which can grow as tall as 30 feet, are called mazzard (a seedling sweet cherry) and mahaleb (*P. mahaleb*). Two dwarfing rootstocks are 'Colt', resulting in a half-size tree, and 'Gisela 5', resulting in a tree only about 10 feet tall. 'Colt' is not very cold hardy and suffers in dry soil. Trees bear quickly and heavily on 'Gisela 5', but they need to be staked throughout their lifetime.

Growing

Especially with sweet cherries, because of their strict preferences in climate, choose your site and tree with care. Good soil drainage and full sunlight are must-haves. Choose a variety adapted to your region. Dwarfing rootstocks, such as 'Gisela 5', coax a tree into bearing at a young age. Be careful with very productive varieties on such rootstocks that the trees do not over-crop when young and get stunted.

Most sweet cherry varieties need cross-pollination, but not all varieties are compatible, so check nursery catalogs to make sure the varieties that you want can pollinate each other.

Pruning

Different species of cherries differ in their growth habits. Train a sweet cherry tree to either a central-leader or modified-central-leader shape (pp. 40–41). Prevent overcropping of productive varieties on dwarfing rootstocks that bear at a young age by heading (see p. 37) new shoots by one quarter each year; this delays bearing by eliminating many of the fruiting spurs that form toward the end of young stems. The spreading habit of a tart cherry tree makes it a natural for open-center form. Nanking and cornelian cherry demand little or no pruning beyond occasional heading cuts for invigoration and occasional thinning cuts to let in light and air.

Once trained and beginning to bear fruit, both sweet cherry and tart cherry trees need only light annual pruning. Both trees bear fruit on young wood and on spurs of older wood, so prune to stimulate just a little new growth. Where winters are frigid, lighter pruning favors flower buds borne on spurs, which survive cold better than those borne on young stems. Spurs on sweet cherries are productive for a decade, whereas those on tart cherries are productive for only three to five years.

Grow It Naturally

- If planting sweet cherries, choose adapted varieties and a site with well-drained soil and an absence of late spring frosts.

- Nanking and cornelian cherries are easiest to grow and most reliable.

Invigorate growth by pruning, as necessary, as spurs on older wood age. Your combined pruning and fertilization efforts should result in about 18 inches of new shoot growth each season.

Fruits cracking as they ripen can be a problem with sweet cherries, less so with tart cherries. Water on the skin is absorbed and causes the fruits to swell and burst. Varieties differ in their susceptibility and the tendency sometimes decreases as a tree grows older.

Pests and Diseases

Sweet and tart cherries are susceptible to a host of pests and diseases. Nanking and cornelian cherries aren't particularly bothered by any of these pests.

BIRDS

Birds are the primary pest problem of cherries, especially sweet cherries. Netting a tree is the only sure way to keep birds at bay, but this is not feasible for a large tree. A less effective alternative is to bother the birds by draping a tree with black cotton thread. Toss a spool back and forth among the branches while holding onto the free end of the thread as it unrolls from the spool. Yellow varieties are less attractive to birds than are red varieties. Nanking and cornelian cherries bear so heavily that there are enough cherries for us and our avian neighbors.

PLUM CURCULIO

Crescent-shaped scars on young fruits, commonly causing them to drop, indicate the work of plum curculio, an insect pest prevalent east of the Rocky Mountains. This pest does her dirty work between bloom time and the following 6 weeks. Spraying Surround would keep her at bay, but removing the white residue (even though it's nontoxic) from fruits would be bothersome. Letting chickens run under trees helps. Or use the traditional control of jarring the tree every morning for that time period and collecting and disposing of the fallen curculios, playing dead, on a sheet.

CHERRY FRUIT FLY

If you find small, white wormlike invaders in your cherries, they are larvae of the cherry fruit fly. Trap flies on balls or pieces of plywood painted bright red or yellow and coated with Tangle-Trap sticky coating, although such traps are more useful for monitoring than for controlling this pest. Ammonium carbonate sprinkled on the traps makes them more effective. Thorough harvest and cleanup of fruits may reduce damage, a job with which poultry, once again, can happily assist. Entrust also controls this fly.

CHERRY LEAFSPOT DISEASE

Rainy spring weather can bring on cherry leafspot disease, symptoms of which are purple spots on the upper surfaces of the leaves. Because the disease overwinters in old leaves, rake them up in autumn to remove sources of infection. Resistance to this disease is found in tart cherry varieties such as 'North Star' and 'Meteor' and sweet cherry varieties such as 'Hedelfingen' and 'Ulster'.

BROWN ROT DISEASE

Wet spring weather also creates favorable conditions for brown rot disease, which turns cherries into fuzzy, gray balls. The disease overwinters on dried up mummies, so dispose of them to reduce the source of infection. Plants are most susceptible to infection during bloom and just before fruits begin to ripen, especially if the fruits have been damaged (by plum curculio, for example). Dormant heading of shoots on very productive varieties makes for less tight clusters of fruit that dry out more readily and hence are less susceptible to disease. Sulfur sprays also are effective.

POWDERY MILDEW DISEASE

Dry weather can bring on powdery mildew disease, the sign of which is a powdery white coating that covers the leaves. As the disease worsens, leaves also become twisted. Sulfur or bicarbonate sprays help control powdery mildew.

BACTERIAL CANKER DISEASE

Cool, wet weather during bloom provides perfect conditions for bacterial canker disease. The bacteria invade frosted blossoms and wounds, including pruning wounds. Look for dark, sunken, elliptical lesions that may exude a smelly, reddish gum. Prune before buds swell in spring so wounds heal before the bacteria become active, sterilize pruning tools between cuts, and avoid bending branches during tree training. Early season copper sprays also keep this problem in check.

Selection of Plants and Varieties

SWEET CHERRIES

'Attika' Fruits are dark red, very firm, and large, with excellent flavor; tree bears at a young age; very productive; a good choice for eastern United States; somewhat resistant to cracking, canker, and powdery mildew; late bloom, late ripening.

'Bing' Common in markets, the fruits are large, firm, meaty, sweet with excellent flavor; tree is not hardy and not suited for eastern United States; fruits tend to crack and susceptible to leaf spot, powdery mildew, and canker; midseason bloom, midseason ripening.

'Black Tartarian' Fruits are almost black, medium, quick to soften, and very juicy when ripe; good flavor; tree is productive; susceptible to canker and cracking, but resists powdery mildew; early bloom, early ripening.

'Compact Stella' Fruits are medium-large, dark red, firm, with good flavor; tree is semi-dwarf and only moderately hardy; reliably productive; a compact form of the variety 'Stella'; self-fertile.

'Hedelfingen' Medium, dark fruit colors before fully ripe, excellent flavor; bears at a young age and is productive; susceptible to canker, somewhat susceptible to cracking, somewhat resistant to leaf spot; midseason bloom, midseason ripening.

'Hudson' Fruit is dark, medium, and very firm, with very good flavor; hardy and productive, a good choice in eastern United States; resistant to cracking and canker, susceptible to leaf spot; late bloom, late ripening.

'Lapins' Fruits are large, with excellent flavor; tree is not very hardy; very productive so needs branch heading to prevent tight fruit clusters; resistant to cracking and powdery mildew, susceptible to canker; self-fertile; early bloom, late ripening.

'Rainier' Fruits are yellow with a blush, firm, large, and very sweet, with excellent flavor; tree is hardy, bears at a young age, and is productive, but not a good choice for eastern United States; tends to crack and susceptible to leaf spot, somewhat resistant to powdery mildew and canker; early bloom, midseason ripening.

'Regina' Fruits are medium-large with very good flavor; precocious and moderately productive, a good choice for eastern United States; resistant to cracking and moderately resistant to powdery mildew and canker; late bloom, very late ripening.

'Stella' Fruit is large, very dark, good quality; productive but not very cold hardy; somewhat susceptible to cracking and canker; self-fruitful and good pollenizer for other varieties; midseason ripening.

'Sweetheart' Fruits are medium, bright red, and very firm, with good flavor; tree is not very hardy; bears fruit at a young age and productive, so shoots need branch heading to prevent tight fruit clusters; susceptible to cracking, canker, and powdery mildew; self-fertile; early bloom, very late ripening.

'Ulster' Fruits are large and dark red, with good flavor; tree is productive, a good choice for eastern United States; some resistance to cracking, canker, and leaf spot; midseason bloom, ripens mid- to late season.

'Van' Fruit is large, very firm, and dark, with good flavor; tree is precocious and very productive, needing annual heading to prevent tight clusters of fruit; resistant to cracking and powdery mildew but susceptible to cherry leaf spot and canker; early bloom, mid-season ripening.

'White Gold' Fruits are yellow with a red blush, medium, with good flavor; tree is very productive, a good variety for eastern United States; some resistance to cracking, canker, and leaf spot; self-fertile; blossoms late, ripens midseason.

TART CHERRIES

'Balaton' Fruits are deep red, firm, and sweeter than most tart cherries, with yellow flesh; tree is vigorous and very productive and bears at a young age; susceptible to leaf spot and brown rot, resistant to canker; early bloom, late ripening.

'English Morello' An old variety whose fruits are dark red with sprightly, aromatic flavor when fully ripe, yellow fleshed, excellent for pies; small, hardy tree with drooping shoots; ripens very late season.

'Kansas Sweet' Duke type; fruits are medium-large, bright red, juicy, and semisweet; tree is upright growing; widely adapted even to warmer zones.

'Meteor' Fruits are bright red and large with red flesh; tree is very cold hardy, small, grows to 10 feet tall, bears at a young age and is productive; some resistance to leaf spot, canker, and brown rot; late bloom, late ripening.

'Montmorency' Fruits are bright red and firm with yellow flesh and have tangy flavor; medium-large tree is productive and widely adapted; susceptible to leaf spot and brown rot, some resistance to canker; early bloom, midseason ripening.

'North Star' Fruits are small and bright mahogany red with spicy, concentrated flavor, hang well when ripe, yellow flesh; very hardy; small tree, grows a maximum of 7 feet tall; productive and bears at a young age; resists leaf spot but is susceptible to canker and brown rot; midseason bloom, midseason ripening.

NANKING CHERRIES

No varieties of Nanking cherries are available, only seedlings, each of which differs from the next to some degree in fruit flavor and color, plant size, and other characteristics.

CORNELIAN CHERRIES

'Black Plum' Very dark red, medium fruits with good, fresh flavor somewhat akin to that of (guess what?) black plums.

'Elegant' Bright red, long, pear-shaped fruits ripen early and are good for fresh eating.

'Pioneer' Dark red, pear-shaped fruits grow up to 1½ inches long and ripen early.

'Red Star' Dark red, oval fruits are 1¼ inches long and ripen late; have a sweet-tart flavor.

'Siretski' Cylindrical, bright red fruits have a sweet-tart flavor.

'Vavilov' Large, oblong fruits have a deep red color and sweet-tart flavor.

'Yellow' Yellow fruits are 1 inch long with sweet-tart flavor.

Citrus

Sweet orange: *Citrus sinensis*
Mandarin: *C. reticulata*
Grapefruit: *C. paradisi*
Lemon: *C. limon*
Lime: *C. aurantifolia*
Kumquat: *Fortunella japonica*

GROWTH HABIT

Shrubs to medium to large trees
Mandarin: 10 feet to 20 feet
Sweet orange: 12 feet to 20 feet
Grapefruit: 15 feet to 20 feet
Lemon: 10 feet to 20 feet
Kumquat: 8 feet to 15 feet
Lime: 15 feet to 20 feet

POLLINATION NEEDS

Mostly self-fertile; in some cases cross-pollination
is necessary or increases yields

LIGHT REQUIREMENT

Full sunlight; some midday shade needed in hot,
desert locations

CLIMATE

Generally, fruits are adapted to USDA Hardiness
Zones 9–10; AHS Heat Zones 9–2. Quite a bit of
variation exists among kinds and varieties; fruit,
especially unripe fruit, is damaged at temperatures
3°F to 4°F above the temperature that damages the
tree itself; approximate low-temperature limits for
plants acclimated to cold are as follows:
Kumquat: 17°F
Mandarin: 23°F
Orange: 24°F
Grapefruit: 24°F
Lemon: 27°F
Lime: 28°F

REGIONS

Relatively easy to grow where winter and summer
temperatures suit the needs of a particular variety;
good in pots in cold regions if moved indoors to a
sunny window or greenhouse for winter

Citrus (and, closely related, kumquat) fruits come in an amazing array of shapes, sizes, and flavors. Flavors are, of course, the main draw for home-grown fruits, and those of citrus range from honey sweet 'Murcott' tangors to puckery 'Bearss' limes, with a whole range of sweetnesses, acidities, and citrus essences in between. Yet this whole group of plants offers much more than just rich flavors. The evergreen trees are ornamental in their own right, and when a tree blooms it fills the air with a heady, sweet aroma. Lest anyone believe the listings that follow encompass the whole world of citrus, more species and kinds exist—too many to mention here. Those interested in broadening their citrus horizons might also want to consider pummelo, citron, sour orange, and many more hybrids among the various *Citrus* species, as well as *Fortunella*.

Citrus are fruits of warm climates. Even within that broad sweep of "warm climates," fruit production and flavor show strong influences of regional and local variations in temperatures and humidity. Generally, and perhaps obviously, a warmer climate will advance bloom and fruit maturity compared to a cooler climate. Generally, and perhaps less obviously, fruits ripening in warmer or more humid regions will have thinner rinds and larger size. Warmer weather during ripening also

Blood oranges have a rich, berrylike flavor.

makes for sweeter flavor. (Sweeter is not always better; in some cases, it reads in your mouth as less rich, or blander.)

The effect of temperature on flesh color is not so straightforward. The red in blood oranges, from anthocyanins (antioxidant pigments), is most intense with only moderate warmth. Heat, on the other hand, brings out the red, from lycopene, another antioxidant pigment, in red grapefruits.

Growing

Like most cultivated plants, citrus thrive best in soils that are moist but not waterlogged. Too dry a soil results in fruit drop and, if conditions worsen, leaf drop. Saline soils also are not to their liking.

Young trees are more susceptible to cold than are mature trees, so make some effort to protect a young'un through its adolescence. When the tree is quite small, you might be able to just throw a blanket over it when potentially damaging cold threatens. It's important, at least, to protect the graft so that if dieback occurs, new sprouts will still be of the desired variety (the portion above the graft union) rather than of the rootstock variety or seedling. Protect the graft by mounding up well-draining soil above the graft union for the coldest part of winter if there's any chance of cold damage. Trunk wraps also provide a bit of protection. If cold kills back a portion of a young or older plant, cut back those damaged portions in late winter, just after growth resumes.

Grow It Naturally

- Plant in well-drained soil to avoid root diseases.

- Keep base of trunk dry by not mulching within 1 foot of the trunk, by sloping ground to keep water away from the trunk, and by not wetting the trunk when using sprinklers.

- Be certain to plant at the correct depth, with trunk no deeper than it was in the nursery or pot.

- In arid regions, paint the trunk of a new tree white to avoid sunburn.

- Ignore diseases or pests that are only skin deep on fruit.

With choice of kinds and varieties, you can have citrus fruits ripening in your yard year-round.

Citrus grow in flushes—that is, bursts of growth—throughout the year, with the largest flush usually in spring. Flowering mostly occurs in spring, the flowers developing where leaves meet stems of a previous flush. However, there are exceptions: kumquats flower in summer and in warmer climates; lemons and limes flower and fruit year-round.

Pruning

Most citrus need little pruning beyond what is necessary to keep the fruit within reach and the plant within bounds. Lemon trees need more severe pruning than other citrus because they can grow to be very large. The best time to prune citrus is in spring, just before the plant blossoms. Occasionally thin out branches to let light and air into the tree canopy so fruiting is more uniform throughout and diseases and insects cannot fester. Pruning trees that tend to alternate bearing more heavily in their "on" year helps even out the feast or famine cycle.

Hedging is another way to keep a tree in bounds and create a different, decorative appearance. Use a hedge shears to shape the plant to the desired form and size. Hedging can be done at various times of the year but sacrifices the fewest fruits if done after harvest but before bloom.

Don't panic if you see a moderate amount of leaf or fruit drop. Even evergreen leaves on citrus drop, mostly in spring, when they are 2 years to 3 years old. Like most other fruit plants, citrus plants typically set more fruit than they can ripen, so they shed a few after fruit set occurs.

Dramatic pruning, called skeletonizing, rejuvenates an old tree that is overgrown and is bearing and growing poorly. This pruning is self-descriptive: Cut growth off and back until what remains is just a simple, low skeleton of branches. The newly bared bark is apt to sunburn, so paint it with a 50–50 mix of white latex paint and water to reflect the sun's rays. Only healthy trees tolerate skeletonizing, which is best done in early spring. Skeletonizing sacrifices the crop for a couple of years.

GROWING CITRUS IN COLD CLIMATES

Cold-climate gardeners can be thankful that citrus plants grow and fruit well in pots. Use a standard potting soil and repot the plants every couple of years, cutting back roots when you do so to allow room for new soil to replace nutrient-depleted soil around the roots. Prune to keep plant size proportional to pot size; ideally, the plant should be about three times the height of the pot. Water regularly, fertilize as needed, and bring indoors for the winter to a sunny window, preferably in a cool room, to give the plants a rest and promote stocky growth. In winter, leaves may yellow in between their veins, an indication of iron deficiency. Usually, these symptoms are not caused by insufficient amounts of iron in the soil but by insufficient root function in cool soil. Symptoms usually clear with warm weather. If not, try acidifying the soil with sulfur to make iron more available, or add iron fertilizer.

Kumquats, 'Calamondin', 'Satsuma' mandarin, and 'Improved Meyer' and 'Ponderosa' lemons are among the best fruits to grow in pots. 'Flying Dragon' is a dwarfing rootstock that can help keep any citrus pot-size.

Pests and Diseases

Citrus plants are not particularly pest prone. Still, aphids, mealybugs, mites, and scale sometimes attack. (See Chapter 4 for more information on these pests.)

The few diseases that sometimes cause problems are related, in large part, to water. Too much water at a plant's feet causes foot rot. Plant in well-drained soil, don't pile mulch up against the base of the trunk, avoid accidentally wounding the plant, and prune for good air circulation.

Moisture up in the tree canopy promotes a few other diseases. Good air circulation and sun go far in limiting greasy spot (looks like, as you guessed, greasy spots), melanose (raised, brown lesions, sometimes in streaked pattern on fruits), and scab (dark rash or worts) diseases. Also avoid watering with a sprinkler. Raking up and disposing of fallen leaves limits the spread of greasy spot and scab. Removing scabby leaves from stems, especially if present on new plants, helps control scab right from the get go. Removing dead twigs and branches eliminates sources of melanose infection. If necessary, use copper sprays for scab, and copper or summer oil sprays to control greasy spot. Melanose is mostly a cosmetic problem, so another control option is to do nothing.

Harvesting

There's only one way to tell whether citrus fruits are ripe, and that is to taste them. Don't go by skin color alone, because some citrus turn color before they are actually ripe and, under certain conditions, fruits might turn green again on the tree after they have turned ripe color. Harvest by clipping off fruit, or by turning the fruit on an angle to its twig and giving it a sharp jerk. Never try to pull fruits straight off the plant, especially if you'd like to store them, because that will leave a hole in the fruit and an invitation for disease.

Acidic fruits, such as lemons, are exceptions to the harvesting by taste rule. Pick these fruits as soon as they are sufficiently large and juicy.

Except for mandarins, ripe citrus fruits store well right on the tree, some kinds and varieties better than others. Or you can pick and store them in the refrigerator. Depending on the kind of fruit, they'll keep well in the refrigerator for a few weeks (grapefruit and mandarin, for instance) to a few months (navel orange, for instance).

Pummelo

Pummelo is a citrus that resembles a grapefruit that's been pumped up to as large as a volleyball, given a very thick skin, and a dryish pulp. Why would anyone grow or eat such a fruit? Because the pulp has a mildly sweet, delectable floral flavor. 'Chandler' is a pink-fleshed variety that was developed at the University of California. The trees grow fairly large and thrive in much the same conditions as grapefruit.

Lurking within the thick skin of this pummelo is a sweet flesh with a fragrant, flowery aroma.

Selection of Plants and Varieties

Citrus varieties are usually propagated by being grafted onto rootstocks (see p. 32), which are often chosen to impart a specific quality to the resulting tree. The fruit is unaffected: a 'Navel' orange will look and taste like a 'Navel' orange on any rootstock. 'Flying Dragon' is a variety of the citrus relative *Poncirus trifoliata* that, when used as a rootstock, makes a dwarf tree that is typically only one quarter the size of a full-size tree. 'Troyer' citrange is a rootstock resistant to root rot, *C. macrophylla* makes a plant adapted to saline soils, and *P. trifoliata* imparts cold hardiness.

The ripening dates for the following citrus varieties should not be considered writ in stone; they vary greatly with climate.

GRAPEFRUIT

In general, grapefruits require long, hot growing seasons for best flavor. Seedy varieties taste best. Fruits generally ripen from late fall through spring and remain in good condition on the tree for a long time.

'Duncan' An old variety with large, white-fleshed, very seedy fruit that is considered to have the best flavor of all grapefruits; tree is large and productive; fruit keeps well on tree.

'Melogold' Pummelo × grapefruit hybrid; seedless, very juicy, sweetish fruit that's easy to peel; needs less heat to advance bloom and fruit maturity than other varieties; large tree; does not keep well on tree.

'Oroblanco' Pummelo × grapefruit hybrid; fruit is medium to large, seedless, sweet, and very juicy; needs less heat than other

No need to harvest grapefruit as soon as it's ripe because it hangs on the tree good for eating for a long time.

varieties; tree is vigorous and large; productive; fruit does not keep well on tree; harvest when rind begins to turn yellow.

'Star Ruby' Fruit is seedless with intensely red flesh that has very good flavor; less acidic than other grapefruits; medium-size tree; erratic production; holds well on tree.

HARDY CITRUS

'Citrange' Sweet orange × *Poncirus trifoliata* hybrid; fruit tastes like a slightly tart sweet orange; ripens late fall; hardy to 5°F to 10°F.

'Ichang Papeda' ('Ichang Lemon') Fruit looks like a lemon with big seeds; can be grown as a shrub or small tree; ripens early fall; cold hardy to below 0°F.

'Yuzu Ichandarin' Natural mandarin hybrid; yellow fruit has large seeds and a mild, sweet, complex lemony flavor; ripens fall to winter; cold hardy to about 0°F.

KUMQUATS AND THEIR HYBRIDS

Kumquats do best in regions with warm to hot summers and chilly autumn nights. One reason for their cold-hardiness is that they don't begin growing until warm weather has settled in, blooming in midsummer.

'Eustis' Limequat (Mexican lime × kumquat); fruit is light yellow when ripe, has an edible rind, and flesh like a lime; tree is attractive, with few thorns; ripens mostly fall to spring; holds well on tree.

'Meiwa' kumquat has sweet, edible skin enveloping a mild flesh.

'Maruma' Fruit is small and round with tart flesh and a thin, sweet peel.

'Meiwa' Similar to 'Maruma' with tarter flesh and sweeter peel, less seedy; tree is small to medium, almost thornless.

'Nagami' Fruit is small, oval, and slightly seedy with a sweet peel and rich, tart flesh; tree is small to medium.

'Nippon' Orangequat ('Meiwa' kumquat × 'Satsuma'); fruit is medium with a sweet rind and slightly tart flesh; small tree; ripens winter to spring; holds moderately long on tree.

LEMON

Included here are true lemons and a couple of lemon hybrids. True lemons are frost sensitive but tolerate cooler growing seasons better than other citrus. Because of potential disease problems, lemons are best suited to drier climates. In warmer climates, true lemons bloom and fruit year-round; in cooler climates, there are two harvest periods, one in fall and the other in late spring.

'Eureka' Fruit is juicy and very acidic, with few seeds; vigorous, thornless tree that can bear fruit year-round; frost sensitive; widely adapted; needs regular pruning; fruit borne mostly on the periphery of the tree.

'Improved Meyer' Lemon × sweet orange hybrid; fruit is aromatic and slightly sweet with excellent flavor and yellowish orange flesh; holds well on tree; tree is small to medium, thornless, productive, and blooms year-round; very ornamental, compact tree with new growth that is tinged purple; hardier than true lemons and tolerant of disease in humid climates.

'Lisbon' Fruit is juicy and very acidic, with few or no seeds; vigorous, dense tree; more adapted to heat and to cold than 'Eureka'; fruit borne mostly on inner branches.

'Ponderosa' Lemon × citron hybrid; fruit is humongous, 2 pounds each, seedy with thick skins; tree is dwarf, thorny, and sensitive to frost; widely adapted; holds well on tree.

LIME

Lime trees are more averse to cold weather than any other citrus.

'Bearss' (**'Persian'**, **'Tahiti'**) Fruit is small to medium, acidic, and juicy with few or no seeds; tree is attractive and has few thorns, grows 15 feet to 20 feet tall, tolerates lack of heat and some cold; holds poorly on tree; harvest when green or yellow.

'Mexican' (**'Key'**) Fruit is small, juicy, and acidic, with intense flavor; 15-foot-tall tree with small leaves and short thorns; sensitive to frost and needs plenty of heat in summer; fruit drops when ripe; harvest when green or yellow.

MANDARINS AND THEIR HYBRIDS

Mandarins are also called tangerines, although this term is sometimes confined to mandarins with red-orange peel. Most mandarins grow best in hot summer climates. Harvest most mandarins when ripe, otherwise the fruit will become dry and puffy. Some mandarins are always seedless, some have seeds only if pollinated, and some are almost always seedy.

'Calamondin' Mandarin × kumquat hybrid; fruit has sweet, edible skin and very tart flesh; small, very cold hardy tree that bears year-round where winters are mild; very productive.

TOP: Enjoy the pleasing flavor contrast from 'Nagami' kumquats' sweet skin and tart flesh.

BOTTOM: 'Improved Meyer' is a hybrid of lemon and sweet orange that results in a sweet lemon.

TOP: Easy peeling and sweet flesh make 'Clementine' mandarins a perfect snack food.

BOTTOM: 'Murcott' is a mandarin with a honey-sweet flavor.

TOP: Navel oranges are excellent for fresh eating, and 'Washington' is one of the best.

BOTTOM: 'Satsuma' mandarins are among the most cold hardy of citrus, the trees tolerating temperatures below 20° F.

'Changsha' Fruit is brilliant orange-red, small to medium, and seedy, with good flavor; very cold hardy tree bears early and is true from seed (doesn't need to be grafted); ripe in late fall.

'Clementine' Fruit is sweet, very juicy, and variably seedy, fragrant, and easy to peel; small to medium tree with weeping habit; better crop with pollinator; holds well on tree; ripens early fall to winter. 'Clementine' is actually not one variety, but a group of varieties that includes the varieties 'Fina', 'Marisol', 'Esbal', 'Oroval', and 'Clemenules'. Fruit quality is best with hot, dry summers and cool winters.

'Dancy' Fruit is small to medium and seedy, with rich flavor, somewhat tart; tree is medium-large with few thorns; needs heat and tends to alternate bearing; ripens early winter to early spring but fruit does not keep well on tree.

'Honey' Seedy and juicy fruit with very sweet flavor; very productive; tree is medium-large and tends to alternate bearing; ripens in late winter; sometimes sold as 'Murcott', which it is not.

'Minneola' Tangelo (mandarin × grapefruit hybrid); fruit is bright orange-red and has a "neck"; rich, tart flavor, too tart if grown without sufficient heat; pollination increases fruit size, production, and seediness; ripens early winter to late spring; holds well on tree.

'Murcott' Tangor (mandarin × sweet orange hybrid); very seedy and very sweet fruit, with thin peel; tree alternates bearing, limbs weighted down with fruit in bearing years often break if not supported; ripens winter to spring and holds well on tree.

'Satsuma' Fruit has mild, sweet, flavor with low acidity; easy to peel, bumpy rind; small to medium tree is very cold hardy (tree to 18°F); ripens in late fall but does not keep well on tree. 'Satsuma' represents a group of mandarins, including the varieties 'Owari', 'Okitsu Wase', and 'Dobashi Beni'.

'Minneola' tangelo has a characteristic "neck" and bright orange-red skin that encloses flesh having a brisk flavor.

'Temple' Tangor (mandarin × sweet orange hybrid); fruit is sweet to tart and seedy; tree needs heat for best flavor and is sensitive to cold, more so than orange or mandarin; ripens early winter to early spring.

SWEET ORANGE

Sweet oranges are divided into three groups: navel oranges, common oranges, and blood oranges. A navel orange has a small, secondary fruit—a navel—at its blossom end. These oranges have a rich, sweet flavor and are easy to peel, but the juice turns bitter. Warm summers with cool nights bring out the best flavor in the fruits. Common oranges are juicier and seedy, and are hard to peel. Their juice retains its good flavor. Blood oranges are named for their reddish flesh and juice, the color depending on the variety, where it's grown, and even its location in the tree. Best color develops with hot, dry summers and cool winters. Even when color is subdued, the fruits develop their rich, sprightly, berrylike flavor.

'Cara Cara' Navel orange; a sport of 'Washington Navel' with excellent berrylike flavor, a beautiful crimson flesh, and a small navel.

'Hamlin' Common orange; almost seedless, low-acidity fruit; good for juice; medium to large tree, widely adapted; ripens fall through midwinter, and keeps well on the tree; cold hardy.

'Moro' Blood orange; dark red pulp with rich flavor, almost seedless; medium-size tree that's very attractive, with fruits mostly on outside of canopy; holds fairly well on tree but eventually develops a musky flavor; ripens early winter through spring.

'Pineapple' Common orange; fruit is seedy with rich flavor, excellent for juice; medium to large, thornless tree is productive and tends to alternate bearing; ripens early winter; drops fruit after ripening.

'Tarocco' Blood orange; juicy fruit with flavor that hints of raspberry; medium-size tree fruits within canopy; has few seeds and is easy to peel; holds poorly on tree; thorny and slow to begin bearing; ripens in winter.

'Valencia' Common orange; fruit is usually sweet and very juicy and holds well on tree (although skin may turn green again); widely adapted, large tree tends to alternate bearing; few seeds; ripens midwinter through summer.

'Washington Navel' This is the original and considered to be the best-tasting navel; seedless and easy to peel; medium-size tree with drooping branches; tends to drop fruit in hot, dry regions; ripens fall through winter.

Currant

Red, white, and pink currants: *Ribes petraeum*, *R. rubrum*, and *R. sativum*
Black currant: *R. nigrum*
Clove currant: *R. odoratum*

GROWTH HABIT
All currants send up new sprouts, called suckers, each year from ground level to create mounded shrubs 3 feet to 5 feet tall and wide. Clove currant: more sprawling than the others; its stems arch to the ground and also sprout from far-reaching, underground runners

POLLINATION NEEDS
Red, pink, and white, and most black currants are self-fruitful; clove currant may fruit better with cross-pollination

LIGHT REQUIREMENT
Full sunlight to shade, except for clove currant, which requires full sunlight

CLIMATE
Red, pink, and white currants: USDA Hardiness Zones 3–7; AHS Heat Zones 7–2
Black currants: USDA Hardiness Zones 3–7; AHS Heat Zones 7–2
Clove currants: USDA Hardiness Zones 4–8; AHS Heat Zones 9–3

REGIONS
All currants are widely adapted within specified climate zones, generally with few notable pest problems

A 19th-century horticulturalist wrote, "The currant takes the same place among fruits that the mule occupies among draught animals—being modest in its demands as to feed, shelter, and care, yet doing good service." Mules are hardly with us these days, but currants are, or should be.

Red, pink, and white currants are different colors of the same fruit, all dangling ripe from stems like short strings of translucent jewels, light shining right through them revealing their small seeds seemingly floating within. Their flavor is tart, excellent for jellies and sauces that might accompany anything from peanut butter on bread to a roast duck. Some varieties, such as 'Red Lake', taste good fresh if allowed to hang longer to sweeten a bit.

Black currants are a whole different animal, with strong, resinous flavor reminiscent of smoothed gin mellowed with a splash of sweetness. They're not enjoyed by everyone. (Dried "black currants" are not, in fact, black currants, but dried 'Black Corinth' grapes, a name bastardized to "black currant.") Black currants are a favorite in jams, sauces, juice, and liqueur. They're also a nutritional powerhouse, oozing with vitamin C and other health-promoting factors.

Clove currants, sometimes called Crandall currants, have their own flavor: sweet-tart with fruitier notes. These are the largest currant fruits of all, plumping up to about ½ inch in diameter. An added attraction is their flowers, which are yellow, 2-inch-long trumpets that suffuse the yard with a delicious sweet and spicy aroma.

Growing

Except for clove currants, currants are bushes of strictly cooler climates, so plant them on a north slope or in shade, especially if your summers get very hot. Clove currants tolerate heat as well as cold, and bear best in full sunlight. Wherever you plant any type of currant, especially if in full sunlight, keep the ground beneath the bushes covered with a thick mulch of some organic material, such as straw or leaves. The plants appreciate the cool soil beneath the mulch, which also suppresses weeds and conserves soil moisture.

Grow currants either as individual bushes or as a continuous hedge. Space individual bushes 6 feet apart. To create a hedge, set plants 3 feet apart. Right after you plant a bush, cut back all but three stems to ground level to stimulate growth of new shoots.

Pruning

You will get the best production from a bush if you prune it every year. Maintain the bush form using renewal pruning. Cut away old wood at ground level and thin out

Clove currant is a tough plant that, in addition to tasty berries, bears exceptionally fragrant trumpets of yellow flowers in spring.

the newest growth to about six stems. Red, white, pink, and clove currants fruit mostly on 1-, 2-, and 3-year-old wood, so always remove wood older than 3 years. Black currants fruit mostly on one-year-old stems, so cut back any stem older than one year either to the ground or to a vigorous, low branch.

Red, pink, and white currants make decorative and edible espaliers that are easy to maintain. All that's needed is straightforward pruning twice each year. For the first pruning, in late spring or early summer, just before the berries start to change color, shorten all shoots growing off permanent arms or cordons to about 5 inches long. For the second pruning, which you do in winter while the plants are dormant, shorten these same shoots to about 1 inch long. The currant espaliers standing shoulder to shoulder on the fence of my vegetable garden each have a permanent framework of a 3-foot-tall T—a trunk and two permanent, horizontal arms—with fruiting shoots, which are the ones that get shortened each year, growing off the arms.

Red, pink, and white currants can also be trained as small trees, not only for beauty but also because certain pest or disease problems may be minimized. Once a single trunk has been developed, with competing branches that sprout along and at the base of the trunk cut away, prune back the top by a couple of inches to induce branching. Do this while the plant is dormant and at the height at which you want the tree's head to develop. Once branches have developed, use renewal pruning (see p. 46) as for a bush (this time a bush perched atop a 2-foot to 4-foot trunk). Stake the plant; it's not really cut out to be a tree.

Red currant espalier in bloom presents subtle beauty that foreshadows the more flamboyant show soon to follow.

Pests and Diseases

Currants usually can be grown without any attention to pest control; however, there are a few pests and diseases to note.

Powdery mildew is a fungal disease that puts a white coating on the new leaves of red or black currants. Plant mildew-resistant varieties such as 'Jonkheer van Tets', 'Minnesota 71', or 'Red Lake', or to combat the fungus, spray sulfur, soap, summer oil, or bicarbonate on your plant. Tree and espaliered currants may experience less mildew, because in these forms there is more distance between new leaves and fungal spores, some of which start the season on old leaves on the ground.

Some of the leaves on a red or white currant bush may turn reddish and puckery, indicating aphid attack. Aphids usually depart or die before causing excessive damage, so ignore their annual arrival and departure.

Borers are insects that may cause an occasional branch to wilt and die back. Cut any infested branch to below where the borer entered (indicated by a swelling), and destroy the branch.

White pine blister rust is a disease that requires two plants to complete its life cycle: a susceptible variety of currant (or gooseberry) and a white pine (or other five-needled pine). The disease causes only minor damage to currants but can kill pines. Red and white currants are not very susceptible to white pine blister rust. Black currants are very susceptible, except for a number of resistant varieties such as 'Consort' and 'Belaruskaja'.

Imported currantworm (currant sawfly) is a pest that quickly strips the foliage from the plant just as leaves open fully in spring, then comes back again to attack newly formed leaves at about the time the fruit is ripening in summer. Besides spraying with soap or Entrust, growing currants as small trees or espaliers might thwart currantworms, which start their feast low in the center of a bush.

Harvesting

No need to rush the harvest of red currants. Ripe berries will hang in good condition for weeks, looking pretty and getting better for fresh eating every day (up to a point, and then they start to shrivel). Harvest all other currants in a timelier manner, especially black currants, which wither and drop soon after ripening. Color, readiness to detach from the plant, and taste dictate when to harvest.

Red currant berries dangle decoratively for weeks from the arms of this espalier.

Selection of Plants and Varieties

CLOVE CURRANTS

'Crandall' The only variety of clove currant available. It is a seed-propagated variety, so not all plants are genetically identical. If they aren't, they can provide the pollen to other clove currant plants that is needed for better yields.

BLACK CURRANTS

'Belaruskaja' Excellent flavor; productive; resistant to rust.

'Ben Alder' Fruits are small, good for juice, and particularly high in vitamin C; resistant to powdery mildew but susceptible to rust; late flowering and ripening; high yields, although ripening fruit sometimes splits its thin skin.

'Ben Sarek' Large fruits; dwarf, productive, bushier variety that yields heavily; resistant to mildew and rust.

'Blackdown' Berries are large and firm, with very good flavor; bushy variety that is tall and wide and resistant to mildew; easy to pick.

'Boskoop': This old Dutch variety produces large, good-tasting fruit.

'Consort' Small fruit; productive; immune to white pine blister rust.

'Kirovchanka' Excellent flavor; compact bush that is moderately productive; resistant to rust.

'Minaj Smyrev' Large berries with excellent flavor; very cold resistant; rust-resistant bush.

'Titania' Large berries with excellent flavor; upright and very vigorous; productive; branches often break from snow or their heavy load of fruit; rust and mildew resistant.

PINK CURRANTS

'Champagne' ('Couleur de Chair' or 'Pink Champagne') This very old variety of currant yields berries with excellent flavor; berries do not keep well.

RED CURRANTS

'Jonkheer van Tets' Berries are very tart and large; productive, upright bush.

'Minnesota 71' Berries are large with good flavor; late ripening; upright and vigorous.

'Perfection' An old variety with large berries and good flavor; moderate vigor; productive; easy to harvest, pick as soon as fruit is ripe.

'Red Lake' Large berries with excellent flavor; upright, productive bush.

'Wilder' Large, flavorful berries; prune more severely than other varieties.

WHITE CURRANTS

'Primus' Creamy white berries have excellent fresh flavor; upright, productive, vigorous bush.

Elderberry

American elder: *Sambucus canadensis*
European (Black) elder: *Sambucus nigra*

GROWTH HABIT
American elder: Large, suckering shrub 6 feet to
10 feet tall and wide
European elder: Large, suckering shrub 10 feet to
20 feet tall and wide

POLLINATION NEEDS
Partially self-fruitful

LIGHT REQUIREMENT
Full sun or light shade

CLIMATE
American elder: USDA Hardiness Zones 2–9;
AHS Heat Zones 8–1
European elder: USDA Hardiness Zones 4–9;
AHS Heat Zones 8–1

REGIONS
No limitations within adapted climatic zones

American and European elderberries, sometimes listed as subspecies of the same species, grow wild over a wide range of both the New and the Old World. Likewise, they can be cultivated just about everywhere. The bushes are especially prominent in bloom, because it occurs after spring's first burst of floral exuberance from other plants has subsided. Their large, flat-topped clusters of creamy white flowers peek out along the borders of woodlands. Yours might also. The flowers have a distinctive, pleasant flavor.

It's not just pretty blossoms for which many people grow elderberries. A number of varieties have been selected for their very ornamental leaves. Some are lacy and green, some are black or yellow, some are two-colored, and some are lacy and black.

Elderberries ripen in late summer, bearing heavy clusters of usually purplish black fruits that weigh down stems as if they were begging to be harvested. In addition to figuring into tasty desserts and beverages, elderberry fruits and their extracts are said to be rich in medicinal properties.

Growing

Elderberries tolerate a wide range of soils as well as sites in full sunlight or partial shade. The bushes send up many suckers from ground level. Space plants 8 feet apart unless you want to grow elderberries as a hedge, in which case, space them about 4 feet apart. Suckers will eventually fill in the space between these close plants.

Pruning

For maximum productivity, prune elderberry bushes annually, in winter. Do this by cutting away the oldest wood at or near ground level to make room for new growth. Also thin out some suckers, saving those that are most vigorous.

Pests and Diseases

Birds may want to share some of the berries with you. Otherwise, elderberry is free from pests.

Harvesting

Harvest berries when they are fully colored and come easily off stems. Wait for the berries to ripen before picking and eating. Elderberries are somewhat toxic when unripe and may cause mild sickness if eaten before their prime. The harvest period lasts a week or two.

The berries lack acidity, so they are insipid and somewhat rank when fresh. Cooked with other ingredients added, though, they make delicious jam, jelly, pie, or juice. Cooking is also a good idea because it destroys any traces of toxin in the fruit. Drying also improves the flavor and diminishes any unhealthful components.

If you're willing to forgo some berries, harvest the blossoms. They can be used to make wine, fritters, and tea.

Selection of Plants and Varieties

AMERICAN ELDER

'Adams No. 2' Bears large clusters of large fruits; bush grows to 8 feet tall, very productive; cold hardy.

'Johns' Very large berries and berry clusters; very vigorous plant, grows up to 10 feet tall.

'Nova' Berries are large and sweet; plant is tall, moderately cold hardy, and very productive; use 'York' as a pollenizer; ripens before 'York.'

'Scotia' Especially good flavor.

'York' Largest of all elderberry fruits; very productive, large bush; late ripening.

EUROPEAN ELDER

'Black Lace' ('Eva') Leaves finely cut and dark purple, almost black; flowers pinkish; bush is compact, 6 feet to 8 feet tall and wide.

'Goldbeere' Yellow fruit.

'Guincho Purple' Leaves emerge purple, turn to green in summer, and then reds and purples in fall, although all this might vary depending on the environment; pinkish flowers.

'Haschberg' Large, juicy berries.

'Laciniata' An ornamental variety with deeply cut foliage, sometimes called fern-leaf elderberry.

'Thundercloud' Deep red to purple leaves; reddish pink flowers.

Fig

Ficus carica

GROWTH HABIT
Suckering, large shrub or small to medium-size tree (10 feet to 30 feet tall), depending on variety, climate, and training

POLLINATION NEEDS
Common-type figs are self-fertile; San Pedro types need pollination for their main crop, not for their breba crop; Smyrna types need pollination for both crops. Pollination, when needed, is from a caprifig, an inedible type of fig whose pollen is carried by a special wasp. Varieties offered to home gardeners are usually of the common type

LIGHT REQUIREMENT
Full sunlight

CLIMATE
USDA Hardiness Zones 8–11; AHS Heat Zones 12–1

REGIONS
Widely adapted, even in colder regions with some protection during winter

Figs have held allure for humans since almost the dawn of civilization. First mentioned in writing about 5,000 years ago in the Middle East, fig cultivation spread to China more than 1,000 years ago, then to Europe and on to the West Indies, Florida, and Peru by the 16th century, and then to my apartment in Wisconsin in the 1970s. I, along with many other people longing to enjoy the fresh fruit, contrived ways to coax figs to fruit in a climate far removed from their native, subtropical habitat. My fig plant grew in a 12-inch flowerpot.

Since then I have harvested figs in northern climates (I once had 35 varieties!) by growing them in large pots that basked in summer sun outdoors and wintered in a cool basement, by swaddling branches of outdoor plants to protect them from cold, and by planting them right in the ground in a minimally heated greenhouse. Depending on the degree of protection, the degree of cold, and the variety of fig, all these overwintering methods can be, and have been, successful because the plants are so accommodating. They don't mind having their roots hacked back periodically, which is good for a plant growing in a pot. Many varieties bear fruit—the so-called main crop—on new, growing shoots, which is good when cold kills back older shoots (that is, as long as the growing season is sufficiently long and dieback has not been excessive). Other varieties bear mostly a so-called breba crop earlier in the season toward the ends of year-old shoots.

Many varieties bear two crops each season, the early breba crop and a later main crop. Fruits of the breba and main crop might even taste and look different from each other. In the case of San Pedro–type varieties, the main crop needs pollination but the breba crop does not.

The fig fruit is, botanically, a synconium, essentially an inside-out stem with flowers on its inside and a small opening—its "eye"—at the far end. That doesn't sound very appealing, although the fruit is juicy and richly sweet, with a lot of character when fully ripe despite its lack of acidity. If you've only known figs in their dried form, you're in for a fresh treat. Still, it can't be only the delectable fruit flavor that has enticed humans to cultivate figs for so long in so many far reaches of the globe. Is it also the plant's large, variably lobed leaves? Its muscular stems with smooth, gray bark? Some primal connection to the distant past?

Growing

Conjure up an image in your mind of an Arabian courtyard or backyard and emulate that habitat in siting your fig, offering the plant abundant warmth and sunlight. Once established, plants can tolerate drought. Those Arabian soils are also lean in nutrients. Avoid excessive fertilization or the plant will put too much energy into growing stems and leaves rather than fruits.

That warm, sunny habitat is especially important when growing figs north of USDA Hardiness Zone 8. In these colder regions, you'll also have to make special accommodations for the plants to get through winter and take advantage of that summer heat and sun.

OVERWINTERING OUTDOOR FIGS

Where winters are cold enough to kill stems back to the ground but the growing season is long enough to ripen figs on new shoots, grow a variety that bears a good main crop. Protect stems when the plant drops its leaves, and if it's reluctant to do so, strip them off in mid to late fall. Shorten the stems to a manageable length; tie them together; and build a wire cage around them, into which you stuff dry leaves or wood shavings as insulation. Top with a waterproof covering. The crop will ripen as long as the stems don't die back or aren't shortened too much; 3 feet to 4 feet of older wood remaining should be sufficient and is a convenient height to cut stems back to before swaddling them. Uncover stems before any growth begins in late winter or early spring.

For even better protection against cold, slowly bend the plant to the ground in autumn, after all its leaves have fallen. Cutting the roots on the side opposite the direction you bend the plant makes bending easier, with little harm to the plant. Weigh the stems to the ground

Grow It Naturally

- In rainy or humid climates, or where dried fruit beetles abound, grow fig varieties with closed eyes.

- Enrich the soil with an abundance of organic materials.

- Generally, just enjoy the plants and fruits; natural growing is easy.

FIG | 121

with some rocks or cinder blocks, then cover them with some insulating material such as dry leaves or straw, a sheet of plastic to keep water off, and additional leaves or straw. The depth of cover needed depends on how cold temperatures become in winter. With enough cover and long enough stems left after fall pruning, the plants will even bear an early breba crop.

A trench into which the stems are lowered offers even more protection than merely laying them on the ground to be covered. Back in Wisconsin, I knew of an enormous fig tree that was lowered into a chest-deep trench late each fall, and then the trench was covered with old doors and topped with leaves. Pulleys lifted the big, old tree each spring, and it bore enormous crops each year.

With stems either on or near the ground, take precautions against rodents, which might find the cover cozy and the stems tasty. Setting traps or having outdoor cats are two obvious solutions to this problem. Again, uncover any protected stems before growth begins in late winter or early spring.

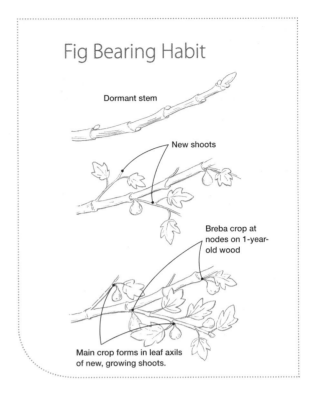

Fig Bearing Habit

Dormant stem

New shoots

Breba crop at nodes on 1-year-old wood

Main crop forms in leaf axils of new, growing shoots.

My Greenhouse Figs

Fig trees planted right in the ground integrate well with other plants in my cool (temperature) greenhouse. In winter, the greenhouse is minimally heated, just enough to keep temperatures above 37°F, which is fine for the lettuce, kale, chard, and other greenery that I grow then and fine for the figs, leafless and dormant, with their stems pruned back. As temperatures warm, with spring going into summer, the greenhouse becomes too hot for the cool-weather greens, but the figs love it. I prune branches in summer when they grow too close to the greenhouse roof, and lop them way back in mid to late fall after leaves drop and the figs have finished fruiting for the season. On varieties that bear a good breba crop, I'll leave a couple of stems long enough for a July harvest in addition to the later main crop.

OVERWINTERING POTTED FIGS

You can harvest a breba crop, a main crop, or both from a potted fig kept indoors during winter. An advantage of sacrificing the breba crop for only a main crop is that you can shorten branches in autumn, making it easier to move the plant through doorways or down a narrow basement stairway—in the case of my potted figs—to some protected area. Keep the plant dormant and leafless through winter by storing it in a cool spot, ideally between 30°F and 50°F, and keeping the soil on the dry side. As long as a plant is leafless, it does not need light.

Once your fig is full size, repot it every year or two in late fall or winter, cutting back its roots, then putting it back into the same pot.

Pruning

Outdoors in the ground, or seasonally indoors in a pot, train a fig either as a bush, with many stems, or as a tree with a single trunk. The bush form is more practical for an outdoor tree in regions where winter cold occasionally kills part or all of the plant back to ground level. Train trees to open-center form (see p. 40 for information on how to train fruit plants).

Figs fruit fairly well with little or no maintenance pruning, but pruning increases production. Prune varieties such as 'Adriatic', 'Alma', 'Brown Turkey', 'Celeste', 'Everbearing', 'Kadota', and 'Magnolia', which fruit mostly on new shoots of the current season (main crop), fairly severely to stimulate new fruit-bearing shoots each year. Thin out stems and cut most of the remaining ones back by three quarters or more. 'King', 'Mission', 'Tena', and 'Ventura' are examples of varieties that fruit on one-year-old stems and on new shoots (breba and main crop) and should not be pruned as severely. Do some thinning and shortening but leave enough stems intact for a good breba crop.

Pests and Diseases

Figs have few pest problems. Where nematodes are common, such as in sandy soils in the Southeast, plant figs near buildings so that their roots grow underneath and out of reach of the pests. Adding abundant organic matter to the soil and watering as needed also helps against nematodes.

Dried fruit beetles can infest fruits and cause them to sour. Where this is a problem, grow varieties, such as 'Eastern Brown Turkey' and 'Celeste', that have small eyes through which the beetles—and other insects—cannot enter.

Wet weather during ripening can be a problem with varieties that tend to split.

Harvesting

Figs do not ripen at all after being harvested, and they also don't travel or keep well, which is all the more reason to grow figs at home if you like them fresh. Wait to harvest until the fruit is fully colored, starting to soften, and beginning to droop. The fruits won't all be ripe at the same time but will individually ripen over a period of many weeks. A tear often wells up in the eye of a dead ripe fig.

If you're blessed with more ripe fruits than you can eat and share, dry them, can them, poach them in wine, or make a homemade version of Fig Newtons®.

Selection of Plants and Varieties

All varieties here are of the common type unless specified otherwise. There are hundreds of varieties of figs, many synonyms for names, and misnaming is rampant.

'Adriatic' Fruit is small to medium with greenish yellow skin and strawberry red pulp; very good flavor; grow mostly for main crop; adapted to cool, coastal areas.

'Brown Turkey' Two varieties parade under this name, one in the eastern United States and one in the western United States; both are brown with pink flesh; eastern 'Brown Turkey' is sometimes called 'Everbearing' or 'Texas Everbearing' and is a relatively cold hardy variety with delicious, small to medium fruit and a small eye; good for the Southeast. California 'Brown Turkey', not very cold hardy and with mediocre, large fruit is sometimes called 'San Piero'; 'Brown Turkey' of either stripe is grown mostly for its main crop.

'Calimyrna' ('Sari Lop') Smyrna type; excellent flavor but rarely grown in home settings because it needs pollination; large yellow fruit with amber pulp; large eye and tendency to split in wet weather; main crop only.

'Celeste' ('Malta') Fruit is small, very sweet, and light brown to violet in color; cold hardy; good variety for the Southeast; grow mostly for main crop but do not prune too heavily.

'Conadria' Pale green fruit with strawberry red flesh, good fresh and excellent dried; small eye; grow mostly for main crop; best in hot climates.

'Green Ischia' ('Verte') Small, green or purplish fruit with pink flesh and relatively closed eye; very good flavor; good breba and main crop; late ripening.

'Kadota' ('Dottato') Fruit is small to medium, a bright greenish yellow, and excellent fresh or canned; some breba crop, large main crop; usually pruned severely for main crop only; fruit has a large eye; needs abundant heat and dry weather.

'King' San Pedro type; fruit is medium with dark green skin, pink flesh, and excellent sweet flavor; adapted to cool, coastal climates; prune lightly.

'LSU Gold' Large yellow fruit blushed with strawberry red; excellent flavor; large eye makes fruit susceptible to spoilage during wet weather; cold resistant.

'LSU Purple' Fruit is medium size with glossy skin varying from reddish to dark purple, depending on light exposure and ripeness; skin checks when ripe, exposing white flesh beneath; light strawberry red flesh with mild, sweet flavor; light breba crop and heavy, long ripening main crop; purple stems; nematode resistant.

'Magnolia' ('Brunswick') Fruit is medium size and has bronze skin and light amber pulp, with large eye and tendency to split; good flavor; grown mostly for main crop.

'Mission' ('Black Mission') Fruits have purple-black skin with amber flesh, those of the breba crop being larger than those of the main crop; small eye and little tendency to split; some breba crop, abundant main crop.

FIG | 123

Gooseberry

Ribes hirtellum, R. uva-crispa

GROWTH HABIT
Suckering, mounded shrubs 3 feet to 5 feet tall and wide

POLLINATION NEEDS
Self-fertile

LIGHT REQUIREMENT
Full sunlight to part shade

CLIMATE
USDA Hardiness Zones 3–7; AHS Heat Zones 7–2

REGIONS
Widely adapted within specified climate zones, generally with few notable pest problems

Gooseberries are a versatile fruit, delicious cooked and fresh. So-called dessert varieties of gooseberry are sweet, and comparable in flavor, depending on the variety, to grapes, apricots, or plums, and culinary varieties make excellent jams and pies (not that the distinction between culinary and dessert varieties is clear-cut).

So why don't most Americans know or appreciate this fruit? Because gooseberry was implicated in the spread of blister rust disease, a malady that attacks and kills white pine trees, an important timber crop. As a result, the planting of gooseberries (and currants) was prohibited by federal law from the early 1900s until 1966. The ban was ineffective because wild types of these fruits abet the spread of disease, because disease spores could travel hundreds of miles under ideal conditions, and because *cultivated* gooseberries are not very susceptible to rust and thus contributed little to disease spread. Still, after being closeted for two generations, gooseberries went off of most Americans' radar.

Not so in northern Europe, where the berry has been appreciated for hundreds of years. That appreciation spurred efforts of both amateur and professional breeders, so that now there are hundreds of gooseberry varieties. Fortunately, gooseberries have staged a comeback on this side of the Atlantic. Seek out the better-tasting varieties and you won't be disappointed.

Gooseberry plants are usually thorny bushes, some upright, some sprawling, depending on variety. Unfortunately, the very best tasting varieties are bushes with the most intimidating thorns. Gooseberries begin ripening soon after the last junebearing strawberries finish ripening

Grow It Naturally

- Do not overfertilize with nitrogen-rich materials or plants will be more susceptible to mildew.

- Unless you're willing to spray (even non-toxic) fungicides or live where powdery mildew is not a big threat, grow mildew-resistant varieties such as 'Poorman', 'Hinnonmakis Yellow', and 'Captivator'.

- Mulch.

TOP: Before pruning, a gooseberry bush has too many old stems and too many new stems.

BOTTOM: After being pruned, this gooseberry bush has just a few each of 1-, 2-, and 3-year-old stems, none of them drooping to the ground.

Growing

Gooseberries are plants of northern climates, tolerating cold winters and enjoying cool summers. If possible, and especially in hot summer areas, plant the bushes on a cool northern slope or in shade. (They are one of the few fruiting plants that grow and bear well without full sunlight.) After planting, blanket the ground with a mulch of leaves, straw, or other organic material to keep the soil cool, moist, and weed free. Renew as necessary.

Pruning

Gooseberries fruit on wood that is 1 year to 3 years old. Prune your bush each winter to leave about a half dozen each of 1-, 2-, and 3-year-old shoots. Cut away, at ground level, any shoots that are more than three years old and thin out one-year-old shoots so that only six of the sturdiest and most upright ones remain. You can tell the age of the wood because it becomes darker and peels with time. Also shorten any stems that arch to the ground.

Gooseberries can also be trained as small trees or espaliers in the same manner as currants, described on p. 116.

Lee's Picks

Gooseberries are among my favorite fruits, and my favorite gooseberries are some of the European varieties, such as 'Achilles' and 'Whitesmith'. These varieties are, unfortunately, very disease susceptible, so I mostly grow my almost-favorites, including 'Poorman', 'Captivator', and 'Hinnonmakis Yellow', which taste very, very good and are disease resistant. One variety not worth growing at all, in my opinion, is 'Pixwell'; among its deficiencies is bad flavor.

Pests and Diseases

A white, powdery coating on young leaves and fruits is a sign of powdery mildew disease, to which some of the best-tasting gooseberry varieties are susceptible. Repeated sprays of sulfur, soap, bicarbonate, or oil helps keep it under control. An even easier way to combat the disease is to plant mildew-resistant varieties, such as 'Poorman', 'Glendale', 'Hinnonmakis Yellow', and 'Black Velvet', all of which also taste very good.

Leaf spot diseases cause gooseberry leaves to develop dark blemishes, then to yellow and drop. Although diseased bushes become unsightly, they usually continue to bear reliable crops. If severe, spray with copper.

Two insects occasionally make an appearance: gooseberry fruitworm, which bores into the fruit, causing it to color prematurely, and imported currantworm, which strips the leaves from the plant just after they unfold. Both pests are easily controlled by sprays applied as soon as you notice damage. Bt sprays are effective against the fruitworms. Insecticidal soap, sprayed right into the center of the bush as soon as new leaves begin to vanish in spring, does in the currantworm. Training gooseberries as small trees (as described for currants) might thwart imported currantworms because they begin their feeding frenzy on leaves down in the center of the bushes and "tree" gooseberries don't have any leaves down there.

Harvesting

Gooseberries cook into delicious jams, pies, sauces, and fools, and for all such purposes should be harvested slightly underripe. For fresh eating, let berries achieve full color and sweetness before picking. When tickled, the ripe berries will drop off the stems into your waiting hand. Some people consider gooseberries at their best with the coolness of morning dew still on them; others prefer to harvest them later in the day, after they have been warmed by the sun.

Picking can be a thorny affair (except with the few thornless varieties). Avoid injury by lifting up a berry-laden branch with a gloved hand (a leather glove is best). Use your bare hand to strip off the berries.

Selection of Plants and Varieties

'Achilles' Among the tastiest and largest of dessert varieties; ripe fruits are red or green, depending on the climate; very susceptible to mildew.

'Black Velvet' Fruit is small and dark red, with very good, rich, wine-y flavor; lanky growth; resistant to mildew.

'Captivator' Fruits are small with a purplish pink skin and very good flavor; resistant to mildew and leaf spot disease and almost thornless.

'Glendale' Deep red, medium berries with very good flavor; resistant to mildew and leaf spots; vigorous bush.

'Hinnonmakis Yellow' Yellow fruits with sweet, delicious flavor that hints of apricot; resistant to powdery mildew.

'Jeanne' Fruits are round and dark red with excellent flavor; bush mostly upright with few thorns; productive; very resistant to powdery mildew; relatively late ripening.

'Lepaa Red' Small, red, somewhat tart fruits; very disease resistant.

'Pixwell' Commonly sold by nurseries, fruits are small, tough, and tart with poor flavor; few thorns; productive; disease resistant.

'Poorman' Fruits are medium, pear-shaped, and reddish, with a delicious, sweet flavor; upright growing and only moderately thorny; resistant to mildew.

'Red Jacket' ('Josselyn') A hybrid that is different from the European cultivar also named 'Red Jacket'; fruit is medium, red, and has very good flavor; resistant to mildew and leaf spots; ripens early season.

'Welcome' Fruits are small to medium and taste similar to the candy Sweet Tarts®; sprawling bush resistant to disease.

'Whitesmith' Fruits are medium-large with thin, pale green skins tinged with yellow; excellent, vinous flavor; bush is upright; very susceptible to mildew.

The tart fruits of 'Lepaa Red' gooseberry are best in jams, tarts, and other culinary delights.

Some gooseberry varieties are large, while others are small; some are red, while others are pale yellow or almost black; some are hairy, while some are smooth; and some are tart, while others are sweet.

Grape

Vinifera (European) grapes: *V. vinifera*
American grapes: hybrids including *Vitis labrusca*,
V. aestivalis, and other American species
Muscadine grapes: *Muscadiniana rotundifolia*
(*V. rotundifolia*)
French hybrid grapes: wine grapes from crosses of
American species and *V. vinifera*, developed begin-
ning in the latter half of the 19th century

GROWTH HABIT
Vine

POLLINATION NEEDS
Except for certain varieties of muscadine grape,
most cultivated grapes are self-fertile

LIGHT REQUIREMENT
Full sunlight

CLIMATE
Vinifera: USDA Hardiness Zones 7–10; AHS Heat
Zones 9–6, but variable, depending on variety.
American grapes: USDA Hardiness Zones 3–7;
AHS Heat Zones 9–2, but variable, depending on
variety.
Muscadine grapes: USDA Hardiness Zones 7–10;
AHS Heat Zones 11–6.
French Hybrids: USDA Hardiness Zones 5–9; AHS
Heat Zones variable, depending on variety.

REGIONS
With choice of appropriate varieties, grapes are
widely adapted

Humans have been enjoying grapes fresh, fermented, dried, and juiced for thousands of years and there are thousands of grape varieties, so just about everyone can grow them. What you need to do is to choose from varieties appropriate to your region and then plant the vines in average soil in full sunlight. Grapes are rather specific in their climatic requirements, but there are types and varieties adapted from the cold reaches of the upper Midwest, Canada, and New England to the sultry Southeast and the arid West.

Vinifera grapes are the grapes of antiquity, originating in eastern Europe and western Asia, and adapted to regions that have mild winters and hot, dry summers. Many vinifera varieties make excellent wine. Climates that do not get very hot in summer maintain acidity in vinifera grapes for the best wines. 'Thompson Seedless' is a familiar vinifera grape, with edible skin and sweet, crisp flesh. Many other vinifera varieties, including 'Thompson' and 'Black Monukka', dry to excellent raisins.

American grapes are adapted to withstand cold winters, humid summers, and indigenous pests found east of the Rockies, where these grapes are native. Some have slipskin—a thick skin that slides off a jelly-like flesh—and a very distinctive, strong, "foxy" flavor (see the sidebar at right), which is enjoyed by some and not by others, typified in the familiar variety 'Concord'. Some of the newer varieties have a meatier texture and a more delicate flavor. American grapes are used fresh, for juice, jam, and jelly and occasionally for wine. Some American varieties grow and bear in the southeastern United States, which has its own disease pressures.

Foxy Flavor

The distinctive, strong flavor of *Vitis labrusca* grapes has long been described as "foxy." The descriptor might have come about because of their musky aroma, reminiscent of foxes, or because foxes enjoy the fruits. The natural flavor compound methyl anthranilate is largely responsible for this foxy flavor. It is interesting that spraying methyl anthranilate on grapes repels birds.

Ephraim Bull grew 22,000 grape seedlings and in 1849 finally came up with a plant that became the familiar 'Concord' variety.

Grow It Naturally

- Clean up black rot mummies on the ground and on the plant in fall.

- Prune!

- Remove dead or infected wood.

- Select a site with plenty of sunlight and good air circulation.

- Choose varieties appropriate to your climate and pest pressures.

Muscadine grapes, which bear small clusters of large, musky, aromatic berries, are native to and ideally suited for the American southeast. Muscadines can also thrive in suitably warm areas of the west, where the weather is not too dry.

About the middle of the 19th century, American grape pests tagging along on American vines that had been brought to France virtually wiped out the grape industry there. French breeders immediately began hybridizing susceptible vinifera grapes with pest-resistant American varieties. The result: so-called French hybrid grapes, which combine the cold-hardiness and pest resistance of American grapes with the colors, flavors, and other characteristics of vinifera grapes that make superior wines. French hybrid varieties were first brought to America in the 1930s, which spurred more extensive growing and breeding of these types of grapes.

American grapes are adapted to the shortest growing season, with French hybrids, viniferas, and muscadines, in that order, requiring an increasingly long growing season.

My Grape Quest

In my yard in the Wallkill Valley, part of New York's Hudson Valley, with its limitations of cold and diseases, top picks for grapes to grow are 'Swenson Red', 'Brianna', 'Vanessa', 'Reliance', 'Edelweiss', and 'Mars'. But that's just me and that's just now; I've tasted or grown a smidgen from among the thousands of varieties of grapes, even the probably hundreds adapted to this little valley within a valley.

Grapes bear fruit on 1-year-old stems, identified by their smooth, tan bark; it's the horizontal stem in this example.

Growing

Success in grape growing can be summed up with two words: *heat* and *light*. (An exception is wine grapes, which produce better wines with cooler summer temperatures.) Provide a grapevine with a site that receives an abundance of both. Grapes have far-reaching roots, so the ideal site should also have deep, well-draining soil. Adjust planting distances according to the vigor of the varieties you plant.

One more term for success with growing grapes: *varietal selection*. Choose a variety adapted to your region.

Pruning

Wild, unpruned vines bear very sour fruits high in trees. To grow the best-tasting grapes and have them easily within reach, train your vines when they are young, and then prune them every year in late winter. Your grapes may bleed sap when you prune them, but bleeding is harmless to the plants.

Grapes bear fruit only on shoots growing off canes, which are stems that grew the previous year. The most fruitful canes are those that are about as thick as a pencil with 6 inches to 12 inches between buds (nodes). The goals of various methods of training and pruning grapes are the same: to leave a suitable number of canes, growing from the main trunk or permanent arms, for fruit the upcoming season; to provide buds that will grow into new, well-placed canes to be saved for fruiting the following season; and to create a form that allows for good light and air circulation.

Some common methods for training grapes are head training, the four-arm Kniffin system, and various cordon systems. Within some of these systems, vines may be either "cane pruned" or "spur pruned." With cane pruning, just a few long canes are left to bear fruit-bearing shoots for the upcoming season. With spur pruning, those fruit-bearing shoots arise from many short canes—each called a spur and only a few buds long—that are left after pruning. What is important is how many total buds are left on the pruned plant; that might be 10 buds on each of 4 long canes or 2 buds on each of 20 spurs. In either case, the crop has been similarly regulated for best quality. Leave 4 or 5 buds per spur on American-type grapes; 2 buds on vinifera varieties.

Cold-Climate Growing Strategies

Elmer Swenson, dairy farmer and amateur (in the original sense of the word, derived from *amor*, to love) grape breeder, has helped many of us in cold climates enjoy home-grown grapes. Working independently and with the University of Minnesota, he bred varieties adapted to the cold temperatures and short growing season of his farm in the upper reaches of Wisconsin. In addition to growing Elmer's very cold hardy varieties, such as 'Swenson Red', 'Edelweiss', 'Briana', and 'Somerset Seedless', attention to the vines and soil can help any variety, anywhere, live up to its cold-hardiness potential.

Soil is a good place to start. Good drainage is essential to cold-hardiness, as is good nutrition and adequate water. Best winter survival is associated with neither excessive nor feeble growth and general absence from stresses such as pests and diseases.

Pruning plays its part in winter survival. For maximum hardiness, prune after the coldest part of winter has past. Prune conventionally, but in two stages, a preliminary shortening followed by a final shortening later on as the weather warms. For the preliminary pruning, select canes to retain and leave 10 to 15 extra buds on each. This two-stage pruning delays budbreak from basal buds, which will bear fruit, so they are less apt to suffer from the vagaries of spring cold. Do the second stage of pruning just before growth begins. Cropping a vine too heavily sends it into winter in a weakened state, so use pruning—canes and bunches—to regulate production which is, of course, tied to a vine's vigor. The more vigor, the greater the crop that can be supported.

Consider protecting a vine by laying it down and burying it with soil or mulch to get it through winter's bitterest cold. For the J-system, plant the vine at an angle and pin the trunk to the ground. Develop a head of canes at the end of the trunk; each fall cane-prune the head and take the whole head off the bottom wire to lay on the ground for protection. For the spur-pruned rose system, head train the vine and spur-prune so that the entire vine can be covered with soil or mulch each fall for winter protection. With either system, uncover vines in late winter, before growth begins.

And finally, consider getting insurance on your vine by training it to multiple trunks, rather than a single trunk. Losing a trunk or two, then, doesn't set the whole plant back to ground level.

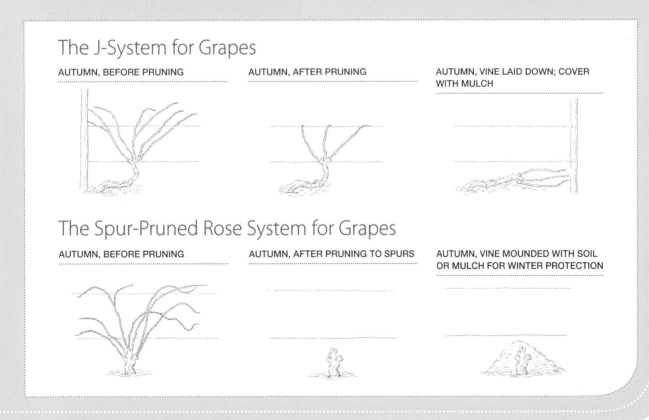

The J-System for Grapes

AUTUMN, BEFORE PRUNING

AUTUMN, AFTER PRUNING

AUTUMN, VINE LAID DOWN; COVER WITH MULCH

The Spur-Pruned Rose System for Grapes

AUTUMN, BEFORE PRUNING

AUTUMN, AFTER PRUNING TO SPURS

AUTUMN, VINE MOUNDED WITH SOIL OR MULCH FOR WINTER PROTECTION

Pruning a Newly Planted Grape Vine

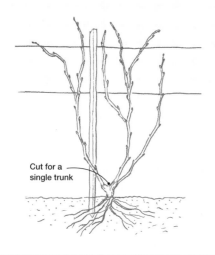

Cut for a
single trunk

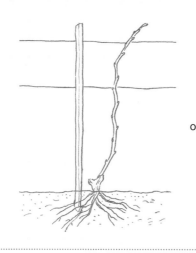

OR

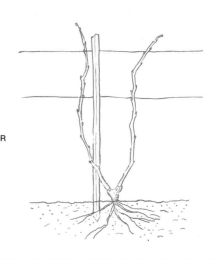

Grape Training, One Way

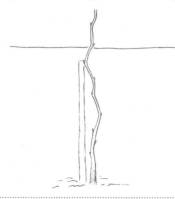

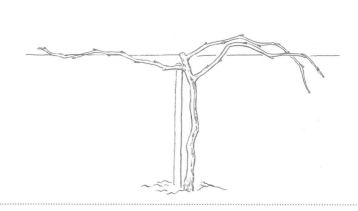

Head-Trained, Cane-Pruned Grape

BEFORE PRUNING

AFTER PRUNING

Head-Trained, Spur-Pruned Grape

BEFORE PRUNING

AFTER PRUNING

Pruning a Mature Grape Vine to the Four-Arm Kniffin System

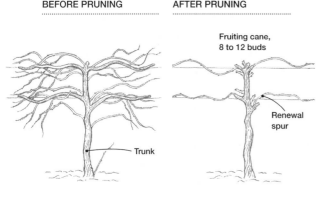

BEFORE PRUNING   **AFTER PRUNING**

Fruiting cane,
8 to 12 buds

Renewal
spur

Trunk

Spur-Pruning a High-Cordon Grape

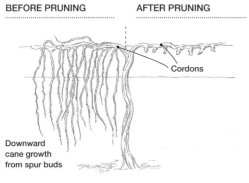

BEFORE PRUNING   **AFTER PRUNING**

Cordons

Downward
cane growth
from spur buds

Space spurs 6 inches to 12 inches apart.
Cut back spurs when they get old.

Pruning a Midwire-Cordon Grape

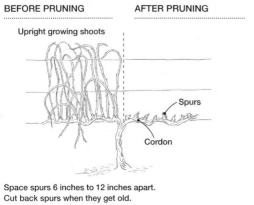

BEFORE PRUNING   **AFTER PRUNING**

Upright growing shoots

Spurs

Cordon

Space spurs 6 inches to 12 inches apart.
Cut back spurs when they get old.

Midwire cordon training lets grape vines bask in sunlight to yield high-quality fruit.

HEAD TRAINING

Head training is useful for varieties with upright growth habits and low vigor. Vigorous or droopy vines trained this way become a tangled mess by season's end. To grasp the idea of head training, picture a low tree with its branches cut almost all the way back every year.

Begin head training by coaxing a single shoot, which will become the permanent trunk of the vine, to grow up a stake about 5 feet high. Remove all other shoots. Cut off the tip of the shoot when it grows just above the top of the stake. Allow side buds along the upper third of the trunk to grow out into shoots to form a head. For vigorous or droopy varieties, each year, prune all canes growing from the head back to one to three buds, which are now "spurs." For nonvigorous varieties, cut back all but four canes (cane pruning) and shorten those canes to about 10 buds each—more if growth was vigorous the previous season, less if it was not. When pruning, either to canes or to spurs, occasionally cut some of the old canes back more drastically to keep fruiting spurs or young canes from originating too far out from the trunk. Also, thin spurs when they become too numerous and dense. Always remove any shoots growing low on the trunk.

THE FOUR-ARM KNIFFIN SYSTEM

The four-arm Kniffin system is useful for cane-pruning varieties that have a trailing habit, such as most American grapes. Build a trellis with two wires—one at 3 feet and one at 5 feet above ground level—strung between two sturdy endposts. (Use nylon monofilament or high-tensile, 9-gauge to 12-gauge steel wire.) Train your young vine to a single trunk up to the top wire. As it grows, select and train two shoots in opposite directions along the bottom wire, and when it reaches the top wire, cut it back and train another two shoots in opposite directions along that wire.

Annual pruning of grapes grown with the four-arm Kniffin system consists of four steps (see the drawings on p. 133). First, choose two pencil-thick canes growing in either direction along the top and the bottom wires and mark them with a ribbon so you do not accidentally cut them off. Second, select wood that you will save as four renewal spurs, two near each wire. Renewal spur wood can be any age, as long as it has two or three plump buds near its base to provide convenient growing-off points for new shoots that will become the following year's canes. Create renewal spurs by cutting back four stems originating near the trunk, two near the bottom wire and two near the top wire, to two buds each. For the third step, cut off all growth except the four canes, the four renewal spurs, and the trunk. And fourth, shorten the fruiting canes you saved to about 10 buds each, more if last year's growth was vigorous, less if it was weak.

CORDON TRAINING

Cordon training is useful for cane- or spur-pruning all kinds of grapes, including grapes on arbors, except where there is danger of freeze injury to the cordon. A cordon is a permanent, horizontal arm growing off the trunk, more usually two arms growing horizontally off the top of the trunk in opposite directions, or just a long, permanent extension of the trunk. Each year, cut all canes along a cordon back to a couple of buds—those canes are now called fruiting spurs—thinning out some fruiting spurs so none is closer than 6 inches to 12 inches apart along the length of the cordon. Periodically, cut a fruiting spur back into older wood closer to the cordon to keep it from, over time, originating farther and farther from the cordon. If a cordon gets injured or decrepit, cut it back and train a new one.

With high cordon training, the trunk rises to about 6 feet, off the top of which grow two cordons trained in opposite directions along a wire. This type of training is very useful for trailing and drooping varieties, such as American and most French hybrid varieties. New shoots droop downward and need to be periodically positioned, perhaps pruned, to avoid tangling and shading of bunches of grapes. Don't let those bunches hide beneath more than three or four layers of leaves. With midwire cordon

Bagging Grapes for Insect, Disease, and Bird Control

1. Snap off the tendril or leaf on the opposite side of the stem of the grape cluster to be bagged.

2. Slide a bag with both sides slit a few inches up around the cluster with either side of the stem sliding into the slits.

3. Fold the top of the bag over the stem and staple it on each side.

training, cordons are trained along a wire 3 feet high, and new shoots are trained upward by weaving them into three more rows of wires strung at intervals up to a total of 3 feet or 4 feet above the cordon wire. Midwire cordon training is useful for varieties, such as vinifera and some French hybrids, that have upright growth habits. Shoots need positioning as they reach the next wire up. Repeat positioning as growth continues.

Grape arbors are notorious for becoming tangled messes of low-quality, disease-ridden berries, a condition easily remedied by cordon-training arbored grapevines. Train a single shoot, which will become the trunk, up to the top of the arbor, then continue its growth—it's now a cordon—across the top. Canes grow off at approximate right angles to the cordon. Each year's pruning involves nothing more than shortening all canes to make fruiting spurs that are a couple of buds' length each and thinning out those spurs so they are 6 inches to 12 inches apart. Periodically cut some of the canes or spurs almost all the way back to the cordon so that, over time, fruiting spurs don't creep too far out from the cordon.

Cordon training is easy and makes for very tasty, highly colored berries and healthy vines. It's all about light and air. In addition to keeping your vine within bounds and opening it up to light and air, pruning also

Removing black, mummified grapes, evidence of black rot, is a natural way to help control this disease.

removes potential fruits. Some varieties benefit from further fruit thinning. Do this by removing whole bunches and, especially where bunches are tight, cutting off some clusters of fruit within or at the end of a bunch. Good light, good pruning, shoot positioning when necessary, bunch thinning, and, if necessary, cluster thinning result in the highest quality fruits, easily accessible, on healthy and cold-resistant vines.

4. No need to bag every bunch of grapes; leave bagged ones for later harvest because they stay in good condition longest.

Pests and Diseases

Diseases threaten grapes, but many problems can be avoided by growing varieties adapted to your region. Four of the most common diseases are: downy and powdery mildew, both of which result in white coatings on fruits and especially leaves; black rot, which starts as a pale brown circle on the fruit and eventually causes the whole fruit to shrivel and darken into a mummy; and botrytis bunch rot, which causes a fluffy, gray-brown coating on the fruit. Resistant varieties, good light, good air circulation, and, if needed, sprays can control these problems. Sulfur, bicarbonate, copper, or light oil sprays control the mildews. For black rot, religiously remove all mummies from the vines in the fall and, if necessary, spray with copper when new shoots are 6 inches long, just before bloom, and again just after bloom. Thinning out berries within a bunch helps avoid botrytis bunch rot.

In mild winter regions of North America, Pierce's disease, a bacterial disease spread by a group of insects called sharpshooter leafhoppers, can kill vines. Symptoms are leaves that start to dry out, beginning at their edges, in midsummer. Muscadine grapes are generally resistant to this disease; among other types of grapes, some varieties are resistant. Also control Pierce's disease by removing nearby plants, such as grassy weeds, wild grapes, blackberries, and stinging nettle, all of which harbor sharpshooter leafhoppers.

Insects sometimes cause their share of trouble. Phylloxera, an aphid-like insect, can kill susceptible vinifera vines by attacking roots. To counter phylloxera, plant resistant varieties or purchase varieties grafted on resistant rootstocks. Grape berry moth goes for the fruits. If you have an extensive enough planting, pheromone disruption can confuse males. Spraying Bt just before bloom

and a week after is also effective against grape berry moth. Japanese beetles are also fond of grapes, making lacework of their leaves. Neem is effective against grape berry moth and Japanese beetle. Surround is effective for Japanese beetles.

And then there are birds and bees and perhaps furry animals.

One way to avoid many or most problems on grape fruit, from insect and diseases to the birds and the bees, is to protect each bunch by sealing it within a bag (see the photos on pp. 134–135). Bagging also lets you leave bunches on the vine longer, to develop full flavor. I use small, white, paper bags, applying them early in the season. I first make a slit a few inches down on each open side of the bag, pull off the leaf or tendril on the opposite side of the stem from a nice bunch, and slide the bag up around the bunch, placing the stem down into the slits. To secure the bag, I fold its top down over the stem, and staple each side. It's really not that tedious, and the vines require little more from me until harvest time.

TIP

HARVESTING HARD-TO-REACH GRAPES

A very useful tool for getting at a hard to reach cluster of grapes, especially when bees also threaten, is a pick-and-hold flower pruner.

Harvesting

Grapes do not ripen after they're picked. The way to tell when grapes are ready for harvest is to look at them, for ripe color and to taste them for sweetness. I find that, with American grapes, at least, the whole bunch snaps easily from the stem when the berries are really, really ripe, which is how I like them.

Bagged grapes are the last to be harvested, and, at their best, they are the most delectable, perfect bunches imaginable. Sometimes a few bagged bunches will be hanging through heavy frosts, the berries on the leafless vines starting to shrivel. They're still quite tasty although not very pretty.

Muscadine berries ripen individually within small bunches, often dropping when ripe. One way to harvest in quantity is to shake the ripe ones down onto a cloth. Hand-picked fruits keep for several days after harvest if refrigerated.

A traditional way to keep grapes (besides making wine, jam, or juice out of them) is to cut perfect bunches with lengths of stems attached, and plunge the cut end of each stem into a narrow-necked bottle or vase full of water that's set on an angled shelf (to keep the bunches from leaning against the bottle) in a cool place.

This ARS pruner, designed to cut and hold flower stems, also does a good job reaching into a tangle of vines to cut and hold a bunch of grapes.

Selection of Plants and Varieties

Grapes are sometimes propagated by cuttings and sometimes by being grafted onto special rootstocks (see p. 32). These rootstocks confer resistance to problems from root pests (such as phylloxera or nematodes) or unsuitable soil (such as soil that's too alkaline) or may be used to increase the vigor of a weak-growing variety or vice versa. Rootstocks also have some influence on a vine's cold tolerance or ripening date. With that said, most grapevines sold for home planting are not grafted because of added expense, because the rootstock/scion combination is very specific to site conditions, and because most table grapes grow sufficiently well on their own roots.

What follows is a mere drop in the bucket from among the thousands of varieties of grapes.

VINIFERA GRAPES

'Black Monukka' Crisp, flavorful, sweet berries good for raisins and fresh, usually seedless; may crack with rain near harvest time so best in drier regions; midseason.

'Cabernet Sauvignon' Red wine grape, clusters small to medium, small berries; very seedy, tough skin, distinctive flavor; very vigorous and productive; ripens late midseason.

'Chardonnay' White wine grape; vine is vigorous and, for a vinifera, moderately cold hardy; very susceptible to botrytis; ripens early.

'Flame Seedless' Small, seedless, red fruits having crisp texture and excellent, tangy flavor; fruits are borne in long, loose clusters; good fresh and for raisins; vigorous and very productive; ripens early.

'Muscat of Alexandria' An old variety with large, loose clusters of dull green, large, juicy, berries having strong muscat flavor; use for wine, fresh, and raisins; moderately vigorous and very productive; medium vigor; good for hot regions but can sunburn in desert; ripens very late.

'Orange Muscat' White wine grape with strong muscat flavor and hints of citrus; susceptible to bunch rot and cracking; moderately vigorous and moderately productive.

'Perlette' Small to medium, seedless grape with crisp flesh, mildly aromatic flavor, and white, waxy skin; compact clusters need thinning; very productive; ripens very early.

'Redglobe' Red, seeded; very large, plum-size grape with crisp texture, mildly sweet and flavorful; ruby red skin; moderately vigorous; ripens late season.

'Sauvignon Blanc' White wine grape with small clusters of pale, yellow berries; vigorous; ripens early midseason.

'Thompson Seedless' Mild, very sweet flavor when home-grown and allowed to ripen thoroughly; good fresh and for raisins and wine; needs abundant heat; borne in very large clusters; very productive and vigorous; ripens midseason.

TOP: 'Alden' is a hardy grape with moderate disease resistance, a meaty texture, and very good flavor.

BOTTOM: Ripe 'Suffolk Red' grapes have a sweet, spicy flavor.

TOP: Large berry size, early harvest, and sweet flavor make 'Sugargate' an excellent muscadine grape to grow at home.

BOTTOM: 'Concord' is an archetypal American grape with a strong, foxy flavor.

AMERICAN GRAPES

'Alden' Large, dark, sweet berries with slight muscat flavor, little or no foxy flavor, excellent for fresh eating; firm, meaty texture; may crack with rain near harvest time; tends to overbear so prune and thin bunches aggressively; moderately cold hardy; moderately disease resistant; ripens early midseason.

'Black Spanish' ('Lenoir') Small, black-seeded grapes form moderately sized clusters; good fresh or processed; vine is vigorous and tolerant to many diseases, including Pierce's disease; black rot susceptible.

'Bluebell' Old variety with very good, foxy flavor for fresh eating, juice, or jelly; medium berries; similar to 'Concord' but has smaller, sweeter berries, better cold-hardiness, and is earlier ripening; makes an excellent, pink juice; very cold hardy; slight susceptibility to black rot, botrytis bunch rot, downy mildew, and powdery mildew; may crack from rainfall near harvest time; sensitive to alkaline soil; ripens early to midseason and holds well on the plant.

'Canadice' Small, seedless red fruits with foxy flavor and edible slipskin; clusters are large and tight; vine is moderately cold hardy; tends to overbear; ripens early.

'Concord' Blue-black fruits, slipskin, and foxy flavor; medium to large berries; vigorous; moderately cold hardy; highly susceptible to black rot and leaf spot; moderately susceptible to powdery mildew and slightly susceptible to botrytis bunch rot, downy mildew, and anthracnose; widely known and grown; ripens mid- to late season.

'Daytona' Berries are nonslipskin, red, and have excellent flavor; low yields; very good disease resistance, including to Pierce's disease; suitable for growing in the South.

'Edelweiss' Pale-gold berries with excellent, very sweet, and foxy flavor, too strong for some palates; grown for fresh eating and wine making; moderately susceptible to anthracnose, botrytis bunch rot, and powdery mildew, and slightly susceptible to downy mildew and black rot; cold hardy and extremely vigorous; ripens early.

'Jupiter' Berries are nonslipskin, large, blue, seedless, firm, and semicrisp; excellent sweet, mild muscat flavor; moderately cold hardy; highly susceptible to downy mildew and powdery mildew, moderately susceptible to black rot, and slightly susceptible to anthracnose and botrytis bunch rot; moderately vigorous; productive; ripens early to midseason.

'Lakemont' Small to medium, sweet, seedless fruits with yellowish green skins; mildly foxy; vine is productive and moderately hardy (more so than its sibling 'Interlaken Seedless', less so than its sibling 'Himrod'); susceptible to downy mildew and, with wet weather during harvest, fruit rotting; productive, needs thinning after fruit set; stores well; ripens early to midseason.

'Mars' Seedless, with a thick slipskin, under which is a sweet, juicy, melt-in-your-mouth flesh with foxy flavor; bunches hold well on the vine even when ripe; slightly susceptible to anthracnose, black rot, botrytis bunch rot, downy mildew, and powdery mildew; productive; thin clusters after bloom; vigorous; moderately cold hardy, ripens early midseason.

'Niagara' White grape sometimes called 'White Concord' and with fruit much like 'Concord' (one of its parents); medium to large berries with pale, yellowish green skin; the flesh is sweet right beneath the slipskin, tart farther in; very foxy flavor; very vigorous; moderately cold hardy; highly susceptible to black

'Lakemont' grape, seedless and mild-flavored, is a stand-in for 'Thompson Seedless'.

'Niagra' is very similar to 'Concord'—except that it is white.

rot and downy mildew, less so to powdery mildew and botrytis bunch rot; ripens mid- to late season, just before 'Concord'.

'Reliance' Seedless, pink fruit with tender skin and excellent, fruity, mildly foxy flavor; bunches hold well on vine; cold hardy; moderately resistant to mildew and black rot; ripens early midseason.

'Suffolk Red' Seedless, red berries borne in long, loose clusters; crisp flesh, with excellent spicy, sweet, mildly foxy flavor; very susceptible to downy mildew; moderately cold hardy; low productivity; ripens midseason.

'Swenson Red' Large, dark red to lavender berries have rich, fruity flavor with little foxy flavor; very sweet and nonslipskin; mostly grown for fresh eating but also good for wine making; highly susceptible to downy mildew, moderately susceptible to botrytis bunch rot and powdery mildew, and slightly susceptible to black rot; keeps well after picking; overly productive so prune stems and thin bunches aggressively; cold hardy; ripens midseason.

'Vanessa' Seedless, red grape with a thin skin, a firm, crisp flesh, and a mild, sweet flavor; highly susceptible to black rot, moderately susceptible to downy and powdery mildews, and slightly susceptible to botrytis bunch rot; moderately cold hardy; ripens early.

MUSCADINE GRAPES

'Carlos' Self-fruitful; medium, bronze fruit that is good fresh or in jelly, juice, or wine; vine is productive and disease resistant; high yield; vigorous, good cold tolerance.

'Hunt' Large, black fruits are very sweet.

'Jumbo' Large, purple fruits ripen over a period of several weeks; very vigorous and productive.

'Scuppernong' The oldest muscadine variety; large fruits have a thick, reddish bronze skin and excellent, distinctive flavor; uneven ripening; vigorous, productive, and reliable.

'Sugargate' Very large, black fruits with excellent flavor; inconsistent yields; moderate vine vigor; good winter hardiness; needs a pollinator.

'Summit' Large, bronze berries with good flavor; vigorous; good disease resistance; good hardiness; needs a pollinator; ripens midseason.

FRENCH HYBRID GRAPES

'Baco Noir' (**'Baco #1'**) Wine grape whose fresh juice tastes almost like blackberry; berries are small and black, tart but not astringent; wine is intensely red; very vigorous and productive, moderately hardy; highly susceptible to black rot, moderately susceptible to botrytis bunch rot and powdery mildew, and slightly susceptible to anthracnose and downy mildew; ripens midseason.

'Seyval' Small, golden yellow berries in large, compact clusters produce a good, neutral, fruity wine; tends to overbear so prune and thin bunches accordingly; highly susceptible to botrytis bunch rot, powdery mildew, and black rot, moderately susceptible to downy mildew, and slightly susceptible to anthracnose; moderately vigorous and moderately cold hardy vine; ripens midseason.

Jujube

Ziziphus jujuba

GROWTH HABIT
Small, thorny tree with a naturally drooping habit

POLLINATION NEEDS
Needs are ill-defined; most varieties do not seem to need cross-pollination, but that may depend on the variety and climate

LIGHT REQUIREMENT
Full sunlight

CLIMATE
USDA Hardiness Zones 6–9; AHS Heat Zones 11–5

REGIONS
Everywhere except places that are too cold, lack sufficient winter chilling (less than 200–400 hours), or lack sufficient summer heat

To most people, jujube, if they have heard the word at all, is a candy. Before their incarnation as a candied mix of starch, gum, and corn syrup, jujubes were actually candied jujube *fruits*. Native to China, the naturally very sweet fruits are the size of small plums. When just ripe, their skin is like smooth, shiny mahogany and their flesh is crisp, reminiscent of a sweet apple. Left to ripen a bit longer, the skin begins to wrinkle as the fruit loses water, and the flesh changes from light green to beige and becomes spongy, at which point it lives up to one of its other names, "Chinese date." The fruits ripen in late summer or early autumn.

Because of its handsome, glossy green leaves, its delicious fruit, and its adaptability to most soils, this medium-size tree traveled long ago from its native home in China to southern Europe and then, in the 19th century, on to America. The tree has been very popular in China, so there are many varieties, some with such descriptive names as 'Dragon's Claw', 'Tooth', 'Bottle', and 'Mellow'.

Jujube gives quick return on your investment of time and money by bearing fruit the same year you plant. Masses of pale yellow flowers burst forth along growing branches. Flowering continues over a long period, often throughout the entire growing season. Even plants that have been damaged from cold often flower and fruit the next year.

Growing

Although it needs a sufficiently long season and abundant sunlight and heat to ripen its fruit, jujube will grow in almost any soil, whether wet or dry, hardpacked or loose. The trees send up suckers, often a few feet from the mother plant, so plant the tree in lawn, where your mower will keep them in check or diligently prune off the suckers. To control weeds and conserve soil water,

mulch around your tree. Avoid tilling because it encourages annoying suckering. Jujubes have no significant pest problems.

Pruning

Jujube trees require little pruning. Encourage a spreading growth habit in young trees. On mature trees, occasionally prune back some older wood and side branches near those cuts to promote new branches to grow and replace them. The fruits do not need thinning.

Harvesting

Because jujubes flower over a long period of time, they also fruit over a long period of time. Harvest them at the brown stage or when they start to shrivel. Harvested fruits will also shrivel and sweeten, although not to the same level of sweetness as those left on the tree.

Ripe fruits keep for a week to a month at room temperature, a month or two at 50°F. (Chilling injury occurs below 36°F.) Dried jujubes keep for about a year under cool and dry conditions.

Selection of Plants and Varieties

'Chin Sze Tsao' Fruits are light brown, small, and very sweet; used to make "honey jujube," the traditional jujube candy; medium-size tree.

'GA866' Crispy fruits are long, broad, firm, and very sweet.

'Honey Jar' Small fruit, honey-sweet and juicy, one of the best for fresh eating; seems to be relatively widely adapted.

'Lang' Pear-shaped, fairly large fruits have sweet flavor hinting of caramel; good fresh, better dried; tree is almost thornless.

'Li' Round, 2-inch-diameter fruit is among the largest of any jujube varieties, often seedless and with excellent flavor.

'Sherwood' Fruits are large with excellent flavor; late ripening; plant is usually thornless with a narrow weeping habit; slow to bear fruit.

'Silver Hill' ('Yu', 'Tigertooth') Large, elongated fruits about 1 inch in diameter; tree has relatively few suckers or thorns; late-ripening; adapted to regions of high humidity; productive.

Grow It Naturally

- Plant in full sunlight.
- Plant in warmest microclimate.

Juneberry

Amelanchier spp.

GROWTH HABIT
Shrubs to medium-size trees

POLLINATION NEEDS
Self-fertile, except white-fruited varieties, which need cross-pollination

LIGHT REQUIREMENT
Full sunlight to part shade

CLIMATE
USDA Hardiness Zones 3–8, varying somewhat with species. Saskatoons (*A. alnifolia*) are the most cold-hardy, many of them adapted to USDA Hardiness Zone 1; AHS Heat Zones 7–1, but variable

REGIONS
Native to every state, but susceptible to some very localized, rather than regional, pest problems

Juneberry is often compared to blueberry. True, it is a blueberry lookalike, but it has its own distinctive flavor. Juneberry has the sweetness and richness of a sweet cherry, along with a hint of almond—delicious, but quite different from (the also delicious) blueberry. The plant itself is good looking, most often planted as an ornamental only because people do not know that the fruit is edible. Its beauty is in its pinkish or white flowers in spring, its blazing crimson autumn leaf color, and its neat, year-round form. Unfortunately, in some places (like my yard), juneberries suffer enough pest problems to negate some or all the "good" they could offer. I've never harvested more than a handful of berries from my half dozen plants. That said, a mere four miles from my house, where the air is less damp than in the valley where I live, the bushes thrive as ornamentals that are loaded early each July with delicious berries. (Plants I grew from cuttings of those healthy plants did as poorly here as did my other juneberry plants.)

Juneberry parades under a number of different names, including shadbush, serviceberry, and sarvisberry. One species, a large shrub, is appreciated specifically for its fruit. That species, *A. alnifolia*, a native of the Canadian prairies and commonly known as saskatoon, has been improved with variety selection and is even grown commercially for its fruit.

Growing

Where juneberry doesn't experience pest problems, it's easy to grow, tolerating a wide range of soils and sunny or partially shaded sites. The plants are somewhat tolerant of salt and drought.

Pruning

Tree species need little or no annual pruning; suckering, bushy species, such as the saskatoon, fruit better if pruned yearly, in winter. The best fruits are borne on stems that are one year to four years old, so each year cut stems that are more than four years old to the ground. Also thin out the youngest stems so that no more than a half dozen of the most vigorous ones remain.

Pests and Diseases

The major pests of juneberries are birds. Mature plants commonly yield enough berries for both human and feathered berry lovers. If you do not wish to share your juneberries with birds, net the plants. Otherwise, grow a white-fruited variety, which birds don't notice.

As mentioned earlier, juneberry, in some plantings, can suffer from a host of problems. Those problems include rust (cedar-quince rust) and brown rot diseases, and curculio and sawfly pests. Often, though, they suffer from few or none of these problems.

Harvesting

Juneberries do not hang around for a long time, so don't put off harvest. Birds will help, enjoying them perhaps as much as blueberries.

Juneberry blossoms open early, with white flowers that sometimes are pink in bud.

Grow It Naturally

- Pests and diseases are localized, so if pests don't become a problem, juneberries are easy to grow.

- If pests are a problem, plant a different type of fruit.

Selection of Plants and Varieties

'Autumn Brilliance' Fruits grow up to ½ inch in diameter; multistemmed large shrub grows 15 feet to 25 feet tall and half that width; large, pink-tinged flower buds, snowy white blossoms that become red fruits; leaves turn a spectacular orange, sometimes red or yellow, in autumn.

'Ballerina' Berries are tender, sweet, and purplish black; can be grown as an upright shrub or small tree, 15 feet to 20 feet tall; flowers are large and the leaves turn purple-bronze in autumn.

'Jennybelle' Adapted to warmer regions, such as the Mid-Atlantic; heavy bearing.

'Paleface' Saskatoon; large, snowy white, mild fruits; pyramidal plant grows to 7 feet tall; few suckers; productive; needs cross-pollination.

'Pembina' Saskatoon; sweet, full-flavored fruits; large bush is upright growing and produces few suckers.

'Regent' Saskatoon; selected from among wild plants in North Dakota, produces very sweet fruit with few seeds, reputedly inferior to that of the better *alnifolia* selections from Canada; bush grows to 6 feet tall; productive; ornamental.

'Robin Hill' Purplish black fruits ¼ inch in diameter; early to bloom, with pink buds that unfold to white blossoms.

'Smoky' Saskatoon; sweet, mild-flavored fruits; bush produces many suckers and grows 8 feet to 10 feet tall.

'Success' Originating in the early 1800s, this is the first juneberry variety to be selected for its fruit; bush grows to be 6 feet tall and 4 feet wide, bearing long clusters of fruit.

'Thiessen' Saskatoon; late-ripening fruits, considered to have the best of flavors; bush grows up to 15 feet tall and wide; bears large berries.

White or pink flowers in spring, crimson foliage in autumn, and a neat growth habit make juneberry as valuable an ornamental as it is a fruit plant.

Kiwifruit

Fuzzy kiwifruit: *Actinidia deliciosa*
Golden kiwifruit: *A. chinensis*
Hardy kiwifruit: *A. arguta*
Super-hardy kiwifruit: *A. kolomikta*

GROWTH HABIT
Vine

POLLINATION NEEDS
Except for a few self-fruitful varieties, kiwifruits need a separate male vine to pollinate up to eight female fruiting vines. Different species do not generally bloom at the same time, so a male of one species cannot naturally pollinate the female of another species, although a very early male (*A. deliciosa*) could pollinate a late-blooming female (*A. chinenses*)

LIGHT REQUIREMENT
Full sunlight or, in hot regions, partial shade for all except *A. kolomikta*, which may grow better in some shade

CLIMATE
Fuzzy kiwifruit: USDA Hardiness Zones 7–9; AHS Heat Zones 9–6
Golden Kiwifruit: USDA Hardiness Zones 8–10; AHS Heat Zones 10–8
Hardy kiwifruit: USDA Hardiness Zones 4–9; AHS Heat Zones 9–4
Super-hardy kiwifruit: USDA Hardiness Zones 3–7; AHS Heat Zones 7–3

REGIONS
Widely adapted, although the ideal location experiences few temperature fluctuations in winter or spring; pest problems are rare within climate zones for each of the species

TOP: Flowers of super-hardy kiwifruit create a mass of pretty, white petals.

BOTTOM: White and, often, pink variegation of super-hardy kiwi's leaves add to the ornamental appeal of this fruiting vine.

Grow It Naturally

- Perfect soil drainage is a must; plant on wide mounds if necessary.

- For best fruit production, prune plants each winter and a couple of times in summer.

- Late frosts in spring can scorch young leaves, but be patient because plants become more frost tolerant with age.

Kiwifruits are Johnny-come-latelies among cultivated fruits, their emerald-green flesh and pineapple-y flavor having captured the hearts of both fruit lovers and gardeners outside of Asia only since the latter half of the 20th century. The plants were introduced to the West primarily as ornamental vines. New Zealand growers were the first to cultivate plants for their fruits, in this case the large, brown, fuzzy kiwifruit.

Although grown as ornamentals since the early 20th century, so-called hardy and superhardy kiwifruits weren't "discovered" for their fruits until near the end of that century. The fruits were overlooked because they are the size of grapes and have smooth, green skins that are hidden by and blend in with the foliage. The skin on these fruits is edible and the flavor is more aromatic and sweeter than that of fuzzy kiwifruits.

Super-hardy kiwifruit plants have pink and silvery leaves that are especially striking. The plants are also more sedate in their vigor and bear at the earliest age of all kiwifruits, sometimes fruiting the year after planting.

Golden kiwifruits have been appreciated outside of Asia even more recently. The fruits are almost the size of fuzzy kiwifruits, and have a peachlike skin and green, yellow, or sometimes reddish flesh. Their flavor is very sweet, smooth, and somewhat tropical, reminiscent of melon, tangerine, or strawberry.

All kiwifruits ripen in late summer or early autumn.

Growing

Kiwifruit plants, even the cold-hardy ones, can be damaged by fluctuating temperatures while dormant, so keep them away from south-facing walls or other areas that tend to periodically heat up in winter. Because the plants need some age to build up their cold-hardiness, protect a young plant with some sort of insulating material such as corn stalks around its trunk or, less attractively, wrap the trunk with foam pipe insulation.

Next, turn to the soil. Kiwifruit plants are prone to crown rot, so choose a site with perfectly draining soil or build a mound on which to plant. The vines tolerate a wide range in soil pH, from 5.0 to 6.5. They are sensitive to soil salinity, so should be fed bulky, organic fertilizers such as compost or manure or, if more nitrogen is needed, soybean meal.

Kiwifruit plants are rampant vines hardly capable of holding themselves up, so they usually need a support on which to climb. Let the plants ramble casually over a pergola or arbor or, for more serious fruit production, erect a T-trellis (see below). In either case, allow about 200 square feet per vine, remembering that you need a separate male vine for pollination.

Along the T-trellis, space plants 15 feet apart and train each plant to have a single trunk starting at the ground up to the center wire of the trellis. When the developing trunk grows just above the height of the wire, cut it back to the wire and train the two shoots that sprout from its two topmost buds to grow in opposite directions along the center wire. These two shoots will form permanent cordons, off which fruiting arms will grow, draped over the outside wires. Each winter during this training period, shorten the developing cordons to leave 2 feet of the previous season's growth.

As insurance against loss of the aboveground portion of the plant to winter cold damage that young plants sometimes experience, you could train a plant to have two trunks instead of one. As the two trunks reach the center wire, train the continuing growth horizontally—as cordons—in opposite directions along and upon reaching the center wire.

Pruning

Because they grow so vigorously and bear fruits only on shoots growing off one-year-old canes, kiwifruit plants need pruning, ideally at least twice a year, in winter and in summer.

WINTER PRUNING

In addition to promoting new growth, pruning is needed to keep the plants from shading themselves. Winter pruning consists of shortening fruiting arms growing off cordons (or growing off older laterals) to a length of about 18 inches and thinning out these arms so they are about 12 inches apart along the cordon. After a fruiting arm is three years old, cut it off completely to make room for a new, young fruiting arm originating closer to the cordon. Otherwise, over time, fruiting arms will creep farther and farther away from the cordon, making the vine ungainly and having to support too much nonfruiting wood. Finally, shorten cordons each winter so that they are no longer than 7 feet.

SUMMER PRUNING

In summer, cut back any overly rampant or tangled shoots and keep the trunk free of new growth. You'll know your vines are getting enough sun if the ground beneath them is spattered with dappled shade.

Male plants are needed only for their flowers. Right after they blossom, prune flowering shoots back to new shoots. This severe pruning can remove about 70 percent of the previous year's growth.

Use these same techniques for kiwi vines clambering up and over decorative arbors. Alternatively, prune less methodically, occasionally whacking back misplaced or congested branches to let the vines happily and haphazardly clothe these structures with their fruits hanging—not as easily accessible or in as prodigious quantity—beneath the leaves.

Kiwifruit Trellis

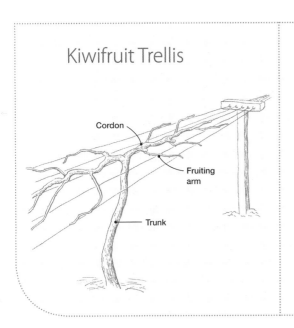

Cordon

Fruiting arm

Trunk

Pruning a Kiwifruit Vine

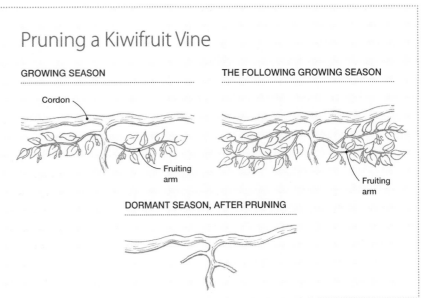

GROWING SEASON

Cordon

Fruiting arm

THE FOLLOWING GROWING SEASON

Fruiting arm

DORMANT SEASON, AFTER PRUNING

Pests and Diseases

Kiwifruits are among the many plants enjoyed by Japanese beetles. Cats also enjoy the plants, which have an effect on them similar to catnip. Protect young plants from cats, if necessary, by fencing the vines in with chicken wire. Mature plants do not need protection from cats.

Harvesting

Kiwifruits ripen in late summer and fall, golden kiwifruits first, followed by super-hardy kiwifruits, hardy kiwifruits, and fuzzy kiwifruits (not that all species could be grown in the same garden). Harvested fruit that is not quite ripe will ripen off the vine, but only after achieving a certain level of maturity. Experience will dictate when to pick, but generally that time would be when the first fruits on the plant start to soften to your touch. Picked before this point, flavor and texture suffer. Sweetness and firmness tell you when a fruit is ripe for picking. Not all fruits on a plant, even in a single bunch, ripen together, so it's best to sample a few fruits for maturity.

Fruit will keep for six weeks for super-hardy varieties, and up to six months for hardy, golden, and fuzzy types, if harvested when firm and stored in a plastic bag with a few holes in it (to allow air circulation) and refrigerated. Let firm fruit sit at room temperature to soften and be ready for eating.

It's a very real possibility that you'll harvest an overabundance of fruit. Consider making kiwi tarts, kiwi jam, and kiwi wine with the excess. Be careful when cooking any of these kiwis; heat can muddy the fruit's vibrant, green color.

TOP: Pruning is needed to reduce the number of stems of this hardy kiwi vine so that it doesn't overbear and so sufficient sunlight bathes each remaining fruiting stem.

BOTTOM: After pruning, this hardy kiwi vine is left with 1-year-old fruiting stems originating at or near the cordon.

Sexing a Kiwifruit Vine

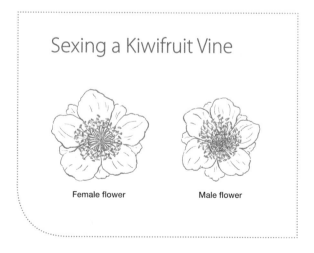

Female flower   Male flower

Selection of Plants and Varieties

FUZZY KIWIFRUIT

'Abbott' Female; elongated, medium fruits; medium to low chilling requirement (50–250 hours) and therefore suitable for regions with short winters; blossoms early; relatively cold hardy.

'Chico No. 3' ('California Male') Male.

'Hayward' ('California Chico') Female; usually the variety you'll find in markets; fruits are large, tasty, and keep well; high chilling requirement (800 hours); moderate productivity and vigor; ripens late season.

'Matua' Male; blossoms over a long period of time.

GOLDEN KIWIFRUIT

'Jintao' Female; fruit is large and long, with almost hairless brown skin and green-yellow flesh that ripens to yellow and orange; excellent flavor; stores well.

For years, kiwis were used strictly as ornamentals to decorate arbors.

Hardy kiwifruits are grape-size but with smooth skins, so you can pop them into your mouth to eat skins and all, just like grapes.

HARDY KIWIFRUIT

'Ananasnaja' ('Anna' or 'Ananasnaya') Female; fruits are relatively large and firm, with excellent flavor; reliably productive; late ripening.

'Dumbarton Oaks' Female; fruit is relatively large, with very good flavor and appearance; moderately good yield; ripens early, about three weeks before 'Ananasnaja'.

'Geneva' Female; large fruit has excellent flavor; early ripening, about three weeks before 'Ananasnaja'.

'Issai' Possibly a hybrid; female; very good flavor; precocious; less vigorous and somewhat less cold hardy than most hardy kiwifruits; plant is somewhat self-pollinating, grow a male pollinizer to increase fruit size and set.

'Meader Male' Male.

SUPER-HARDY KIWIFRUIT

'Aromatnaya' Female; medium fruit; productive; early ripening.

'Sentyabraskaya' Female; fruit is medium-large; productive; early ripening.

Mango

Mangifera indica

GROWTH HABIT
Wide-spreading tree; can grow from 8 feet
to more than 50 feet tall

POLLINATION NEEDS
Self-fruitful

LIGHT REQUIREMENT
Full sunlight

CLIMATE
USDA Hardiness Zones 9–10; AHS Heat
Zones 12–8

REGIONS
Best adapted to tropical regions with pronounced
drier or cooler season; not adapted to consistently
wet climates

When a mango is good, it is very, very good, and when it is bad, it is horrid. Very, very good means silky, smooth, juicy flesh that hints of peach. A bad mango has stringy flesh and a flavor that more than hints of turpentine. Mango is sometimes called the peach of the tropics; perhaps peach should instead be called the mango of the north. In fact, mangos and peaches each have their own, unique flavor and aroma.

Like a peach (I'm from the north, so can't help starting here), mango has lustrous, lance-shaped leaves that droop decoratively downward along the stems. The leaves, on some varieties at least, start out coppery colored. A mango tree can grow very large; or not, in the case of some varieties.

Mango is in the same family as poison ivy, and some people experience an allergic reaction to the fruit's skin. Volatiles given off from burning mango wood also cause discomfort to some people. No need to shy away from mango, though. Just don't eat near the skin or burn the wood. If it puts your mind more at ease, mango's family also includes cashew and pistachio, as well as ornamentals such as smoke tree and sumac. A healthy mango tree will bear fruit for over a century.

Growing

Start with a good tree and growing mangos will be an easy proposition. A good tree is, first of all, one that grows in a pot deep enough to accommodate its taproot, or is a plant whose taproot has been shortened a few weeks before being transplanted to encourage development of new feeder roots. A good tree is also of a variety adapted to the climate. Especially in humid climates, such as in Florida and Hawaii, choose varieties resistant to anthracnose disease.

That "good" tree could be either a grafted one or one that you started as a seed. Although varieties of most fruits do not come true from seed, some mangos have polyembryonic seeds, each one giving rise to a number of seedlings. In certain kinds of mangos, including the varieties 'Nam Doc Mai', 'Fairchild', and 'Piña', most of those seedlings will be genetically identical to the parent. Get a seed growing by eating a fruit and then removing the leathery coating around the seed with a pruning shears or a sharp kitchen knife. Plant the seed immediately, on edge and covered with ¾ inch of soil, either in a deep pot or at the tree's permanent location in the ground. Thin out or separate the seedlings after they sprout, discarding the weakest one(s). A grafted tree

that you buy or make (see p. 32) will, of course, be of a named variety.

Micronutrient deficiencies (see p. 25)—and the resulting off-color leaves or atypical growth patterns—may arise in mango plants grown in alkaline soils. Avoid such problems by using bulky organic fertilizers, especially composts and manures. Adjusting soil pH to between 5.5 and 7.5 also helps keep nutrition on track. Avoid excessive fertilization of a mature tree with nitrogen fertilizers, or you'll get a lot of shoot growth rather than large crops.

Mango flowers appear in branching clusters of hundreds, even thousands, of flowers, very few of which need to set fruit for a full crop. Mango bursts into an abundance of blooms two or more times during the year, and often after a period of dry or cool weather. Fruit set is poor during cool (less than 55°F) or moist weather. Fortunately, with repeated bursts of flowers each year, opportunities exist for fruiting after subsequent bursts.

Pruning

Once planted, mango needs little pruning beyond heading cuts (see p. 37) in its youth to promote branching, and thinning cuts (see p. 37) to avoid overcrowding of future limbs. Pull off any fruits on a young tree so the plant can put its energy into growing shoots and leaves. The best-tasting and highest yield of fruits is borne on branches that receive the most sunlight, so occasionally prune mature trees so light can get in among the branches. Grafted trees start bearing quickly, often one year or two years after planting; don't let them bear for the first couple of years.

Grow It Naturally

- In humid climates, grow a disease-resistant variety.

- Prune occasionally to keep branches from becoming too dense and shading the interior of the plant.

After a decade, a tree can get into the habit of bearing well only every other year. Pruning during an "on" year, by removing branches that would have borne fruits, might have some effect in evening out the feast or famine cycle.

Drastic pruning can quickly bring an overgrown tree down to a reasonable size (see p. 44). This pruning sacrifices the crop for the year, but the tree soon starts bearing again. Paint the once-shaded limbs that remain with a 50/50 mixture of white latex paint and water to avoid sunburn.

Pests and Diseases

Wet weather during or after flowering can result in anthracnose, a disease that either destroys the flowers so few fruits form or pocks fruits with large, dark splotches. The splotches coalesce, sometimes causing the fruits to crack and eventually rot. Leaves are also prone to infection and exhibit similar symptoms. Avoid or control this disease by planting resistant varieties, pruning and siting for good sunlight and air circulation, and, if necessary, spraying natural pesticides. Neem oil is an environmentally friendly spray option; copper is less so.

Powdery mildew is another potential disease problem, this one more prevalent in areas with little rainfall. Symptoms are a powdery covering on leaves, flowers, or fruits. The first line of defense is to plant a disease-resistant variety, such as 'Carrie'; the second line of defense is to prune and site for good sunlight and air circulation; and the third line of defense is to spray neem oil, sulfur (which can sometimes also damage the plant), or bicarbonates.

Harvesting

Depending on the climate and the variety, mangos ripen three months to six months after flowering. Some hints to when a fruit is ripe are its full "shoulders," smooth skin, and shriveling stem. The color of its skin will also change, the background becoming lighter green and the foreground turning the variety's characteristic color, which might be yellow or blushed with some shade of red. Ripe fruit also softens like a ripe peach. At this point, the fruit stem will snap easily off the tree with a slight pull.

Fruits picked just slightly underripe will ripen at room temperature after harvest. Sacrifice one fruit to cut open and check the flesh for timing. The more yellow near the seed, the sooner full ripening will occur. Do not store ripe or slightly underripe fruit below 50°F.

Avoid getting the sap on your skin when harvesting (or pruning). It can be an irritant.

Selection of Plants and Varieties

'Alphonso' Skin is green or yellow with a slight red blush; flavor is excellent, rich, with hints of citrus; smooth flesh; vigorous tree; moderately productive; recommended for Florida.

'Angie' Yellow skin with orange-red blush; excellent flavor that hints of apricot; small tree, easily maintained at 10 feet high; disease resistant; early ripening.

'Carrie' Yellow fruit with excellent flavor; dwarf tree; disease resistant; early ripening; harvest fruits when fully ripe; recommended for Florida.

'Edgehill' Fruit is green with red blush, sweet and smooth; upright tree; recommended for California.

'Fairchild' Small, pale yellow fruits with spicy, rich flavor and no fiber; small tree, easily kept to 10 feet or grown in pots; productive; disease resistant; recommended for Hawaii.

'Glenn' Fruit is yellow to pink or red with mild, peachy flavor and no fiber; small tree; productive; disease resistant; early ripening; recommended for Hawaii.

'Julie' Fruit is sweet and tangy with good flavor, slightly stringy; dwarf tree, grows well in pots; reliable production; susceptible to disease; recommended for Hawaii.

'Nam Doc Mai' Fruits are yellow with a slight blush; excellent flavor, sweet and aromatic, with silky smooth, juicy flesh; small to medium tree is very productive; disease resistant; ripens over an extended season; recommended for Florida.

'Piña' Small, orange-yellow fruit with sweet, almost fiberless flesh that hints of pineapple; upright tree; recommended for California.

'Valencia Pride' Fruit is large with excellent, sweet flavor and no fiber; large tree.

Medlar

Mespilus germanica

GROWTH HABIT
Small tree, grows up to 8 feet tall and 6 feet wide

POLLINATION NEEDS
Self-fruitful

LIGHT REQUIREMENT
Full sunlight

CLIMATE
USDA Hardiness Zones 5–8; AHS Heat Zones 9–4

REGIONS
Adapted throughout regions within its cold-hardiness and heat zones

Medlar is the perfect fruit for a small garden. The tree is small and self-fruitful, so it doesn't need cross-pollination to bear fruit. Its pretty, white flowers look much like wild roses and open up against whorled backdrops of already unfolded leaves. The blossoms open late enough to almost never be bothered by spring frosts and almost every blossom sets fruit, so a single tree yields a lot of fruit. And medlars keep well, so there's no rush to eat them all at once.

So what if the fruit is strange looking? Picture a small, russeted apple whose calyx end (opposite the stem) is flared open. J. C. Woodsford described the fruit in *The Gardeners' Chronicle* (1939) as "a crabby-looking, brownish-green, truncated, little spheroid of unsympathetic appearance." Despite its appearance, the fruit is delicious, with the spicy flavor of applesauce along with winey overtones. The fruit has an odd quirk, described under "Harvesting" on the facing page, something that gets it to that delicious stage. Because of that quirk and its strange appearance, medlar is a fruit that you'll probably never see offered for sale, which is all the more reason to grow it at home.

Growing

Medlar trees fruit best in full sunlight and well-drained soil. Trees are propagated by grafting (see p. 32) on pear, quince, hawthorn, juneberry, or seedling medlar rootstocks. Because the rootstock is used only to propagate the plant, not dwarf it, plant the tree with the graft union below ground and let the medlar scion eventually form its own roots.

Pruning

Medlar is truly a carefree fruit. Little pruning is needed beyond what is necessary to train a young tree to a nice, open shape (see p. 40) and the removal of dead or crossing branches. The young plants are very precocious, typically bearing their first fruits within three years. Prune off the tips of short branches to remove some flower buds and allow the tree to channel more energy into growth rather than fruit. On the mature tree, prune out dead and crossing branches and thin out spindly wood to let light and air in among remaining branches.

TOP: Medlar is a perfect tree for a small yard because it never grows large, does not need a pollinator, and is attractive in every season.

BOTTOM: Each white medlar blossom opens relatively late so is framed in a verdant whorl of leaves.

Pests and Diseases

Medlar shares some problems common to apple and pear, such as rust and fire blight disease. These potential problems rarely cause enough damage to medlar to warrant control.

Harvesting

Harvest medlar in autumn, at about the same time as the tree's leaves are dropping. But wait, don't eat the fruit yet! Fruits need to "blet" before they're ready to eat. (Yes, this is medlar's odd quirk!) Bletting is a natural ripening process during which the fruit softens, sweetens, and becomes less astringent. The best place for bletting

to occur is on a shelf in a cool room; the cooler the temperature, the longer the time before the fruit is ready to eat. Once the skin has darkened and the flesh has softened and browned, the fruit is ready to be enjoyed. It is delicious folded with cream; mixed with egg, cream, and milk to make a refreshing gelato; cooked with eggs, sugar, cinnamon, and ginger and poured into a pastry shell; or…just plain, unaccompanied.

One problem with the fruit, for some people, is that the flesh, when ready for eating, is brown and mushy, and lacking visual appeal. This is why D. H. Lawrence, evidently not a fan, described the fruits as "wineskins of brown morbidity." Look past its lack of aesthetic beauty; you will not be disappointed.

Fruits left clinging to branches outdoors also blet, as will those that drop beneath the tree. Depending on the weather, such fruits may or may not match the quality of medlars bletted in a cool room, but there is something to be said for being able to walk by your medlar tree on a wintry, perhaps snow-covered day and enjoy a fresh-picked fruit. For more civilized pleasure, follow the lead of the great British wine connoisseur George Saintsbury, who wrote (*Notes on a Cellar-Book*, 1920), "The one fruit which seems to me to go best with all wine, from hock to sherry to port, is the medlar."

When "bletted" and ready to eat, medlar tastes like rich apple-sauce with wine-y overtones even if it does look disagreeable.

Selection of Plants and Varieties

'Dutch' ('Monstrous') Large fruits, 2 inches to 3 inches in diameter; vigorous tree with an almost weeping growth habit.

'Nottingham' Small but tasty fruits; productive old variety; tree has an upright growth habit.

'Royal' Characteristics intermediate to 'Dutch' and 'Nottingham', both in fruit size and tree form.

Mulberry

Black mulberry: *Morus nigra*
Red mulberry: *M. rubra*
White mulberry: *M. alba*

GROWTH HABIT

Black mulberry trees are small to medium size and often grown as bushes; white and red mulberry trees are medium-large

POLLINATION NEEDS

Self-fruitful

LIGHT REQUIREMENT

Full sunlight

CLIMATE

Black mulberry: USDA Hardiness Zones 7–10; AHS Heat Zones 9–4
Red mulberry: USDA Hardiness Zones 5–8; AHS Heat Zones 9–3
White mulberry: USDA Hardiness Zones 5–8 (very variable, with just a few varieties that can grow outside of this range); AHS Heat Zones 9–3

REGIONS

Adapted throughout regions within their cold-hardiness and heat zones

Wild mulberries abound over much of the country, but a backyard tree is more convenient and, if of an appropriately selected variety (for your climate), will have better-tasting fruits than its wild counterparts. Note that the species names and common names of mulberries bear little relation to the color of these blackberry-shaped fruits. White mulberries, for instance, might produce white, lavender, or even black fruits.

The best tasting of all mulberries—and perhaps the best tasting of all fruits—is black mulberry. It is native to western Asia and, unfortunately, best adapted only to dry, mild winter regions such as found in Mediterranean climates. The berries have an intense flavor, as if coming from a fruit five times its size, and a sweetness that is offset with a perfect balance of zing. Black mulberry also grows well in a pot, moved indoors to a cool, dark room for winter, or in a greenhouse.

Red mulberry is native to America, but has naturally hybridized with white mulberry, introduced from Asia over a century ago and now also wild here. Both red mulberry and white mulberry are sweet—very sweet, even too sweet—on many trees. Some varieties of red mulberries and white mulberries, and their hybrids, have a nice flavor balance that approaches that of black mulberry.

Growing

The weedy nature of mulberries—white mulberries are the second most common weed tree (a "weed" being any plant in the wrong place) in New York City—is testimonial to their tolerance for a wide range of site conditions. For best fruiting, plant a mulberry tree in full sunlight. Avoid planting mulberries near walkways, driveways, decks, and terraces or stains from fallen fruit will find their way indoors on shoes or bare feet.

Pruning

Beyond planting and perhaps a little training, a mulberry plant needs little further care. You can train the plant as a large shrub with many stems, or as a tree with a single trunk (see Chapter 3). Some mulberry varieties have a naturally weeping habit. Black mulberry can be espaliered by developing a main decorative framework of branches and, each year in early August, shortening all shoots growing off those branches to about 6 inches

long. Periodically cut these shoots back heavily in late winter so the 6-inch-long fruiting stems don't, over time, move too far off the main framework of branches, making the plant bigger and bigger and obscuring the tracery of the main branches.

Pests and Diseases

Birds are the main pests of mulberries. Once a plant grows large, however, it bears enough fruit to satisfy both humans and birds.

Harvesting

Black mulberry is late to begin growing in spring and similarly late to begin ripening its fruits—for a mulberry, that is. Its fruits ripen in July and August.

Harvest of white mulberries, red mulberries, and their hybrids begins early in the season, soon after spring strawberry season ends. With some varieties, the ripening season can go on and on over a large part of the summer. To harvest in quantity, spread a clean dropcloth or sheet on the ground, and shake branches.

'Illinois Everbearing' is quick-growing and quick to begin bearing.

'Illinois Everbearing' is a mulberry variety that tastes almost as good as black mulberry and can be grown almost everywhere.

This small, potted 'Geraldi Dwarf' mulberry is already bearing fruits.

Selection of Plants and Varieties

'Black Persian' Black mulberry with delectable flavor; this variety may go under other names.

'Geraldi Dwarf' White mulberry; very good flavor; compact tree suitable for USDA Hardiness Zones 5–8.

'Illinois Everbearing' Probable hybrid of white and red mulberry; very good flavor, almost matching black mulberry; cold hardy; very vigorous; ripens over a long period.

'Kokuso' White mulberry; firm fruit with very good flavor; tree low and wide, easy to pick; very cold hardy; ripens early and lasts for only a short period.

'Oscar' White mulberry; very good flavor, rivaling black mulberry; wide, spreading tree.

'Pakistan' White mulberry; fruit is very long, sometimes over 3 inches, with firm flesh and excellent flavor; not cold hardy below 25°F.

Papaya

Hawaiian papaya: *Carica papaya*

GROWTH HABIT
Herbaceous plant has the form of a palm tree; grows up to 30 feet tall

POLLINATION NEEDS
Many varieties, including 'Solo' and its seedlings, are self-fruitful

LIGHT REQUIREMENT
Full sunlight; partial shade for babaco papayas in hot areas

CLIMATE
USDA Hardiness Zones 9–12; AHS Heat Zones 12–10

REGIONS
Throughout tropical regions

Papaya fruits can look like small to humongous melons and have a mild, melonlike flavor. That mild-mannered flavor really comes alive when given some zest with a spritz of lime juice. Note that papaya is sometimes called "pawpaw" (discussed on p. 162). The two fruits are not at all related.

The papaya plant has three very interesting features. First, although it has the form of a palm tree, a single trunk capped with a whorl of leaves, the plant is herbaceous, never developing a woody trunk and not living a very long time. Its lobed leaves and pendulous fruits create a bold, tropical look. Second, the flowers need pollination to set fruit, and a single plant might bear male, female, or hermaphroditic flowers, or some combination of the three. During its life, a plant's sex might change. Fruits from female flowers are rounder and thinner-walled than fruits from hermaphroditic flowers.

The third interesting fact about papaya is that it is among the few fruit plants grown from seed. Fruiting begins within a year from seeding, making me hopeful that someday breeders will develop a papaya that could be sown indoors in late winter, grown in a sunny window through early spring, transplanted outside into the garden once warm weather settles in, and harvested later in summer. Just like tomatoes.

Growing

Gather papaya seeds as you eat the fruit. Put them in a colander and rub and wash them to remove their arils (gelatinous coating). The seedlings don't transplant well, so sow a group of them at their permanent home or in a good-size pot. At optimum germination temperature, about 80°F, seeds sprout in two to five weeks. Once plants are up and growing well, thin the group down to the sturdiest plants by clipping off the weak ones rather than pulling them out. Otherwise you may disturb the

roots of the plants that remain. When moving the plant to a larger container or open ground, be especially careful not to disturb the roots.

Whether finally planted in a container or in open ground, papaya roots need perfect drainage and warm soil. In a container, this means adding extra perlite or other aggregate. In open ground, if drainage is less than perfect, plant on a raised mound or install ditches or drainage tile to draw off excess water. This is not to say that the plants enjoy dry soils. Plenty of water is needed to plump up the large, juicy fruits. Papaya must be grown in well-drained soil, watered, as needed, and mulched.

The ideal site for a papaya plant is warm (between 70°F and 90°F) and protected from strong winds. Even light frosts cause damage, as do extended cool temperatures, which also adversely affect the fruits' flavor. Strong winds lead to bruised fruits and can topple the top-heavy plants.

Even under the best of conditions, papaya plants peter out after three to four years. Have new seedlings ready to replace old ones.

Pruning

Pruning papaya is rarely necessary. If the growing point of a plant is injured, a few new branches will develop. Plants fruit best on a single trunk, so remove all but one—the sturdiest—of those branches. Individual leaves eventually age and die. Remove them to lessen the chance of diseases and fruit scarring. Scarring can also occur if fruits are overcrowded, so thin them when they're young.

Pruning sometimes rejuvenates trees that are declining. Cut the trunk down to about 18 inches and on a slant just above a node so that water doesn't collect in the stump. New sprouts develop and bear quickly (but so do seedlings, which makes drastic pruning of limited value).

Grow It Naturally

- Relatively few problems in home settings.
- Perfect drainage is a must.

Pests and Diseases

Papaya's pest and disease problems are generally insignificant in home settings with healthy, naturally grown plants. Among the worst pest is the papaya fruit fly, a yellow and black fly that lays eggs through the skin into the fruit's seed cavity, where the larvae feed and ruin the fruit. The easiest way to control this pest, where it has been a problem (generally in southern Texas, southern Florida, and Central and South America), is to thoroughly enclose individual fruits in paper bags as soon as flowers have dropped. Either use large bags or successively remove and replace bags with larger ones as fruits get bigger.

Viruses cause various mottling or distortion of leaves. Stay ahead of these problems by starting new plants from seed every few years to replace older plants, which likely pick up infections and generally become less productive anyway.

Harvesting

Harvest mature papayas when their skins yellow and their flesh softens slightly. At that point, the seeds within should be dark brown. Eat the fruit immediately, or store at cool temperatures (50°F to 60°F) for no longer than a couple of weeks. Papaya will continue ripening after harvest only if picked near maturity. The optimum postharvest ripening temperature is about 75°F.

Unripe, green papaya fruits hold promise for a tasty future when the fruits yellow and soften at maturity.

Selection of Plants and Varieties

'Betty' Excellent flavor; very tender flesh; quick to bear.

'Bluestem' Thick flesh; rich flavor; good for growing in Florida.

'Graham' Small to medium fruit with excellent flavor; good for growing in Texas.

'Kamiya' Small to medium fruit; yellow-orange skin and flesh is firm, juicy, and very sweet; dwarf, productive plant.

'Solo' Orange flesh and excellent, rich flavor; 1-pound to 2-pound fruits; seedlings produce only hermaphroditic and female flowers. This variety, along with its seedlings—'Sunrise', 'Sunset', 'Waimanalo', and others—is self-pollinating and inbred, so it grows relatively identical seedlings.

'Sunrise' Flesh is firm, reddish orange, and very sweet; average-size fruit, typically 1½ pounds; precocious, begins to fruit at a height of about 3 feet.

'Sunset' Orange-red skin and flesh; very sweet; dwarf and productive plant.

'Vista Solo' Flesh is orange to yellow-orange, high-quality fruit in hot climates; medium to large fruits; self-fertile; compact growth habit.

'Waimanalo' Flesh is thick, firm, orange-yellow in color; quality of fruit and flavor is high; 1-pound to 2-pound fruits; begins bearing when less than 3 feet tall; fruit stores well.

Pawpaw

Asimina triloba

GROWTH HABIT
Small to medium-size pyramidal tree can grow up
to 25 feet tall

POLLINATION NEEDS
Requires cross-pollination

LIGHT REQUIREMENT
Full sunlight

CLIMATE
USDA Hardiness Zones 4–8; AHS Heat Zones 8–5

REGIONS
Adapted throughout regions within its cold-
hardiness and heat zones

One of my few regrets to living where winters are frigid is not being able to grow tropical fruits. But I can grow "bananas"—Michigan bananas, Hoosier bananas, or any-state-it's-native-to bananas. These "bananas" are really pawpaws, a native, banana-like fruit that laughs off cold in spite of its many tropical aspirations. Pawpaw has a texture like banana and a flavor that is a pleasing mix of banana, vanilla custard, avocado, mango, and pineapple. Or, described another way, it tastes like crème brûlée (without the fat and sugar).

The fruit's tropical aspirations do not end with flavor and texture. The pawpaw tree sports large, lush leaves, and its fruits ripen in clusters, as do bananas. The pale green fruits, about the size and shape of medium mangos, even get speckled black as they ripen, as do bananas. The plant's botanical roots are in the tropics. Pawpaw is the northernmost member of the mostly tropical custard apple family, and the fruit does indeed resemble custard apple in flavor.

Although native from Pennsylvania down to Florida and west to Nebraska, pawpaws grow happily well beyond their native range. They are among the easiest fruits to grow.

Growing

Get your pawpaw trees from a nursery that sells named varieties (that is, ensures grafted trees) and has experience with this unique fruit tree. A named variety ensures that you are picking fruits that have certain, known qualities and ripening times. Grafted trees also bear their

Pawpaw trees have large, lush leaves that look very tropical.

first fruits at an earlier age than do seedlings, typically within two years to three years versus eight or more years for trees grown from seed. Pawpaws have taproots so don't transplant as easily as most other fruit trees; hence the need for growing the plant in a deep pot or for careful digging and transporting of a bare root plant.

Pawpaw flowers are not all that attractive to insects, so hand-pollination sometimes helps on small plants with few flowers. When the balls of thread-like anthers are loose in the flowers, dab the bristles of an artist's brush back and forth between flowers of two different varieties of pawpaw. You get a lot for very little effort because each flower can give rise to a cluster of fruits.

Abandon playing the birds and the bees on larger trees because it is unnecessary and might result in limbs breaking under their weight of fruit. The multiple ovary of a pawpaw flower can morph into as many as nine fruits.

Grow It Naturally

- Pawpaw experiences relatively few problems.

- Near the northern limits of its growing, plant varieties, such as from the 'PA-Golden' ('Pennsylvania Golden') series, that ripen fruit in shorter seasons.

Pruning

Pawpaws require little or no pruning once they have been trained to a sturdy framework of branches. They naturally tend to a central-leader form (see pp. 40–41). If flowering becomes too sparse on a mature tree, head back some branches to stimulate new shoot growth, which will flower and fruit the next year.

Pawpaw is a suckering tree, and the suckers often sprout a few feet from the mother plant. Fruits produced on suckers will be different from those borne on the mother tree if the mom is grafted. Suckers also can crowd each other, so cut them off, or run them over with the lawn mower if the trees are growing in lawn.

Pests and Diseases

Pawpaws generally have no pest problems worth noting.

Lee's Picks

'PA-Golden' and 'SAA-Zimmerman' are my favorite pawpaw varieties.

Harvesting

Pawpaws ripen in late summer and autumn. Pick them as soon as they soften a little or let them hang on the plant until they drop. Individual fruits on a single tree ripen over the course of a couple of weeks, more or less depending on the weather, rather than all at once. Use leafy or wood chip mulch beneath your trees to make a padded landing for plummeting fruits (as well as to promote a good root environment). In peak season, collect dropped ripe fruits every day or two.

On and off the plant, pawpaw fruits undergo a rather dramatic transition in flavor, from firm, mild vanilla custard–like to very sweet, soft, and rich, often with the flavor and color of café au lait.

Eat fully ripe fruits within a few days. Firm ripe fruits, if kept cool (around 40°F), store for up to about a month. Inside each fruit is a double row of lima bean–size brown seeds. They are inedible, as is the skin. The best part of the fruit, though, is the flesh right around each seed.

The way to eat a pawpaw is to halve the fruit, then scoop out the creamy flesh with a spoon. If no spoon is handy, just squeeze one and then the other of the halves, pushing and mushing the pulp up out of the skin and eating it before it drops off.

For something fancier, pawpaw can contribute its texture and flavor to ice cream, cookies, drinks, and pies.

Selection of Plants and Varieties

Note that even for a selected variety much variation exists within a tree for fruit size and flavor.

'PA-Golden' ('Pennsylvania Golden') Includes four varieties, differentiated as #1, #2, #3, and #4; all are medium size, have yellow skin and golden flesh with excellent flavor; among the earliest to ripen.

'Rappahannock' Fruit is medium, with firm texture and relatively low percentage of seeds; skin is pale yellow-green and flesh is yellow; sets fruit in clusters of three or less; prune off excessive vertical growth that this cultivar tends to develop; ripens midseason.

'Rebecca's Gold' Kidney-shaped 3-ounce to 6-ounce fruit with yellow flesh.

'SAA-Zimmerman' Medium, smooth fruit with excellent flavor; ripens midseason.

'Shenandoah' Large fruits with firm yet custardlike creamy yellow flesh that have a relatively small percentage of seeds; mild flavor appeals to many people; ripens in clusters of one to three; ripens mid- to late season.

'Sunflower' Fruit is large with few seeds and average flavor; may be self-fertile; moderate vigor and reliable production; late ripening.

'Susquehanna' Among the largest and sweetest of pawpaws; fruit has a very rich flavor and few seeds; ripens mid- to late season.

Peach and Nectarine

Peach: *Prunus Persica*
Nectarine: *P. Persica* var. *nucipersica*

GROWTH HABIT
Small, spreading tree about 10 feet tall and wide; some dwarf varieties do not grow taller than 3 feet

POLLINATION NEEDS
Most varieties are self-fruitful

LIGHT REQUIREMENT
Full sunlight

CLIMATE
USDA Hardiness Zones 5–9; AHS Heat Zones 9–4

REGIONS
The best regions for tree longevity, production, and lack of pest problems are those with steadily cold winters, no late frosts in spring, and warm, dry weather through summer

Peach blossoms provide a cheery, pink welcome into spring.

Grow It Naturally

- Prune aggressively each spring just before blossoms open so branches can bathe in sunlight and air, and to stimulate new growth for next year's crop.

- Thoroughly remove and dispose of any infected or infested fruit during and at the end of the growing season.

- Plant disease-resistant varieties.

- Keep bark healthy. Paint it white in winter to protect the tree from sunburn, and avoid damage such as from mowing.

- Maintain vigorous growth with mulches and, if needed, fertilizer.

Maria called me one August day to come and visit her and her fig trees. Maria is originally from Italy, very short, very sturdy, and 80-something years old, and soon we were also looking at her chestnut trees, Romano beans, broccoli rabe, and more plants. As I was getting ready to leave, she preferred, in her thick, Italian accent, "You wanne some o' my peaches?" The peaches looked small, fuzzy, a bit greenish, and speckled with brown spots. Still, it was an offer I couldn't refuse, even if she did refuse my offer to climb her rickety wooden ladder to fill a small basket. That basket she filled held some of the most flavorful peaches I'd ever eaten, peaches not only sweet, but with rich, peachy flavor and pleasant, fibery texture. The fruits oozed old-fashioned peachiness.

To savor peaches and nectarines at their best—drippy, aromatic, and bursting with flavor—you must raise them yourself. The trees never grow large and are very ornamental with their showy pink blossoms and lustrous, drooping leaves. They bear fruit quickly, often in their second year.

Although the botanical name (*Persica*) implies origin in Persia (modern-day Iran), peaches are actually native to China. Long ago, peaches were carried westward, through Persia, on to ancient Greece, and then to Rome. Romans spread cultivation of the peach throughout their empire. Seeds were brought to America in the 16th century, where they found a welcome reception. Native American tribes, such as the Havasu in the Southwest, soon began cultivating orchards of peaches, and in the Southeast, peaches even formed wild stands (called "Tennessee naturals").

Nectarines and peaches are practically the same fruit, differing by only a single gene. It's not uncommon for a branch on a peach tree to mutate and start bearing nectarines, and vice versa.

Growing

To keep your tree healthy, productive, and bearing the best-quality fruit, choose a site carefully. Peaches and nectarines bloom very early in the season, so the ideal site does not warm up too early in spring. Also critical to success is full sunlight, perfectly drained soil, and summer warmth.

Peach or nectarine growing is a chancy proposition in less-than-ideal sites. Still, a tree-ripe peach or nectarine of a flavorful variety is such a treat that resigning yourself to occasional, or more than occasional, crop failures may still make planting the tree worthwhile

(I'll settle for two out of five good years). And anyway, the trees are beautiful in bloom in spring and then pretty all season long; in good years, fruits make them even prettier.

Pruning

Train your young tree to an open-center form (see pp. 40–41), then prune every year. To promote rapid healing of pruning wounds, and so that you can notice and remove branches injured by winter cold, prune as soon as possible after the tree awakens—while the tree is in bloom is an ideal time.

Peach and nectarine trees bear only on 1-year-old stems, so annual pruning, which stimulates new growth that season for fruit-bearing shoots the following season, is a must. It is also important because it thins fruits, especially if you want the biggest and best-tasting peaches and nectarines.

Use a combination of heading and thinning cuts (see p. 37) to stimulate new growth as well as to keep the tree low and open to light. Invite light and air into the canopy by removing vigorous upright stems, thinning remaining stems, and occasionally cutting back stems into two- or three-year-old wood. Cut back drooping stems as well as any very short stems because they typically produce small fruits. The combined effects of pruning and fertilizing should stimulate 3 feet of new growth on young trees and 18 inches to 24 inches of new growth on mature trees. When you've finished pruning a peach or nectarine tree, you should have removed enough wood so that a bird could fly right through the tree without touching any of the branches.

Doughnut Peaches

Around 1980 I was fortunate enough to be working in the Fruit Laboratory of the U.S. Department of Agriculture in Beltsville, Maryland, where, besides doing research, we got to be among the first in the United States to taste some really fine fruits. Among my favorites were the 'Peen Tao' peaches. These small, flattened fruits are honey-sweet and look liked flying saucers or doughnuts. (They first arrived on American shores in the 1800s, but evidently impressed few people at that time.) Besides having good flavor, doughnut peaches are easier to eat neatly than are conventional peaches. Just hold the center and rotate the fruit as you eat it.

Since then, other doughnut peaches have been bred, including 'Saturn' (white fleshed), 'Sweet Bagel' (yellow fleshed), 'UFO' (white fleshed, firm when ripe, subtropical), and 'Galaxy' (white fleshed, large fruit).

Doughnut peaches are generally less cold hardy and more susceptible to pests and diseases than are other peaches.

Even after you remove potential fruits by pruning, you'll probably have to thin fruits after they set. While the fruits are still small, remove excess so that none is closer than 8 inches to its neighbor. This tedious job will show its worth when you bite into fruit later that season.

Pruning a Peach Tree

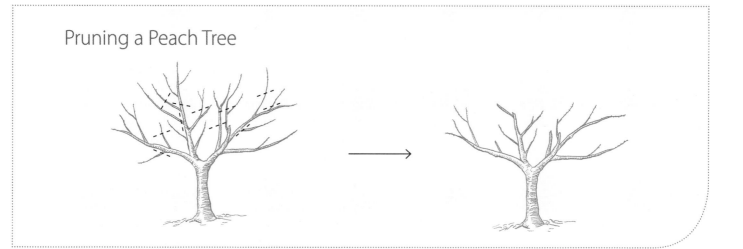

Pests and Diseases

East of the Rocky Mountains, plum curculio, an insect that damages developing fruits and leaves a tell-tale crescent-shaped scar, is common. Injured fruits usually drop or become susceptible to disease. Curculios are mostly active during the six-week period beginning around petal fall. Keep curculios at bay by spraying three layers of Surround before bloom and then renew the spray every seven days to ten days, more frequently after rains, throughout that six-week period. Another option is to hit the limbs or the trunk of the tree with a padded mallet every morning to jar the curculios off the fruit. Spread a sheet or tarp on the ground underneath the tree to catch them and provide an easy means for disposal. Keeping poultry, which eat curculios, beneath the trees also offers some control.

Oriental fruit moth is another insect pest that attacks peach and nectarine fruits, leaving a large hole where it enters. This insect also bores into young stems, causing them to wilt at their tips. Besides spraying, this pest has been controlled by mating disruption (on plots greater than 3 acres) and by *Macrocentrus ancylivorus* parasitoid wasp. Spraying of Surround, Entrust, or Bt can be effective, although wiping Surround residue (edible but disconcerting) off the skin of a fuzzy peach is challenging.

Especially in the Southeast, catfacing of fruits can be a problem. These sunken, corky lesions are caused by plant bugs, such as the tarnished plant bug. The insects live among weeds and plant debris, so clean up areas adjacent to trees in addition to spraying, if necessary.

Fruits that become covered with a fuzzy gray fungus are infected with brown rot disease. Infected fruits, called mummies, darken, shrivel, harden, and often remain hanging in the tree. Remove all mummies from the ground and the tree, because they are a source of the next year's infections. The disease also attacks twigs, so prune off and dispose of twigs that show the dark, sunken cankers from brown rot. Brown rot is one more reason for thinning peach and nectarine fruits. A few peach varieties are resistant, including 'Early Redhaven', 'Garnet Beauty', 'Harbrite', 'Harcrest', 'Harrow Beauty', 'Glohaven', and 'Elberta'. Nectarines are generally more susceptible to brown rot than are peaches; 'RedGold' and 'Midglo' have some resistance. Spraying copper or sulfur around time of bloom and again before fruits begin to ripen also helps control brown rot.

Dark spots pitting the surface of fruits are symptoms of bacterial spot, another disease more prevalent in moist climates such as those of the eastern United States. Besides spraying copper during dormancy and spring, choosing resistant varieties also can limit this disease. 'Candor', 'Earliglo', 'Harbelle', 'Harbinger', 'Redskin', 'Redhaven', 'Harrow Diamond', and 'Harrow Beauty' are peaches with some resistance; 'Mericrest', 'RedGold', and 'Midglo' nectarines have some resistance. The bacteria overwinter in dark, gummy branch tips and diseased twigs; prune them away when you notice them to help reduce future sources of infection.

If the leaves on your peach tree are reddish, puckered, and curled, peach leaf curl disease is the culprit. Again, resistant varieties ('Elberta', 'Redhaven', and 'Candor', to name a few) and spraying copper help limit the disease. Cold winters kill the fungus.

If large branches or entire trees are wilting, suspect bark cankers or borers. Cankers are caused by a combination of factors, including wounds and winter cold damage, the latter the result of lack of cold-hardiness or late fertilization. Borers are insects that generally attack weakened trees or trees that have already had their bark damaged, as by lawn mowers or cankers. Kill a resident borer, if already present, by jabbing a stiff wire into the hole in the bark to the borer's residence. The beneficial nematode *Steinernema carpocapsae* is a borer killer, and Entrust or Surround sprays are effective against borers. Also prune off and dispose of twigs with canker disease.

Harvesting

"If you don't like my peaches, baby don't shake my tree," goes an old blues tune. It used to be that you just shook your tree to get ripe peaches (or nectarines) to drop. Back then, though, these fruits were mostly used to make brandy and feed pigs. Some commercial peaches and nectarines are still harvested by shaking the trees, mechanically, but for the best fresh eating, more finesse is needed.

Before picking, wait for the background color to turn yellow on yellow varieties and pale green, almost white, on white varieties. The fruit should also have softened, less so for some of the newer, firmer varieties. Cradle the ripe-looking, perhaps softening fruit in the palm of your hand, give it a twist and a lift, and off it should come. Some varieties release more easily than others. The final and best part of the ripeness test is to take a bite.

Not all fruits will be ripe on any tree at the same time. Plan on three or four pickings over the course of a couple of weeks.

Selection of Plants and Varieties

Peaches and nectarines grow readily from seed, and many seedlings bear high-quality fruits at a relatively young age. As a result, there are many, many varieties of peach, less of nectarine, with new ones rapidly being developed. Maria's trees, mentioned earlier, were seedlings from pits she had planted, another one of which I am now growing. Many new peach and nectarine varieties are developed with a nod to better pest and disease resistance and flavor, and to extend the northern and southern limits of growing these fruits. Choose a variety adapted to your area, in terms of tolerance for winter cold and chilling requirements. Consider also a variety's productivity and pest resistance. In humid regions, look for resistance to bacterial spot and brown rot diseases. Disease and insect pests generally are more prevalent east of the Rocky Mountains.

Also, of course, consider fruit quality. The best white-fleshed peaches and nectarines taste as if they have been drenched in honey and have less peach or nectarine flavor. Many newer varieties, for better or worse, aren't as drippy as older varieties because of a "stony hard" gene that keeps the fruit firm when it is ripe. Peaches and nectarines are either freestone or clingstone, depending on whether the pit adheres to the skin. Freestone peaches generally have high-quality, smooth, melt-in-your-mouth flesh. The firm flesh of clingstone varieties clings well to the pit and holds together better than freestone varieties for cooking.

Choosing a rootstock is another important part of selecting peaches or nectarines that might grow best in your yard. 'Lovell' is a rootstock suitable for soils that tend to be wet in winter. In dry, sandy soils where nematodes might cause problems, 'Nemaguard' is one rootstock of choice. 'St. Julian A' and 'Siberian C' are semidwarfing rootstocks good for cold areas with fluctuating spring temperatures. 'Krymsk 1', a new dwarfing rootstock still being tested, seems to be tolerant of cold, drought, and waterlogging, and creates about a half-size tree. There are also others, although nurseries may not offer a broad selection from which to choose.

Genetic dwarfs are varieties that are naturally dwarf. Many mature at 4 feet tall or less. They generally bear lower-quality fruit and are more disease susceptible than other varieties.

Listed here is just a handful of popular peach and nectarine varieties. Your local Cooperative Extension office can suggest the best (which might also be the newest) varieties for your yard.

PEACHES

'Babcock' White flesh, freestone; sweet, juicy, and aromatic; low acidity; thin aggressively for good fruit size; low chill, 300 hours.

'Belle of Georgia' White flesh, freestone; excellent flavor; very productive; susceptible to brown rot, resistant to bacterial spot; very cold hardy; ripens midseason.

'Bonanza II' Freestone; fruit is large with orange-red skin and sweet yellow flesh; low chill, 250 hours or less; genetic dwarf grows to a maximum of 6 feet.

'Contender' Large, firm, yellow-fleshed freestone fruit with excellent flavor; resistant to bacterial spot, susceptible to leaf curl; productive.

'Desert Gold' Yellow flesh, semi-freestone; medium fruit with good flavor; susceptible to diseases; low-chill variety requiring 300 chilling hours.

Dr. Elwyn Meader standing next to some super-dwarf peaches he bred to withstand harsh New England winters.

'Madison' is a good-tasting peach well suited to regions with cold winters and late spring frosts.

'Galaxy' Clingstone, doughnut peach (p. 167); has cream-colored skin with a red blush; white fleshed with a sweet taste and firm texture; low chill.

'Loring' Yellow flesh, freestone; large fruit with very good flavor; skin has a bright red blush over yellow background; vigorous; resistant to bacterial spot, susceptible to leaf curl; flower buds somewhat tender to winter cold; ripens midseason.

'Madison' Medium freestone fruit with very good flavor and tender, yellow flesh; productive; resistant to leaf curl and bacterial spot; very cold hardy in winter and can tolerate spring frosts; late ripening.

'O'Henry' Freestone; large fruit with excellent flavor and firm, yellow flesh; high yields; very susceptible to bacterial spot; ripens midseason.

'Redhaven' Medium fruit; skin red over yellow; freestone flesh is sweet, yellow and fine textured, very good flavor; vigorous; cold hardy; susceptible to brown rot, resistant to leaf curl and bacterial spot early; widely adapted; ripens midseason.

'Reliance' Yellow, freestone, good flavor; dark red splashed with yellow; very cold hardy and tolerates spring frosts; resistant to leaf curl and bacterial spot; ripens midseason.

'Saturn' White flesh, freestone, doughnut peach; sweet, low acid, sometimes with rose-like aromatics; red skin with creamy white background; buds very cold hardy; leaves resistant to bacterial spot.

'Sugar Lady' Skin is dark pinkish red over a cream background; freestone white flesh is moderately firm, very aromatic, and sweet with little acid and very good flavor.

'Summer Pearl' Pinkish skin; white, freestone flesh is very sweet and aromatic; susceptible to bacterial spot.

'Sunhaven' Yellow, freestone flesh is flecked with red; fruit is large with excellent flavor; vigorous; productive, resistant to bacterial spot, susceptible to brown rot; ripens very early.

'Tropic Snow' White flesh, freestone, large fruit with excellent flavor; pale yellow skin with red blush; low chill, 150–200 hours.

'Tropic Sweet' Yellow, freestone flesh; very sweet with excellent flavor; large fruit; productive, strong tree; self-fruitful; low chill, 150 hours.

NECTARINES

'Arctic Star' Semi-freestone; snow-white flesh, low acid, super-sweet; beautiful dark red skin; ripens very early season; low-chill variety needs 300 chilling hours.

'Earligrande' Medium to large fruit has yellow, semi-freestone flesh with yellow, red-blushed skin; firm, fine-textured fruit with excellent quality and flavor; heavy producer; chilling requirements low at 200 hours.

'Fantasia' Large, yellow, freestone flesh; skin is bright yellow with red blush over half the fruit; vigorous; productive; moderately susceptible to brown rot and bacterial spot; ripens late season.

'Hardired' Yellow, freestone flesh; good flavor, tolerant of bacterial spot and brown rot; very cold hardy and tolerant of spring frosts.

'Mericrest' Medium fruit with yellow, freestone flesh; excellent flavor; resistant to brown rot and bacterial spot, productive; very cold hardy; ripens midseason.

'Midglo' Very firm, medium to large fruit; yellow, clingstone flesh has excellent flavor; semi-resistant to brown rot and bacterial spot; ripens midseason.

'Morton' Bright red skin and juicy, white, clingstone flesh; small to medium fruit; brown rot resistant; ripens early.

'Panamint' Yellow, freestone flesh; aromatic, intensely flavored with a nice acid-sugar balance; low chilling requirement of 275 hours; resistant to bacterial leaf spot; ripens midseason.

'RedGold' Fairly firm yellow, freestone fruit; resistant to brown rot and bacterial spot; fairly cold hardy; ripens mid- to late season.

Pear

European pear: *Pyrus communis*
Asian pear (nashi): *P. pyrifolia*, *P. ussuriensis*, and
P. × *bretschneider*

GROWTH HABIT
Depending on rootstock and variety, trees grow
from 8 feet to 30 feet tall

POLLINATION
Generally require cross-pollination, although some
varieties are self-fruitful in certain regions

LIGHT REQUIREMENT
Full sunlight

CLIMATE
European pear, USDA Hardiness Zones 2–9; AHS
Heat Zones 9–3
Asian pear, USDA Hardiness Zones 4–9; AHS Heat
Zones 9–3

REGIONS
As long as plants experience sufficient winter
chilling, pears are widely adaptable, with few pest
problems

Pears come in two "flavors": European and Asian. European pears, which are most familiar in American markets, are typically buttery, sweet, and richly aromatic. They're also pear shaped. Asian pears, sometimes called nashi, have turned up in American markets more recently. They're typically round and have crisp flesh that explodes with juice when you take a bite. Their flavors are sweet with a delicate, floral aroma and sometimes a hint of walnut or butterscotch. Because of their firm flesh and usually round shape, Asian pears are sometimes known as apple pears.

Both Asian and European pears have been cultivated for thousands of years, and within each type exist thousands of varieties. As the various species met in America in the 19th century, breeders hybridized them, infusing the European pear with the disease resistance or cold-hardiness of some of the Asian pears.

Among tree fruits, pears of either flavor are easy to grow. But growing and ripening a European pear to its highest state of perfection is an art. The best one I ever tasted was at the conclusion of a horticultural conference at the venerable East Malling Research Station in England, when we were led into an elegant, large, wood-paneled room, up the center of which ran a hulking, oak banquet table. Nothing more than a few bowls of perfectly ripened 'Comice' pears, ours for the tasting, sat on the table. I reached for a pear, took a bite, and quickly had to make my way to the far end of the room to keep the ambrosial juice from marring the staid surroundings.

Lee's Picks

'Magness', 'Comice', 'Seckel', 'Chojuro', and 'Yoinashi' are among my favorite varieties. I'm constantly cutting back undesirable trees and grafting with new varieties and have not waded among the thousands of other varieties—yet. Some contenders include 'Beurre d'Amanlis', 'Aurora', 'Dana Hovey', 'Clara Frijs', 'Flemish Beauty', 'Patten', 'Vermont Beauty', 'Tyson', and 'Beurre Superfin'.

Growing

Cultivation of European and Asian pears is essentially the same, with just a few subtle differences. Both need full sun and soil that is at least reasonably well drained. Pears can tolerate wetter soils than many other tree fruits.

Asian and European varieties generally cannot pollinate each other because their bloom times, with few exceptions, do not overlap. Further complicating matters, certain varieties cannot be used to cross-pollinate each other at all, such as 'Seckel' and 'Bartlett', 'Seckel' and 'Patomac', 'Shinsui' and 'Kosui', and 'Shinseiki' and 'Seigyoku'. And 'Magness' has sterile pollen, so two other varieties are needed for everyone to bear fruit.

Grow It Naturally

- Plant disease-resistant varieties where diseases are a particular problem.

- Prune diseased wood whenever you see it.

- Remove watersprouts by hand in summer.

- Avoid excessive pruning or fertilizing; it promotes overly lush growth that is susceptible to fire blight disease.

Pruning

Prune a pear tree every year, while the plant is dormant. On a young Asian pear tree, do only the minimum amount of pruning necessary to train the plant to an open-center or modified central-leader form (see pp. 40–41). European pears have an upright growth habit that lends itself more to the modified central-leader or central-leader form. During the training period, bend branches down to an angle within 30 degrees of the ground to promote good form and early fruiting. Asian pears are precocious, sometimes fruiting in their third season, whereas European pears are slower to come into bearing.

Once a tree reaches bearing age, prune it lightly every year (as you would do with an apple tree; see the illustrations on p. 72). Thin out overly vigorous stems, which mostly originate higher in the tree, and head back weak twigs, which are mainly found lower in the tree. Pear trees bear fruits on spurs, short stems that grow only ½ inch each year, so they do not need to make much new growth every year to remain fruitful. Asian pears fruit best on spurs only 2 years to 3 years old, so they need to be thinned out and headed back more aggressively to maintain a steady supply of young spurs. European pear spurs are good for about 10 years. When a whole branch on either kind of pear becomes decrepit, head it back severely to make room for and stimulate growth of a replacement. The combined effects of fertilizer and pruning should coax about 2 feet of annual growth on a young tree, 1 foot of growth on a mature tree.

European pears, especially, are prone to growing many watersprouts, which shade the plant, are not fruitful, and are prone to disease. Cut them back when pruning or, even better, grab them in your hand and rip them off with a quick downward jerk while they are still green and growing during summer.

Pears, especially Asian pears, are good candidates for espalier.

Each flower bud on a pear tree opens to a cluster of flowers, so pear trees, left to their own devices, usually will overbear. Thin fruits to about 5 inches apart. Thinning Asian pears is very important, spelling the difference between a harvest of ho-hum pears and ones that elicit a "Wow!"

TOP: Pears blossom and fruit on long-lived spurs, which are growths that branch and elongate only a fraction of an inch each year.

BOTTOM: Symptoms of fire blight disease are blackened leaves that remain attached to stems, the ends of which curl over.

Pests and Diseases

In most yards throughout the country, pears can be grown successfully without any attention to pest control. Occasionally, a few pests warrant attention and action.

FIRE BLIGHT

The main bugaboo in pear growing is the bacterial disease fire blight, readily identified by stems whose ends curl in shepherd's crooks with blackened leaves, looking as if they have been singed by fire, remaining attached. During winter, the disease rests in dark, sunken cankers evident on the bark. Still, fire blight does not show up everywhere (I've never had it on any of my two dozen pear trees) and there are many resistant varieties. Fire blight can be satisfactorily controlled with diligent, frequent pruning. During the growing season, cut diseased wood back into 6 inches of healthy wood, sterilizing pruning shears between cuts by wiping the blades with alcohol, Listerine, Lysol, or Pine-Sol. In winter, prune off any infected wood or stems you missed during the growing season. No need to sterilize shears between cuts during winter pruning.

Because fire blight most readily attacks succulent growth, avoid excessive fertilizer or pruning, both of which can overstimulate a tree. One way to slow down an overly vigorous tree is to grow grass right up to its base to suck up extra water and fertilizer. (Do not do this with young trees, though, or you may stunt them.)

PSEUDOMONAS BLIGHT

Cool, wet springs foment pseudomonas blight, which has symptoms similar to fire blight, except that the cankers do not ooze, as do fire blight cankers, in spring. Control pseudomonas blight by planting resistant varieties and by pruning as for fire blight. If further control is necessary, spray copper early and late in the season.

PEAR SCAB

Cool, wet summers promote pear scab, the symptoms of which are round, brownish spots on leaves and brown, corky areas on fruits and twigs. Clean up and dispose of or bury infected leaves at the end of the season, and prune away infected twigs in winter to help control scab. Sulfur sprays also protect pears against scab, especially if they're applied in the season. The first line of defense, of course, is to plant scab-resistant varieties such as 'Harrow Delight', 'Magness', 'Moonglow', and 'Comice'.

STONY PIT

Stony pit is a virus that attacks some pear varieties, resulting in dimpled or pitted fruit with a grain of hard flesh at the pit or point of dimpling. The disease is transmitted through infected scion wood during propagation. Severity varies from year to year, even within a tree. Varieties differ in their expression of this disease; 'Beurre Bosc' is among the most susceptible. Other problems, such as tarnished plant bug injury, cork spot, and boron deficiency, cause similar symptoms. Healthy nursery plants and resistant varieties avoid stony pit caused by the virus; other causes are not as prevalent.

Perry

Perry is fermented pear juice, an old-fashioned beverage whose origin lies in France but reached its heyday in 16th- and 17th-century England, especially in the western part of that country. The juice itself was not your mother's—or grandmother's—pear juice. Pears for perry are botanically *P. nivalis*, a hardy and long-lived species, and most are too astringent for fresh eating. Perry is made in much the same way as is hard cider except that perry pears need to sit and ripen for a few days after harvest, and the pomace likewise needs to sit to reduce tannins. The end product is quite different from cider because perry pears have more sugar as well as more unfermentable sugars, more citric acid, and different kinds of tannins. And because, of course, the raw material is pears, with their unique flavor profiles. Especially with some perry pear varieties, fermentation can be sluggish.

Traditionally, perry has been a very variable product, reflecting the kinds of pears that figure into the mix, how the mix was fermented, how the fruits were grown, and the vagaries of a particular season. The drink was very much a home- or farm-made beverage, varying as much in alcohol concentration as in flavor. After experiencing a lapse in interest and various attempts to industrialize the product in the 20th century, perry is undergoing a renaissance. Part of that renaissance lies in the rediscovery of some of the traditional perry varieties. 'Arlingham Squash', 'Green Horse', 'Moorcroft', 'Rock', and 'Taynton Squash' are among the varieties that have contributed to vintage-quality perries for over three centuries. A few varieties of perry pears are considered dual purpose, for both perry making and for fresh eating. Among those varieties are 'Blakeney Red', 'Brown Bess', and 'Thorn'.

'Chojuro' is a productive Asian pear with bold flavor.

PEAR PSYLLA

Pear psylla is an insect that weakens the tree by sucking out its sap. Also, the psylla excretes honeydew that coats the leaves and becomes colonized by a superficial black fungus. If extensive enough, that black coating shades the plant and can be mistaken for fire blight. Differentiate between fire blight and this superficial mold by rubbing a leaf; if the black color wipes off, the problem is not fire blight. Control this sucker by spraying oil, insecticidal soap, or Surround.

Harvesting

First, the easy harvest: Asian pears. Harvest them when they are fully colored and detach easily. Roll them upward with a twist. Taste is the final test; if flavor is not up to snuff, let the fruits hang longer. These pears keep well in a refrigerator anywhere from a couple of months to almost a year, depending on variety.

European pears must be harvested when underripe. They ripen from the inside outward, so their interiors become brown mush if the fruits are allowed to fully ripen on the tree. The fruit must, however, be mature before it is picked. The first clue to fruit maturity is a subtle lightening of the skin's background color. Look closely at the raised pores on the skin (called lenticels); they will become brown and corky at harvest time. Lift and twist the fruit. If the stalk separates easily from the stem, the fruits are ready for harvest.

You're not yet in pear heaven. European pears need to be kept cool for a while before they can begin ripening: a few days for early-ripening pears, a few weeks for late-ripening pears. Keep them cool longer if you intend to store them.

Take some pears out of cold storage a few days before you want them for eating and put them in a cool room, ideally at a temperature of 60°F to 70°F. They are ready to enjoy when you apply pressure near the stem with your finger and feel a slight give. Before you take your bite, realize that a lot goes into creating that perfect pear: variety choice, pruning, fruit thinning, timely harvest, skillful ripening, even the weather. 'Bartlett' and 'Beurre Bosc', for example, taste best if temperatures are high during the two months preceding harvest; 'Anjou' likes it cool.

If you've mastered the art of pear growing, harvesting, and ripening, and the weather cooperated, your reward will be fruits that are juicy and sweet with characteristic aromas that might include varying proportions of almond, rose, honey, and musk. Still, to quote Ralph Waldo Emerson, "There are only 10 minutes in the life of a pear when it is perfect to eat." But what a sensuous 10 minutes.

'Magness', an offspring of the also delectable 'Comice', is among the best flavored of all European pears.

Selection of Plants and Varieties

Full-size pear trees grow very large, but a number of semi-dwarfing and dwarfing rootstocks are available. Quince is one such dwarfing rootstock, producing a tree that eventually grows only about 8 feet tall. Some pears are graft-incompatible with quince, in which case a tree can be made by first grafting a short length of stem of a quince-compatible variety of pear on the quince rootstock and then a quince-incompatible variety on the quince-compatible pear interstem (see p. 78). A series of rootstocks, designated OH×F (they are hybrids of 'Old Home' and 'Farmingdale' pears), also offer various degrees of dwarfing as well as resistance to fire blight disease. Rootstock resistance to fire blight does not prevent a grafted scion from getting the disease but at least prevents the disease from traveling internally to kill the whole tree. The most dwarfing of this series, producing a tree comparable in size to that on quince rootstock, is OH×F.51. Pyro.2-33 is another fire blight resistant rootstock that induces precocity and dwarfing of about 50 percent.

Be careful about using dwarfing rootstocks with Asian pears. These pears are very productive. Heavy crops coupled with a dwarfing rootstock on a young plant leads to stunting. Usual rootstocks are *P. calleryana* in mild winter regions or more vigorous OH×F selections, such as OH×F.69, OH×F.87, or OH×F.40, elsewhere.

The following is a selection of a few varieties from among the thousands of European and Asian pears.

EUROPEAN PEARS

'Bartlett' Familiar in markets, 'Bartlett' (known as 'Williams' in Europe) has a smooth, yellow skin and a very good, sweet, musky flavor when grown, picked, and ripened well; tree is productive and reliable; likes hot summers; very susceptible to fire blight, moderately resistant to leaf spot and scab; cannot cross-pollinate with 'Seckel'; ripens early to midseason; stores well for about two months; some red sports exist, such as 'Max Red Bartlett' and 'Sensation'.

'Beurre Bosc' Usually has a russet skin, crisp texture, and sweet, spicy flavor; productive; needs good soil and drainage; susceptible to fire blight, leaf spot, scab, and stony pit; ripens late season; keeps for three to four months.

'Beurre Superfin' Medium to large fruit with smooth, greenish yellow skin and sweet, spicy flavor; refrigerate for one month before taking it out to begin ripening; ripens mid- to late season; does not store well.

'Collette' Large fruit with rich, aromatic flavor and yellow skin that has tiny, reddish brown speckles and a rosy cheek; ripens early and continues to do so for weeks.

'Comice' Considered perhaps the best flavored of all pears; large fruit with greenish yellow skin having a slight blush and russet; bruises easily; production is erratic; resistant to scab, susceptible to fire blight and leaf spot; refrigerate for at least one month before taking it out to begin ripening; late; keeps for about four months.

'Harrow Delight' Very good flavor, similar to 'Bartlett'; productive; resistant to fire blight and scab; susceptible to leaf spot disease; ripens early and keeps for about a month.

'Highland' Dull, brownish yellow, slightly russeted fruit is smooth and juicy with sweet, rich flavor; productive and widely adapted; ripens mid- to late season; stores for about three months.

'Magness' Among the best tasting of European pears ('Comice' is one parent); sweet, juicy, aromatic, and soft, with a greenish yellow skin having dark spots and light russet; medium fruit; resistant to fire blight and scab, susceptible to leaf spot; slow to come into bearing, low yielding, and cannot pollinate any other pears; ripens midseason and keeps for about four months.

'Moonglow' Medium, soft, yellow fruit with good, mild flavor; resistant to fire blight, leaf spot, and scab; widely adapted; precocious; ripens early and keeps for about four months.

'Orcas' Medium to large, slightly lumpy fruit with sweet, mild flavor; productive; resistant to scab; ripens early to midseason.

'Seckel' ('Sugar Pear') Fruits have a sweet, spicy flavor and a yellowish brown skin with a pale russet and a red cheek; tree is widely adapted and naturally small; resistant to fire blight, susceptible to scab and leaf spot; cannot pollinate 'Bartlett'; ripens midseason and keeps for about three months.

'Warren' Excellent flavor, comparable to 'Magness' and 'Comice' (and very possibly a sibling of 'Magness'); resistant to fire blight and scab, susceptible to leaf spot; low yields; sterile pollen; ripens midseason and stores for about four months.

ASIAN PEARS

'Chojuro' Strong-flavored flesh with a slightly astringent skin; flat and russeted fruit; productive; susceptible to fire blight and pseudomonas blight; ripens midseason and keeps for about five months.

'Hosui' A golden brown pear with a sweet, rich flavor; round fruit; tree has a somewhat weeping form; productive; susceptible to fire blight and pseudomonas blight; ripens early and keeps for one month to two months; moderately low chilling requirement of 450 hours.

'Korean Giant' ('Olympic') Fruit is round with russeted skin; tastes honey sweet with hints of butterscotch and caramel; low productivity; resistant to fire blight, susceptible to pseudomonas blight; late ripening, too late for northern regions; keeps for about five months.

'Kosui' Bronze skin and sweet flesh of excellent flavor; ripens early and stores for a couple of months.

'Nijisseikei' ('Twentieth Century') Common in American markets, this variety has an especially thin, tender skin and a sweet, juicy flesh; tends to bear crops in alternate years; productive; susceptible to pseudomonas and fire blight; ripens early to midseason and keeps for about five months.

'Seuri' Large pear has an excellent, spicy flavor that hints of walnut; very productive; moderately resistant to fire blight, susceptible to pseudomonas blight; ripens late season but does not store well.

'Ya Li' ('Duckbill Pear') Old, pear-shaped variety, aromatic with a sweet flavor; good for growing in warm regions; susceptible to fire blight and pseudomonas blight; ripens late and stores for six months or more; low chilling requirement of 300 hours.

'Yoinashi' Large, russeted fruit with excellent flavor suggesting brown sugar and butterscotch; moderately productive; susceptible to fire blight and pseudomonas blight; ripens midseason and keeps for about five months.

EUROPEAN-ASIAN HYBRID

'Kieffer' Introduced in the 19th century and widely planted; most suitable for cooking or canning, poor quality for fresh eating; fruits are large and yellow; widely adapted and disease resistant; ripens mid- to late season.

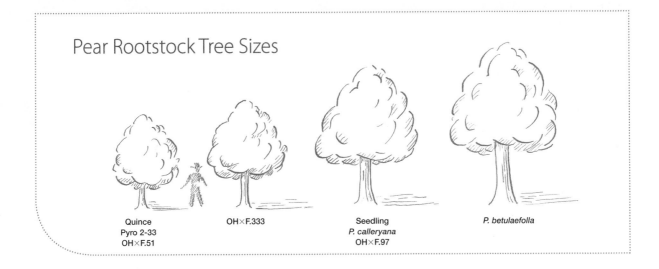

Pear Rootstock Tree Sizes

Quince
Pyro 2-33
OH×F.51

OH×F.333

Seedling
P. calleryana
OH×F.97

P. betulaefolla

Persimmon

Kaki (Asian) persimmon: *Diospyros kaki*
American persimmon: *D. virginiana*

GROWTH HABIT
Kaki persimmon is a medium-size tree; American persimmon is a medium to large tree

POLLINATION NEEDS
Variable, depending on variety

LIGHT REQUIREMENT
Full sunlight

CLIMATE
Kaki persimmon: USDA Hardiness Zones 7–10; AHS Heat Zones 10–7
American persimmon: USDA Hardiness Zones 4–10; AHS Heat Zones 9–4

REGIONS
Adapted throughout regions within its cold-hardiness and heat zones

Ahhhh, food of the gods. That's the translation of *Diospyros*, the botanical name for persimmons. American persimmon, usually the size of a golf ball and some shade of orange, has the taste and texture of a dried apricot that's been soaked in water, dipped in honey, and given a dash of spice. Kaki persimmons are larger, red or orange, and shaped like anything from a tomato to an acorn, or they're lobed. They are juicier than American persimmons, with a similarly sweet, though less rich, flavor. Kaki flesh is either crisp like an apple or smooth like jello.

Both American and kaki persimmons are among the easiest of fruits to grow. In a backyard, pests rarely cause problems and the trees' other needs are minimal. American persimmon doesn't even need regular pruning! The plants blossom relatively late in the season, so they fruit reliably without danger from late frosts. And for all this good taste and low maintenance, the trees also look nice throughout the growing season and especially in autumn, when the brightly colored, ripening fruits are peeking out from among the leaves. After the leaves drop, some varieties cling to their fruits for your continued visual and tasting pleasure.

Growing

Having been cultivated for hundreds of years, kaki comes in thousands of varieties. Not so for American persimmon, the first variety of which—'Early Golden'— was selected and named in 1880 during a flurry of interest in native fruits in America. More than a century later, American persimmons are still not well known, except

TOP: 'Szukis' American persimmon ripening on branches in late summer foreshadows good flavor soon to come.

BOTTOM: American persimmon looks pretty all season long with its languid, blue-green leaves and bark that resembles alligator skin.

Grow It Naturally

- Persimmons have few or no demands as far as pruning or pest control so are relatively easy to grow naturally.

- Plant an adapted variety—one that tolerates your winter's cold and will ripen within the growing season for your region.

Lobed fruits of 'Honan Red' kakis have very sweet, rich flavor.

'Tamopan' is a kaki with a fleshy cap and refreshing, sweet flavor.

to a few aficionados and in places where the trees grow wild. If you want to grow American persimmon, get a named variety. Many wild American persimmons don't taste good. If you live near the northern limits for growing American persimmon, not all varieties may ripen within your growing season. A well-chosen, named variety ensures that you'll get good-tasting fruit that will ripen where you live.

Wild persimmons are dioecious, but a number of named varieties of both kinds of persimmons bear fruit without the need for a separate male pollinator tree. Pollination puts seeds in their otherwise seedless fruits and, with some varieties, can change fruit flavor or texture.

Persimmons have a taproot, so purchase a tree growing in a deep pot or one that has been transplanted, with care, in spring. The black roots look like they are dead; they are not.

Pruning

Once a persimmon tree has been trained to a sturdy framework of branches as a central or modified central leader form (see pp. 40–41), little further pruning is

necessary. Aside from removing misplaced, dead, or diseased branches, head some branches each winter to stimulate new growth (see p. 37), on which fruit will be borne the following season. Also head back enough young wood to reduce the crop load and keep bearing limbs in near the trunk. If fruit set is very heavy, especially with kakis, thin the fruits by hand after they have set. American persimmon naturally drops some stems that have borne fruits, so it is somewhat self-pruning.

Pests and Diseases

In general, you'll experience few, if any, pest or disease problems when growing persimmons, though occasionally they might arise in areas where persimmons are wild. Dead and dying branches on the tree and some dead branches on the ground could be symptoms of damage from persimmon girdler. Closer inspection reveals a circular ring where the branch is or has been cut, as if a tiny beaver were at work. Keep this pest in check by gathering and burning or otherwise disposing of dead, dying, and fallen branches.

Persimmon borer leaves a black gum ooze and particles of bark near the base of the tree, and hollowed out or bored roots. Vigorous growth is least attractive to persimmon borers, as is the case with most plant borers.

Spotting on leaves could be a symptom of persimmon anthracnose, a disease to which certain varieties, such as 'Morris Burton' and 'Runkwitz', are resistant.

Persimmon wilt is a fungal disease occasionally found in the southeastern United States, causing trees to wilt and then die from the top down. Cold winters, late freezes, or bark injuries trigger the problem. Cut down and burn infected trees.

Harvesting

Eating an unripe persimmon is extremely unpleasant, a sensation I'd describe as having a vacuum cleaner in your mouth (due to the unripe fruit's stringency). Or, as Captain John Smith (of Pocahontas fame) stated: "If it is not ripe it will draw a man's mouth awrie with much torment." The captain did go on to say that "when it is ripe, it is as delicious as an apricot."

Wait to harvest American persimmons and so-called astringent (astringent until they are ripe, that is) varieties of kakis until fruits are fully colored and soft. Pick fruits of kaki varieties that are nonastringent (edible while firm) as soon as they are fully colored. Kakis and, to a much lesser extent, American persimmons, can be picked underripe and ripened indoors. You can speed the ripening process by putting near-ripe fruits into a bag with an apple. Drying the fruit also removes its astringency.

Clip ripe kakis from branches. American persimmons either drop when they're ripe or can be pulled off. Damaging American persimmon fruits during harvest is inconsequential because they don't keep or travel well anyway. Eat them soon after picking or freeze the pulp (freezing also removes some astringency).

Contrary to popular myth, frost is not necessary to ripen a persimmon. Both events just happen to occur late in the growing season.

After leaves fall in autumn, 'Szukis' American persimmon clings to its fruits for my picking and visual pleasure.

Selection of Plants and Varieties

The most important consideration when selecting persimmons is to plant a tree adapted to your climate so that it survives your winters and has a sufficiently long and warm season in which to ripen its fruits. In coldest areas, grow American persimmons, making sure that the varieties you plant will ripen within your growing season. American persimmons grow wild throughout much of the eastern United States, and wild trees might meet American persimmon trees' pollination needs for those varieties that require it.

In warmer regions, you can grow astringent kakis, and, in still warmer areas, nonastringent kakis. Within each of these categories of kaki are varieties whose fruits are influenced by pollination ("pollination variant") and varieties whose fruits are unaffected by pollination ("pollination constant").

When pollination is needed, you will have to either plant a separate (nonfruiting) male tree or graft a male branch onto your female tree.

Abbreviations for kaki varieties:

PCA = pollination constant, astringent

PVA = pollination variant, astringent

PVNA = pollination variant, nonastringent

PCNA = pollination constant, nonastringent

AMERICAN PERSIMMONS

'Early Golden' Fruits have good size and quality; anthracnose resistant; provide a male pollinator for best yields; ripens late in the season.

'John Rick' One of the largest and most attractive American persimmons; the red pulp is delicious; ripens late.

'Juhl' ('Yates') Large, clear, yellow skin with a red blush on the skin and black specks in the pulp, good flavor; does not need pollination; ripens early.

'Meader' Fair quality; very cold hardy; does not need pollination; ripens early, but loses its astringency slowly.

'Mohler' Very high quality; sweet fruit up to 2 inches in diameter with a pale orange skin; does not need pollination; very early ripening; fruit drops as it ripens.

'Szukis' Transparent, orange-colored skin encloses sweet, rich, and nonastringent flesh; fruits are 1½ inches in diameter; extremely cold hardy and prolific; bears some male flowers, no pollinator needed; ripens early; most fruits cling to tree after ripe, well after leaves fall.

KAKI PERSIMMONS

'Eureka' PCA; medium-large, round fruits are deep red and of excellent quality; one of the most cold hardy kakis.

'Fuyu' ('Fuyugaki') PCNA; large, orangish red fruits with excellent flavor; does not need pollination, but yields more consistently with pollination.

'Giboshi' ('Smith's Best') PVA; delicious fruit is shaped like a top; seeded fruit is the color of chocolate; one of the most cold hardy kakis.

'Giombo' PCA; fruit is large, broad, conical, and yellow; excellent flavor; very productive; very cold hardy (USDA Hardiness Zones 5–6).

'Hachiya' PCA; fruits are large, orangish red, cone shaped, and have excellent flavor.

'Honan Red' PCA; small, slightly lobed fruits are deep red and excellent fresh or dried; flesh is rich, sweet, and smooth.

'Kawabata' PCNA; large, yellow fruits are of excellent quality; cold hardy for an NA type of kaki.

'Saijo' ('Very Best One') PCA; small, bell pepper–shaped, yellowish orange fruits are very sweet and juicy; productive; very cold hardy (USDA Hardiness Zones 5–6).

'Suruga' PCNA; fruit is large, orange-red, and flattened, with a very sweet, excellent flavor.

'Tamopan' PCA; large, orange fruit with a fleshy "cap"; flesh is orange-colored, juicy, and sweet but not rich.

'Tsurunko' ('Child of the Stork', 'Chocolate Persimmon') PVNA; small to medium fruit, cylindrical shape, orange-red skin over a dark brown flesh; flavor is sweet and rich; female plant that also produces many male flowers. (Other varieties are called 'Chocolate Persimmon' as well.)

Pineapple Guava (Feijoa)

Acca sellowiana (formerly *Feijoa sellowiana*, and still often referred to by this botanical name)

GROWTH HABIT
Small tree or large shrub that grows up to 10 feet to 15 feet tall and wide

POLLINATION
Mostly needs cross-pollination, and even varieties billed as self-fruitful yield more, bigger, and earlier fruits with cross-pollination

LIGHT REQUIREMENT
Full sunlight, except in desert regions where partial shade from midday sun is needed

CLIMATE
USDA Hardiness Zones 8–10; AHS Heat Zones 12–9

REGIONS
Pineapple guava is easy to grow wherever there's a sufficiently long growing season and winter temperatures turn cool (50 hours or more of chilling), but not too cold; best flavor where summers are not scorching hot

Petals of pineapple guava are edible, fleshy, and very sweet.

Both the flowers and the leaves, pale green below and darker green above, make pineapple guava a prime candidate for luscious landscaping.

"Torpedo-shaped and green," the remains of the flower being the torpedo's propellers, does not describe a fruit that would make most mouths water. But let's not eat with our eyes. How about a fragrance of pineapple with a bit of strawberry? That should entice any mouth closer to the fruit. And then a taste: A pleasantly grainy flesh with a jellylike inner portion that has a sweet-tart flavor of pineapple with hints of strawberry and mint. Delicious.

If the fruit's flavor isn't enough of a draw, check out the flowers. The whorl of four to six white petals are brushed pale purple on their upper sides, and from the center of that whorl bursts forth a bottlebrush of yellow-tipped red stamens. Those petals are edible, not merely edible like many "edible" flowers, but fleshy and refreshing with a super-sweet, minty flavor. To eat,

simply pluck them off and enjoy. Or sprinkle them on a salad or ice cream. You can "have your cake and eat it too" because the flowers can go on to become fruits even after you eat the petals if you pinch them off without damaging any other parts of the flower.

Pineapple guava's evergreen leaves, pale downy green on their undersides and darker green on top, set the whole bush shimmering in breezes. Grown as a hedge or as individual shrubs, the plants are both ornamental and tasty additions to any yard.

Pineapple guava is native to the tropical and sub-tropical highlands of South America. It's cold hardy to about 12°F. If too cold a climate precludes planting pineapple guava in your yard, grow it in a pot.

Grow It Naturally

- Within is climatic limitations, pineapple guava is very easy to grow naturally. It's also a decorative plant in its own right.

Growing

Pineapple guava is a low-maintenance plant, needing not much more than well-drained, slightly acidic soil and full sunlight. The plant tolerates some salt in the soil or air, so it does well in coastal regions. Ideal summer temperatures are between 80°F and 90°F. In desert locations, partial shade from midday sun is needed for best fruit quality and so the fruits avoid sunburn. Expect your first crop three years to four years after planting. Pineapple guava is remarkably free of pest and disease problems.

Pruning

This plant demands little pruning. Train it as either a small tree or a multitrunked shrub. Plants are sometimes propagated by grafting (see p. 32), in which case cut out any sprouts growing below the graft.

A good time to prune is right after the plant flowers. Then you can enjoy the appearance and/or flavor of the blossoms. If you prune before flowering, anytime between fall and early spring, don't lop off the end of too many young branches. Flowers arise in the leaf junctures of those young branches, so such pruning would drastically reduce yields.

Expect lower yields if you grow pineapple guava as a sheared hedge. Growing the hedge informally and maintaining it with mostly thinning cuts and a few heading cuts (see p. 37) as needed gives better yields.

This delicious fruit could not survive my USDA Hardiness Zone 5 winters, so I grow plants in 18-inch-diameter pots and enjoy the fruits of my extra labors. This extra care includes repotting the plants every year or two in autumn; shearing back roots and pruning tops (again, with mostly thinning cuts) to keep the plants a manageable size for moving indoors and out; moving plants indoors to a cool, bright location in winter (a large, south-facing window in my unheated basement); and keeping them watered all summer.

Harvesting

For best flavor, harvest pineapple guava when it's fully ripe. You'll know that stage has been reached because about six months will have elapsed since flowering and, more telling, ripe fruits will start dropping to the ground. This bearing habit makes a good case for mulching the ground beneath the plant with a soft, organic mulch to cushion the fruits' fall. Alternatively to letting them drop at their whim, every few days give the branches a shake and then collect the fallen fruits from the ground. Fruits will keep under refrigeration, especially if picked firm and mature but before they drop, for up to one month.

Eat a pineapple guava either by peeling away the skin and slicing or biting into the fruit, or by halving it and scooping out the refreshing flesh with a spoon. Peeled and sliced, the fruits are a lively addition to a fruit salad. If you're not going to eat any sliced pieces immediately, dip them in diluted lemon juice to keep them from browning. The high pectin content and tart flavor of the fruit is ideal for making jellies and preserves.

Selection of Plants and Varieties

A number of pineapple guava varieties have been named, although very few are available. Often the plants are sold as unnamed seedlings. Pineapple guavas are generally considered to need cross-pollination or to be partially self-fruitful, so for best yields, plant two different varieties or seedlings, or a seedling and a variety.

'Coolidge' Fruits are variable in size, with fair quality; bush is reliable and productive; reputedly self-fertile; ripens late season.

'Edenvale' ('Improved Coolidge') Large fruit with excellent flavor; bush grows slowly but is productive; self-fertile; ripens late season.

'Mammoth' Fruits are medium to large with very good flavor; vigorous plant; partially self-fertile; ripens mid- to late season.

'Nazemetz' Large fruit with excellent flavor; self-fruitful; ripens late season.

'Pineapple Gem' Small fruit with very good flavor; grows poorly in coastal locations; partially self-fruitful; ripens late season.

'Triumph' Fruit is small to medium with excellent flavor; bush is vigorous; partially self-fertile; ripens midseason.

Plum

European plum: *Prunus domestica*
Japanese plum: *P. salicina* mostly
American plum: *P. americana*, *P. angustifolia*,
P. munsoniana, and other species native to America.
Japanese-American plum: hybrids involving various
species of Japanese and American plums
Plumcots: hybrids of mostly plum and some apricot
(sometimes called Pluots®, a name legally reserved
for plumcots developed by Zaiger Nursery)

GROWTH HABIT

Small to medium-size trees; the Japanese and
European types are the largest, the American types
are the smallest, almost shrublike; hybrids are
intergrade between their parents

POLLINATION NEEDS

European plums are mostly self-fertile; Japanese-
American plums, American plums, and plumcots
require cross-pollination with the same kind of plum
or, for hybrids, one of the hybrid's parent types;
Japanese plums mostly require cross-pollination

LIGHT REQUIREMENT

Full sunlight

CLIMATE

European plum: USDA Hardiness Zones 4–8;
AHS Heat Zones 8–3
Japanese plum: USDA Hardiness Zones 6–10;
AHS Heat Zones 9–3
American plum: USDA Hardiness Zones 3–8;
AHS Heat Zones 8–1
Japanese-American plum: USDA Hardiness Zones
(variable); AHS Heat Zones 8–2
Plumcot: USDA Hardiness Zones 5–9; AHS Heat
Zones 9–3

REGIONS

Expect pest problems east of the Rocky Mountains, especially in more humid regions

Plums are not supposed to taste like lemons. Pick one off a market shelf, and it probably will. Pick one off a tree in your yard, and it will be sweet with a rich, fully developed flavor. Or perhaps it will be tart, but a rich tartness that comes with full ripeness, perfect for baked goods and jams. Plums are among the most diverse fruits, offering something for everyone.

Plums encompass a number of species, and with so many species, it's no wonder that there are so many types of plum fruits. They are stone fruits (within the flesh is a shell—the "stone"—enclosing a seed), closely related to peach, nectarine, apricot, and cherry and have even been hybridized with some of these relatives. Plum-apricot hybrids are known as "plumcots" or "apriums," depending on the amount of plum or apricot in a particular variety's parentage. Plum flavors span the whole spectrum from supersweet to pleasantly tangy to downright puckery (good for cooking), and their colors range from yellow to red to blue to almost black. Some plums are no bigger than cherries, whereas others are as large as apples.

The sweetest of the lot are plumcots and European plums. Oval, blue varieties of European plums are appropriately called "prune plums" because that's one of their destinies; like other European plums, they're also excellent for fresh eating. Damson plums are a subspecies of European plums (sometimes put in their own species, *P. insititia*) whose tart flavor comes into its own primarily in preserves, jams, and pies. European plums do not like hot climates. Plumcots do.

Japanese plum fruits are large, roundish, and very juicy, with amber or red flesh and red, yellow, or almost black skin. Their flavor is sweet-tart. As compared with European plums, which are upright trees that bloom around the same time as apples and do not set heavily, Japanese plums bloom early and set fruit heavily on spreading limbs. The plants and fruits tolerate heat well.

American plum species, in general, bear small, red or yellow fruits with tough, tart skins. Plants of hybrid plums are generally bushy and very cold hardy, and the fruits vary in quality from those suitable only for cooking to those that taste good fresh. Many American species and their hybrids grow well in southern locations as well as in northern ones.

Plant a plum tree, or two, or more, and you'll be enjoying the delicious fruits of your labor in three years or four years.

Growing

All plums require a site that has well-drained soil, is in full sunlight, and is free or protected from late spring frosts. Space plants according to their eventual size, which ranges from 15 feet tall and wide for an Oriental plum to only 6 feet tall and wide for some hybrid plums.

Pruning

Train your young Japanese plum or plumcot to an open-center form (see pp. 40–41). European and American hybrid plums may be trained to open-center or central-leader form, depending on their natural growth habit.

Plums bear fruit both on the previous season's shoots and on short-lived spurs of older wood, so they need only a moderate amount of annual pruning to maintain a slow but steady supply of new bearing wood. Pruning and fertilization combined should stimulate new shoots to grow about 3 feet each season on a young tree, or about 18 inches of growth on a mature tree. Prune also to keep the plant open to light and air and to remove diseased or damaged wood.

In most cases you do not have to thin plum fruits. However, the large fruits of Japanese plums, which

Grow It Naturally

- Prune off black, tarry growths of black knot a few inches back into healthy wood.

- Plant in a sunny site and prune to allow for good sunlight and air circulation.

- Clean up mummified fruits (from brown rot) in fall.

- Spray sulfur and Surround every 7 days to 10 days during the six weeks after bloom for reasonably good pest and disease control.

- Grow disease-resistant varieties such as 'Shiro', 'AU-Rosa', and 'AU-Roadside'.

- Move to California or the Mediterranean.

are typically borne heavily, can weight down a branch to the point of breaking, so thin these fruits to 5 inches apart when the crop is heavy. Another way to prevent limb breakage is by shortening long branches loaded with fruits. Thin European plums only if fruit set is very heavy.

Pests and Diseases

East of the Rocky Mountains, plum curculios might lay their eggs on developing fruits, leaving crescent-shaped scars and usually causing the fruits to drop. Fruits that do not drop are ruined, either from feeding of the larvae or from diseases entering through the scars. Curcs are active in the six weeks after bloom, during which time they can be knocked out of the trees; every day give limbs a sharp jar with a padded mallet, being careful not to damage the bark. The insects play dead after dropping so can be collected and disposed of on a sheet spread beneath the limbs. Poultry allowed to run beneath the trees also provide some control. Three sprays of Surround applied to build up a thick layer before bloom and renewed every 7 days to 10 days during the curculios' six-week active period, more frequently if it rains, also control this pest.

Plums that become covered with a fuzzy, gray fungus, then darken and shrivel to become mummies, have brown rot disease, prevalent in humid weather. Limit this disease by planting a variety with some resistance and by removing and disposing of mummies and twigs with disease cankers, both of which provide inoculum for the next year's infection. Insect feeding allows easier fungus entry. Early sulfur sprays, at one-week intervals, also control brown rot, especially if the sulfur is mixed with Surround, which also helps control insects. Fruits are mostly susceptible early in the season and then again beginning a couple of weeks before ripening.

Brown, sunken pits in fruits are symptoms of bacterial leaf spot, a disease common in the southeast. On leaves, this disease causes angular, dark spots. The best control is to plant a resistant variety, such as 'AU-Rosa', 'AU-Roadside', 'AU-Amber', 'Green Gage', or 'Ozark Premier'. Applying copper spray when the plant is dormant and then again in spring also offers control.

Plum leaf scald disease is prevalent in the southeast, scorching the edges of leaves, stunting and killing branches and, eventually, whole trees. Cold temperatures limit this disease's northward spread. No cure exists, so dig up infected trees, which also prevents further spread of the disease, and plant a more resistant variety such as 'AU-Rosa' or 'AU-Amber'.

Wilting branches could be a sign of canker, also called valsa canker, a disease that invades wounds and then

Plums put on a beautiful—and, with some varieties, also fragrant—show of flowers in spring.

'Methley' is a productive plum bearing juicy fruits with excellent, sweet flavor.

Plumcots and Pluots

Plumcots—hybrid fruits that are half plum and half apricot—have been around for many years. They occasionally occur naturally, and the great plant breeder, Luther Burbank, bred a handful of them in the early 20th century. Flavor and marketing pushed plum-apricot hybrids into the fore in the late 20th century when plant breeder Floyd Zaiger introduced his varieties, 'Plum Parfait' and 'Flavorella'. In an effort to put a new face on plumcots, which had had a bad reputation for being hard to grow and ship, Zaiger named his hybrids Pluots. Pluots are actually complex hybrids distinguished only by being mostly—not necessarily half—plum, of which there are many species. To further muddy the waters, Pluot is commonly being used as a generic term for any and all plum-apricot hybrids, which some people also call plumcots.

grows beneath the bark. Also look for dark sunken areas of bark and, eventually, black pimples on bark. Prune off cankered branches with clean cuts that heal quickly (see p. 38), and paint bark with a 50–50 mixture of white latex paint and water to prevent winter bark injury.

A thick, tarry coating on branches is a sign of black knot disease. Diligently prune off diseased portions of the plant. Resistant varieties include 'AU-Rosa', 'AU-Roadside', 'AU-Amber', 'Crimson', 'Santa Rosa', 'Fellenberg', and 'Shiro'. Japanese plums are generally resistant.

Harvesting

You know a plum is ready to pick when it becomes fully colored, softens, and tastes great. At this point, the fruit will not keep very long, perhaps a week refrigerated. What a sweet dilemma it is to be inundated with ripe, fresh plums, trying to figure out what to do with all of them. Certain varieties ripen over a short period of time, so a yield from even a single tree can easily put you in this position. Remedies include canning, making jam, drying, sharing, and, of course, eating a lot of plums.

'Gracious' is very cold hardy and very delicious.

Selection of Plants and Varieties

Dwarfing rootstocks are available for plums, but even full-size plum trees do not grow very large. 'Krymsk 1', a new dwarfing rootstock still under test, seems to be tolerant of cold, drought, and waterlogging, and creates about a half-size tree. Choose a special rootstock if your site has a particular problem or need ('Citation' for wet soil and dwarfing, or 'St. Julien A' for hardiness and dwarfing, as examples.)

Refer to nursery catalogs for the pollination needs of specific hybrid plums. USDA Hardiness Zones are listed only when different from the usual range for that type of plum.

AMERICAN PLUMS

'**Alderman**' Large, red fruits with excellent flavor; productive and precocious, need thinning; ripens midseason.

'**La Crescent**' Small to medium yellow fruit with excellent flavor hinting of apricot; ripens early.

'**Redglow**' Large, red fruit with excellent flavor; skin is thick and tart; ripens late season.

'**Toka**' Fruit is medium size, pointed, and apricot-orange with a yellow, spicy flesh; good pollinator for Japanese-American plums and other American plums.

JAPANESE PLUMS

'**AU-Roadside**' One of the AU (Auburn University) series of plums developed in Alabama for growing in the southeast; fruits are soft and dark red, with excellent flavor; resistance or tolerance to black knot, bacterial canker, bacterial fruit spot, plum leaf scald, and brown rot; requires 650 chilling hours.

'**AU-Rosa**' One of the AU series of plums; medium to large fruit with dark red skin and flesh, very good flavor; very resistant to diseases; moderately vigorous and productive; requires 750 chilling hours.

'**Elephant Heart**' Large, purple, heart-shaped fruits with flavorful, dark red, freestone flesh; very juicy; needs cross-pollination; USDA Hardiness Zone 5; ripens late season.

'**Gulf Beauty**' Small fruit with bright red skin and yellow flesh; has very good, sweet flavor; precocious, productive, and very disease resistant; adapted to southeastern United States; low chill, 250 hours; ripens early and over a four-week period.

'**Gulf Rose**' Medium fruit with golden skin speckled with magenta; red flesh is crisp with a nice balance of sweetness and tartness; resistant to bacterial disease; adapted to the southeast; low chill, 275 hours.

'**Methley**' Round fruit with dark red skin and red flesh; sweet and juicy with excellent flavor; productive; self-fruitful but yields better with cross-pollination; wide adaptation; USDA Hardiness Zone 5; ripens early and over a long period.

'Ozark Premier' Fruits are very large and red, with a juicy, tart, yellow flesh and good flavor; resistant to bacterial spot and bacterial canker; cold hardy and productive; fruit keeps well on tree but not in storage; adapted to growing in the southeast but can flourish as far north as USDA Hardiness Zone 5; requires 750 chilling hours; ripens midseason.

'Santa Rosa' Large purple fruit with clingstone, amber flesh; excellent tart flavor; productive and widely adapted; winter buds are tender to cold; partially self-fruitful; USDA Hardiness Zone 5; requires 300 chilling hours; uneven ripening (good for home garden); ripens early in the season.

'Satsuma' Small to medium fruit with dark red skin and juicy, sweet, red flesh; very productive so needs thinning; skin sometimes cracks if it rains near harvest time; USDA Hardiness Zone 4; ripens early to midseason.

'Shiro' Light green-skinned fruit with yellow flesh is juicy and sweet with a mild, excellent flavor; productive; resistant to bacterial spot and black knot diseases; somewhat self-fruitful; widely adapted; USDA Hardiness Zone 5; requires 600 chilling hours; ripens early to midseason.

'Wickson' Heart-shaped, large fruit has yellow skin with a red blush and very sweet, yellow flesh; vigorous; self-fruitful and productive; needs a pollenizer; requires 500 chilling hours; ripens midseason.

JAPANESE-AMERICAN PLUMS

'Gracious' Oval fruit with yellow-orange, firm, sweet, and juicy flesh; USDA Hardiness Zone 3.

'Pipestone' Large red fruit with somewhat stringy, yellow flesh and excellent flavor; tough skin; cold hardy, productive and reliable, but pollen-sterile, so cannot pollinate itself or other plums; USDA Hardiness Zone 3; ripens early.

'Superior' Large, dark red, russeted skin and yellow flesh that has excellent flavor; fruits need thinning; vigorous and productive; ripens early.

EUROPEAN PLUMS

'Green Gage' (**'Reine Claude'**) Old variety, named after the wife of Francis I of France; heart-shaped fruit with a green skin and a rich, sweet, juicy, amber flesh; productive, sometimes bears only in alternating years; widely adapted because of low chill requirements and cold-hardiness; ripens midseason.

'Imperial Épineuse' A prune plum excellent for fresh eating or drying; sweet, meaty, and richly flavored; skin is mottled dark and light purplish red; brown rot resistant.

'Mount Royal' Fruits are dark blue and medium with very good flavor; semi-dwarf tree; resistant to bacterial spot and black knot; very cold hardy; self-fruitful; ripens early.

'Shropshire Damson' A damson with small, oval fruit, yellow, flesh, and dark blue skin; skin is very tart but fruits are excellent in jellies, jam, and pastries; resistant to canker and bacterial spot, susceptible to black knot; self-fruitful; keeps well on tree when ripe; ripens late.

'Stanley' A prune plum with large, oval fruit, blue skin, and yellow flesh; good flavor; susceptible to brown rot; productive and precocious; cold hardy; widely adapted; ripens midseason.

HYBRID PLUMS

'Dapple Dandy' (sometimes sold as **'Dinosaur Eggs'**) Plumcot; large, red and yellow speckled fruit with pink flesh and very sweet flavor; susceptible to disease; requires 450 chilling hours; late ripening.

'Flavor King' Plumcot; medium fruit with reddish purple skin and red flesh having excellent spicy flavor; susceptible to disease; blooms late; requires 700 chilling hours ; ripens mid- to late season.

'Flavor Supreme' Plumcot; medium fruit with excellent, red flesh; susceptible to disease; early bloom; 550 chilling hours.

'Opata' Japanese-American hybrid known as cherry plum (*P. salicina* × *P. besseyei*); fruit is small, purple skin with yellow flesh; good fresh, fair for preserves; very cold hardy and very productive; shrubby plant; pollinate with another cherry plum.

'Sapa' Japanese-American hybrid known as cherry plum (*P. salicina* × *P. besseyei*); fruit is small, dull, reddish purple in color with deep purple-red, juicy and sweet flesh; good fresh and excellent for cooking; tree is small, spreading, shrublike, cold hardy, and very productive; pollinate with another cherry plum.

'Sapalta' Japanese-American hybrid, cherry plum (*P. salicina* × *P. besseyei*); red-purple skin with almost black flesh, small; semi-freestone; good fresh, fair for preserves; very cold hardy and very productive; shrubby plant; pollinate with another cherry plum.

'Shiro' is a Japanese plum with wide adaptation.

Pomegranate

Punica granatum

GROWTH HABIT
Tree or multistemmed bush grows 15 feet to
20 feet tall

POLLINATION
Partially self-fruitful

LIGHT REQUIREMENT
Full sunlight

CLIMATE
USDA Hardiness Zones 7–10; AHS Heat Zones
12–1

REGIONS
Pomegranate has few pest problems within its
adapted climate zones, but fruits best in dry
regions with abundant summer heat

Pomegranate oozes fruitiness. Break open the ripe fruit and the sparkling arils (an aril is the extra covering around a seed; flavorful and juicy in the case of pomegranate) beckon you back in time, to indulge in refreshment that melds the best of citrus, berries, and wine. Humans have enjoyed pomegranates for millennia. The abundant seeds reinforce the primitive effect, a tease, just like man's original fruit, doling out juiciness and flavor not all at once but in small portions around each seed. On a more mundane level, that primitive quality precludes eating pomegranate, unless prepared beforehand, in formal settings.

Long since its wild beginnings in Persia and central Asia, perhaps also India, the fruit was carried by humans eastward to China and westward to countries bordering the Mediterranean. Missionaries brought pomegranates to the New World, to northern Mexico as early as the beginning of the 16th century, whence cultivation spread to California and beyond. Pomegranate has come a long way; interest in the fruit is on the upswing due to good marketing and touting of its possible health benefits. No matter, it tastes good.

This large shrub or small tree is also notable for its copper-colored foliage in spring and, more flamboyantly, its traffic-stopping large, red (sometimes white or pink), funnel-shaped flowers. The flowers bloom over a relatively long period in spring; in cool climates, flowering could last all summer. Some varieties are strictly ornamental, with double flowers that don't set any fruit at all.

Pomegranate flowers open with frilly petals that usually are fire-engine red, but sometimes pink, or white.

Growing

Abundant sun and summer heat are most important to success with pomegranate. Pomegranate is a subtropical plant that fruits best with an annual rest, typically brought on by cold weather. In tropical climes, a period of drought or leaf removal can coax a pomegranate plant to sleep. Humid weather is not to its liking, especially during bloom, when rain can interfere with fertilization and fruiting, and during harvest time, when fruits might split. In warm, humid climates, varieties such as 'Christina' and 'Mariana' fruit well.

For a freestanding plant, space a pomegranate 15 feet from other plants, except for a dwarf variety like 'Agat', which can be 5 feet from its neighbors. To grow it as a hedge, space plants 6 feet to 10 feet apart.

Enthusiasts of pomegranate have long tried to push the limits to which it can be grown. Humidity, rain, and cold or cool temperatures present challenges. Pomegranate is much more cosmopolitan when it comes to soil. Although fruiting is best in a near neutral pH soil that is well aerated and consistently moist, the plant tolerates a pH from 5.5 to 8, salinity, some degree of waterlogging, and drought. Under such conditions, the plant will survive, but may not yield many or any luscious orbs. Consistent soil moisture is especially important, and particularly near harvest time, otherwise fruit bursts open.

'Eversweet' pomegranate, with pink flesh inside, is, as the name says, ever sweet.

Cover the bent branches with plastic to keep out moisture and top them with leaves, straw, or other insulating material to fend off winter cold; how low a temperature it is protected to depends on the depth of cover. Uncover the plant and prop stems back up when temperatures are no longer below pomegranate's cold-hardiness limit, surely before the buds start awakening.

Another alternative in cold climates is to grow the plants in pots, leaving them outside in the heat of summer and bringing them indoors to a cool, protected location for winter. Dormant plants are leafless and don't need light in winter. Come spring, you can move the plants back outdoors into the sun to get them started growing as soon as possible. If a late frost threatens, they can easily be brought indoors until the threat passes.

A final cold-climate option is to grow pomegranates in a greenhouse, either in the ground or in pots, in which case hand-pollination might be needed.

Getting a pomegranate through winter in a marginal climate is one thing; the plant also needs enough summer heat to ripen its fruits. The varieties 'Sverkhranniy', 'Sumbar', and 'Granada' are notable for ripening their fruits early, so are adaptable to climates with shorter summers. Most early ripening varieties are soft-seeded and sweet even if they don't keep that well.

The plant is not demanding in its feeding. If growth seems weak, nitrogen is probably all that is needed to nurse it back to health. Apply nitrogen at the rate of ½ pound to 1 pound actual nitrogen per plant per year, which could be supplied organically by scattering 7 pounds to 14 pounds of soybean meal beneath the plant in winter. An even better solution is to maintain organic mulch underneath the tree or shrub year-round. That mulch should supply all or most of the plant's nutrient needs, especially if the mulch is compost applied 1 inch deep and scattered evenly at least as far as the spread of the branches. Organic mulch also helps the soil hold moisture, lessening the chance of fruit splitting.

GROWING POMEGRANATE IN COLD CLIMATES

Staving off winter cold damage on pomegranate trees can begin with painting trunks with a 50–50 mixture of white latex paint and water. You might rely on a snow cover to protect the branches of a dwarf variety such as 'Agat'. Protect taller varieties through winter by bending their branches to the ground after their leaves drop.

Pruning

Grow pomegranate with one or a few trunks. In areas where pomegranate is not reliably cold hardy, multiple trunks provide insurance because if a few of them die back during winter, there will still be trunks on which fruit will grow the following spring. Do not allow more than six young stems to become trunks, as too many will crowd each other and result in decreased production and quality. The fruit will also scar from rubbing and be more susceptible to diseases from self-shading. Every year, remove any root suckers unless one or more is needed to replace a damaged trunk or trunks.

Pomegranate fruits are borne mostly on spurs on 2-year- to 3-year-old stems. Light annual pruning is needed to encourage growth of new fruit spurs to replace those that become decrepit, as well as to prevent crowding. Watch out for the sharp thorns when pruning. More drastic pruning—cutting back a few or all trunks and selecting new shoots as new trunks—rejuvenates an old, weak, or neglected plant.

If left hanging too long following rainy weather, pomegranates are likely to split open.

Pests and Diseases

Pomegranate is remarkably free of pest and disease problems so is easy to grow naturally, especially on home grounds. Heartrot, caused by an *Alternaria* fungus, an occasional problem, is most severe when there is high humidity or rainfall during bloom. The infection occurs within the fruit, rotting it, with little evidence of transgression on the outside. There is no known cure, except perhaps to diligently discard all infected fruit and old fruits still hanging from stems at pruning time.

Insects occasionally crawl into the calyx end (opposite the stem end) of pomegranate fruits. If this becomes a problem, grow varieties with closed "eyes," such as 'Kazake', 'Sirenevyi', and 'Salavatski'.

If sunburn is a problem, spraying with Surround provides an effective sunscreen.

Harvesting

Expect your first harvest two years to three years after planting, with full production beginning after about eight years. Depending on the variety and the season, most pomegranate varieties ripen their fruits five months to seven months after blossoming. You'll know the fruit is ripe by its color change, the metallic sound it emanates when tapped, and its flavor. Pick fruits when they're ripe, because after that they are likely to split, especially in humid or rainy weather. Varieties resistant to splitting include 'Kazake', 'Salavatski', 'Nikitski Ranni', and 'Christina'. Don't just pull ripe fruits off the plant; clip each one individually, close to the fruit. No ripening takes place after harvest, although slight drying might concentrate flavors and make the fruit sweeter. Except for early-ripening varieties, fruits keep for many months at 85 percent humidity and 40°F to 45°F.

Pomegranates have all sorts of gustatory uses besides being just split open and eaten. The arils can be used in salads or sprinkled with rose water and a little sugar and eaten as a dessert.

Juiced, pomegranate makes a delicious drink or, concentrated with sugar or by itself, an equally but differently delicious syrup known variously as pomegranate molasses, pomegranate syrup, or by its Persian name *rob-e anar*. Juice a pomegranate either by removing the arils and squeezing them in cheesecloth, or with a citrus press (not a citrus reamer, which will pick up too much of the taste from the spongy membrane to which the arils are attached). For juice on the go, roll and press a whole pomegranate on a flat surface and then massage it, using enough force to extract the juice without breaking the skin. Then, poke or bite a small hole in the side, and suck out the juice with your mouth over, or a straw in, the hole.

'Kazake' is resistant to splitting and is one of the most cold-hardy varieties of pomegranate.

Selection of Plants and Varieties

Pomegranate varieties range from tart to sweet-tart to sweet, with flavors reminiscent of citrus, cherry, and wine. Some varieties have hard seeds, some semihard, and some have seeds so soft you hardly notice them. In general, the more cold-hardy varieties are those that have harder seeds. Flavor components, as well as fruit colors, are not immutable; they vary with growing conditions, with hot sunny days and cool nights generally bringing out the most lively colors and flavors. (Thanks to Jeff Moersfelder, curator of the USDA pomegranate collection, for some of the suggestions for, and descriptions of, the varieties.)

'Agat' Medium-large fruit with a tart taste; soft-seeded; low-growing plant; productive.

'Christina' Dark red skin with pale pink arils; bears well even in humid regions.

'Desertnyi' Light orange skin with coral red arils; excellent sweet-tart balance with lots of citrus-y orange overtones; very soft seeds.

'Eversweet' Red skin with pink arils and juice; always sweet, even before fully ripe; medium-soft seeds; widely adaptable and ripens over a long season.

'Gissarskii Rozovyi' Skin and arils are pink; very good flavor, sweet-tart with a good mix of cherry and citrus.

'Granada' Medium, dark red fruit; sweet, with only a very slight tart taste; medium-hard seeds; very similar to 'Wonderful', of which it is a sport, except early ripening.

'Kazake' Medium fruit, whose skin is yellow with some pink and green; crimson red arils; very good, sweet-tart flavor, and juicy; large seeds; productive; crack resistant, closed eye; keeps well; among the most cold-hardy varieties of pomegranate.

'Marianna' Red-skinned fruit with red arils; bears well even in humid regions.

'Nikitski Ranni' Pink skin with a green background; large medium-hard-seeded arils; good sweet-tart balance; juicy; productive; resistant to cracking.

'Parfyanka' Red-skinned fruit with red arils; excellent, distinctive, complex flavor reminiscent of tangy wine or a cherry lifesaver; soft seeded.

'Salavatski' Very large red or pink fruit with pink arils; sweet tart; medium-hard seeds; resists splitting; may sunburn; closed eye; very cold hardy.

'Sin Pepe' ('Pink Ice', 'Pink Satin') Medium to large red or pink fruit with light pink arils; very good, sweet flavor reminiscent of fruit punch or watermelon; very soft seeds.

'Sirenevyi' Large fruit with pink skin that ripens to red, has dramatically contrasting dark purple arils; complex, very good, sweet flavor; soft seeded.

'Sverkhranniy' Yellow skin splashed with a soft red; light red arils; sweet flavor; soft seeded; productive; very early ripening.

'Utah Sweet' ('Sweet') Small to medium pink fruit with pink arils; very sweet taste and very juicy; very soft seeded; productive; widely adapted, even to relatively cool summer climates.

'Wonderful' Large purple-red (deep red) fruit with dark red arils; delicious, tangy flavor, sweet-tart leaning to tart; seeds are small and medium soft; very productive plant; the leading commercial variety in California.

Quince

Cydonia oblonga

GROWTH HABIT
Small tree or large shrub

POLLINATION NEEDS
Self-fruitful

LIGHT REQUIREMENT
Full sunlight

CLIMATE
USDA Hardiness Zones 5–9; AHS Heat Zones 9–3

REGIONS
As a relative of apple and pear, it shares some of their pest problems, which are generally more prevalent in eastern regions, but to a lesser degree

Transport yourself back in time, way back, almost to the "beginning" (day six), and what fruit do you come upon? The "forbidden fruit," of course, which many people contend was not an apple but a quince. Quince, closely related to apple, looks like a downy 'Golden Delicious' apple on steroids and is generally considered too dry, sour, and astringent to eat raw. Cooked, however, a quince turns rosy pink and becomes sweet, soft, and juicy, with a sprightly flavor perfumed with the likes of pineapple, guava, and spice.

I occasionally hear about quinces that are good for eating raw, special varieties found in the Black Sea region of Russia and Turkey ('Aromatnaya') or from the Majes Valley in southern Peru ('Karp's Sweet'). Subdued descriptions like "quite pleasant," directives such as "slice very thin," and a one-time taste of one of these varieties keep me skeptical as to their fresh quality. I could be wrong. For now, though, I prefer to add pizazz to an apple pie with quince or to eat it as jelly or stewed. Quince is also good to mix into other fruit jellies because it provides natural pectin, for gelling.

There's no question about the plant's beauty, though. Large white or pinkish blossoms unfold relatively late in spring and the brightly colored fruit itself dresses up the branches at the other end of the season, long into autumn. My favorite quince plants are the exquisitely trained, picturesque, gnarly trees, formal but not overly so, in the Cloisters Garden of the Metropolitan Museum of Art in New York City.

Don't confuse this edible quince with a couple of other "quinces." So-called flowering quince (*Chaenomeles japonica*) is a familiar thorny, ornamental shrub decked in salmon-pink flowers (some varieties have white or red flowers) in spring. Chinese quince (*Pseudocydonia sinensis*) is also sometimes grown as an ornamental. Flowering quince and Chinese quince require heroic culinary efforts to render them edible, but are sometimes cooked and eaten. The best eating of the lot, though, is *Cydonia oblonga*.

Growing

Give quince a site in full sun, with well-drained, moderately fertile soil. For best-quality fruit, surely if you're going to try for good-tasting, fresh fruit, don't let the plant suffer from lack of moisture, especially later in the season as fruits are ripening.

Pruning

Quince can be trained to grow either as a shrub or as a small tree with one or multiple trunks (see p. 38). Either way, shape the plant in its youth to a permanent framework of spreading limbs that will be bathed in sunlight and air. Once the plant has been shaped, prune it lightly every year to keep the center open, to remove dead and diseased wood, and to stimulate a little bit of new growth. A foot or two of new stem growth every season is about right.

Pests and Diseases

Quince is closely related to apple and pear, and is potentially affected by many of the same pests. Usually, however, pest problems aren't serious enough to warrant control, especially with a good site and good growing conditions.

Keep a special eye out for fire blight disease, which shows up as blackened leaves that remain attached to stems, the ends of which curl over in characteristic shepherd's crooks. In summer, diligently prune any diseased wood back into 6 inches of healthy wood, sterilizing pruning shears between cuts with a wipe of

Grow It Naturally

- For best flavor and minimal disease, plant where there is full sunlight and good air circulation.

- Prune so branches are never congested.

- Avoid rust disease by removing nearby cedar trees (not feasible where cedars are native and plentiful).

Quince welcomes the season with large, white flowers that open against a backdrop of already unfolded leaves.

alcohol, Listerine, Lysol, or Pine-Sol. Fire blight bacteria overwinter in dark, sunken bark cankers, so also prune below any of these in winter. Avoid stimulating overly lush growth, from excessive fertilization and/or pruning, because such growth is most susceptible to fire blight. Unchecked, the disease can kill a plant.

Cedar-quince rust disease, showing up as rust-colored spots on leaves, requires both a susceptible cedar (*Juniperus communis*, *J. Virginiana*, *J. sibirica*, and *J. communis* var. *depressa*) and quince on which to complete its life cycle. The spores travel several hundred feet, sometimes miles, from cedars to quinces, so removing cedars near your quince is a feasible control only where susceptible cedars are not native or plentiful. Infection takes place only early in the season, before shoots have grown more than a few inches long. Spray copper just as buds are swelling, and two more times at 7-day to 14-day intervals if pruning to let branches bathe in air and sunlight is not sufficiently effective. New infections do not spread from old infections.

Harvesting

Even though you'll probably be cooking quinces, wait until they are thoroughly ripe—that is, fully colored—before harvesting them, especially if you're going to be eating them fresh. You'll want to put off harvest anyway because the fruits look so pretty hanging from the branches. Don't worry about cold; frost won't harm them. Despite the hardness of the fruits, they bruise easily, so handle them with care.

Even after you harvest the fruit, there's no need to rush to eat them. Ripe, they keep quite well even at room temperature, ripening more as they sit, and for months in cold storage. There's no need to rush eating quinces because their mere presence is most pleasant; sitting in bowls on your kitchen counter, they'll suffuse the room with their spicy fragrance. A traditional (and natural) way to freshen up a closet or drawer is with a resident quince fruit stuck full of whole cloves and hung from a string.

These picturesque, old quinces, trained as trees, each take up little space in the enclosed garden of the Cloisters of the Metropolitan Museum of New York.

Selection of Plants and Varieties

'Aromatnaya' Medium fruit with pineapple-y flavor, enjoyed fresh by some people; disease resistant.

'Champion' Large, roundish to pear-shaped, greenish yellow fruits of delicate flavor; flesh is tender, yellow, and only slightly astringent; productive.

'Ekmek' Pear-shaped fruit with yellow flesh that is crisp, juicy, and mild flavored; productive; popular in Turkey, where it's used fresh, dried, and in jam and syrup.

'Karp's Sweet' Sweet, juicy, and nonastringent, especially when grown in warm climates, where it originated.

'Orange' ('Apple') Fruit is large to very large, round, smooth skinned, and bright yellow; flesh is very tender and yellow-orange with excellent flavor; a good variety where summers stay cool.

'Pineapple' Large, round, golden fruits, with a flavor that hints of pineapple; tender, white flesh with slight astringency; tree is cold hardy, productive; low chilling requirement of 300 hours.

'Smyrna' Very large, pear-shaped fruits with a golden yellow skin; flesh is mild and tender, with excellent flavor; tree has unusually large leaves.

Raspberry

Rubus spp.

GROWTH HABIT
Bush about 6 feet tall, spreads by tip layering or root suckers

POLLINATION NEEDS
Self-fruitful

LIGHT REQUIREMENT
Full sunlight

CLIMATE
Red and yellow raspberries: USDA Hardiness Zones 3–6; AHS Heat Zones 8–4
Black raspberries: USDA Hardiness Zones 3–8; AHS Heat Zones 8–1
Purple raspberries: USDA Hardiness Zones 5–8; AHS Heat Zones 8–5

REGIONS
Raspberries can grow just about anywhere within their climate zones with minimal problems

Black raspberries, also called blackcaps, are wild treats in many places.

Raspberries are easy to grow, bear their first fruits the same year or one year after they're planted (and bear a full crop the year after that), and taste great fresh or in pies, jams, spreads, syrups, dressings, and sorbets. They also are highly perishable and delicate when ripe. No store-bought raspberry, picked firm and of a variety that must withstand the rigors of picking and shipping, can match those tender, flavorful morsels you can pluck each morning from your own yard. This makes a great case for having your own patch of raspberries not too far from your front or back door.

Raspberries come in a variety of colors—red, yellow, black, and purple—each kind with its own distinctive flavor. Red and yellow raspberries, which are different colors of the same fruit, are most familiar. There are, of course, flavor differences between the various varieties of red and yellow raspberries, but reds do not as a group taste different from yellows. As compared with red raspberries, black raspberry fruits are drier, richer in flavor, and, of course, black. Purple raspberries are hybrids of red and black raspberries, and, like black raspber-

ries, tend to have firm fruits that are richer, tangier, and seedier than those of red raspberries. (The purples are a bit too tangy for me except for in jams and pies.)

If you're crazy for raspberries, you could be eating them almost all summer and on into fall by choosing appropriate kinds and varieties, including so-called everbearing types. Not to mention frozen raspberries for winter.

Growing

Raspberries are easy to grow provided you give them a good site and diligently prune them every year. That's all! Except in searingly hot climates, where the plants enjoy a bit of afternoon shade, raspberries fruit best in full sunlight. Their soil needs to be well drained, slightly acidic, and rich in organic matter. Do not plant near wild raspberries, blackberries, tomatoes, peppers, eggplants, or potatoes, or in ground where you recently grew these plants, because they all share disease problems with raspberry. Such isolation may prove impossible in a small yard. If so, still plant raspberries; in a sunny site, with good soil and attention to pruning, you'll probably still reap good crops. In general, purple and black raspberries are more prone to diseases than are red and yellow raspberries—but they're still easy to grow.

PLANTING IN ROWS

Most raspberries are easier to manage if you support the canes in some way. You may already have a fence calling out to be dressed up with raspberries. Lacking that, the most straightforward way to prop them up is on a trellis. To make one, sink a sturdy post into the ground at each end of your proposed row of raspberries and string two

Grow It Naturally

- Prune religiously and correctly.

- For the easiest growing, plant everbearing (fallbearing) red or yellow raspberries.

This raspberry bed has just finished bearing its summer crop so could be pruned now.

Canes that bore fruit have been removed, and the remaining row of young canes has been narrowed and thinned.

or three lengths of 12-gauge wire between the posts, with the top wire about 5 feet aboveground and the others lower down. There's no need for any exactitude with the placement of these wires because their purpose is nothing more than to keep canes off the ground and prevent them from flopping around. Set 3 feet apart in rows 6 feet apart, wandering roots of red and yellow raspberries will eventually fill in the empty spaces and make a dense row of plants. Plant black or purple raspberries 3 feet apart in rows 8 feet apart. No trellising is necessary with any red or yellow raspberry that has stiff, upright canes, such as 'Heritage', or with black or purple raspberries trained low. Some semi-erect and more sprawling plants will need trellising. If a plant's canes are unruly, prop them up.

PLANTING USING THE HILL SYSTEM

Another way to grow raspberries is in the hill system. Where's the hill? There isn't one. This "hill" means nothing more than a cluster of plants growing together in a small area. Space hills 5 feet to 8 feet apart in all direc-

tions, with a sturdy post on which to tie the cluster of plants at each hill. I find it easier to keep my black raspberries tidy if they're planted in hills; the same would be true for purple raspberries.

Tip

BLACK RASPBERRY VERSUS BLACKBERRY

How do you distinguish between a black raspberry and a blackberry? Pick it! The core stays on the plant when you pick a ripe black raspberry, but stays in the fruit of a blackberry. Perhaps it's easier to remember black raspberry's other name, blackcaps, which is what the hollow berries look like after picking.

By weaving together raspberry canes remaining after pruning, I can leave them longer for larger yields.

GROWTH HABITS

Knowing something about how a raspberry plant grows and fruits highlights the necessity and how-to of pruning these plants. Growth habits vary among raspberries, but left to their own devices (which we're not going to let them do) all types will spread to form impenetrable thickets. As roots of red and yellow raspberry plants spread, buds on those roots sprout to make new, unbranched canes. Purple and black raspberries have arching canes (depending on their heritage, some purple raspberries are more upright) with side branches, all armed with stiff thorns. These plants spread by tip layering, hopscotching along as the tips of their canes arch over, touch the ground, and root to make new plants, which, in turn, hopscotch and root to make more new plants, and so on.

All raspberries have perennial roots and biennial canes. In most cases, the canes just grow their first year and fruit and then die their second year. You don't have to resign yourself to years of raspberry feast and famine, because while second-year canes are fruiting, new canes are growing that will fruit the following year.

Canes of one type of raspberry, the so-called everbearing type, begin to fruit near their tops toward the close of their first season, which is why they're sometimes also called fallbearing raspberries. Around midsummer of the next season, those same canes finish fruiting lower down. The result is everbearing raspberries.

Well, almost everbearing, with two crops per season: a midsummer crop on second-year canes and a late summer and fall crop on first-year canes.

Pruning

Annual pruning is a must to keep raspberries from becoming overgrown and diseased. It also makes picking the berries much more enjoyable as the branches splay out their fruits for your picking pleasure.

Prune red and yellow raspberries in three easy steps in late winter: First, cut all second-year canes (those that fruited the previous summer) away at their bases. It will be obvious which canes are second-year because they'll be dead or dying. Even better, cut these canes away right after they finish fruiting in summer to give new growing canes more elbow room; the second-year canes look old and ragged then too and show remains of fruit stalks. Next, thin out new canes, leaving those that are sturdiest and healthiest. In a hedgerow planting, cut down to the ground any canes escaping beyond a 12-inch-wide swathe and, within that swathe, prune so individual canes are no closer than 6 inches apart within that 12-inch-wide swathe. In hills, remove all but six new canes per hill as well as any sprouts trying to establish themselves between hills. When you have

Fruiting Habit of Raspberries

SUMMERBEARING RED AND YELLOW RASPBERRIES

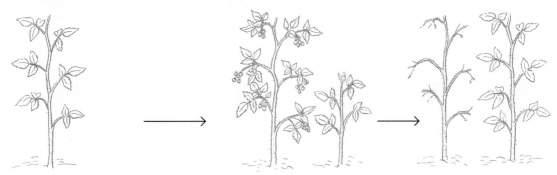

First season: The plant produces only stems and leaves.

Second season: Last year's canes bear fruit, then die; new canes will fruit the following year.

EVERBEARING RED AND YELLOW RASPBERRIES

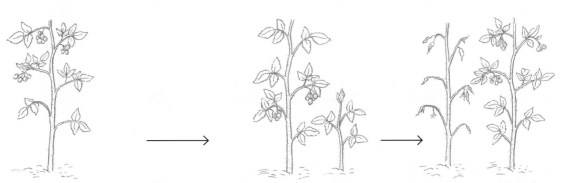

First season: Fruits are borne at the tops of new shoots in late summer and fall.

Second season: Early summer fruits are borne lower down on last year's canes, which then die; new canes bear in late summer and fall.

BLACK AND PURPLE RASPBERRIES

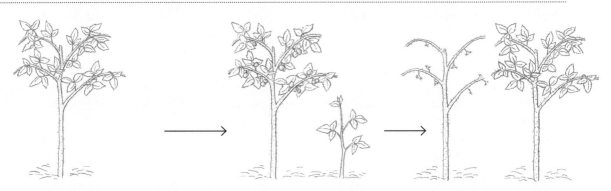

First season: The plant produces only stems and leaves.

Second season: Last year's canes bear fruit, then die; new canes will fruit the following year.

Pruning Summerbearing Red and Yellow Raspberries

Dormant plants   2-year-old cane   1-year-old cane

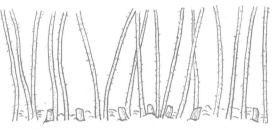

1. Remove 2-year-old canes.

2. Thin excess 1-year-old canes.

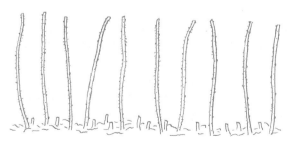

3. Shorten remaining canes.

Pruning Black and Purple Raspberries

Fruiting cane

New cane

1. Pinch out growing tips throughout summer.

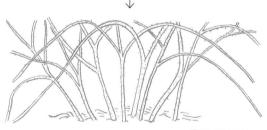

Dormant season

2. Remove canes that have fruited.

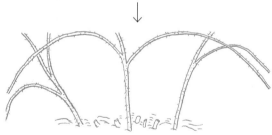

3. Thin excess 1-year-old canes.

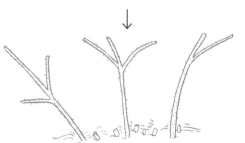

4. Shorten laterals.

finished pruning, you'll likely look at your patch and feel like you've cut away too much. You haven't.

Finally, top the canes to a height of about 6 feet or, depending on your trellising, whatever height you need to keep the canes neat and prevent them from flopping around. I leave my red raspberry canes long, bending them over and weaving them together onto the top wire to let them retain more length and hence bear more fruits.

Follow the same steps in pruning everbearing raspberries, except prune back the tops of the remaining first-year canes to just below the height where they finished fruiting the previous fall. You'll know where this point is because the remains of old fruit stalks will still be dangling from the canes.

An even easier way to prune everbearers is to mow the whole patch to the ground each fall. This sacrifices the summer crop but helps avoid problems with winter-kill, deer damage, and diseases that overwinter on canes.

Prune black and purple raspberries as described for summerbearing red and yellow raspberries, with two additional steps. First, during the summer nip out the tip of any cane as it reaches a height of 2 feet to 3 feet, using pruning shears or your fingernails. This stimulates growth of branches, on which fruits are borne the following year. The other additional step, in late winter, is to shorten each of those branches to about 12 inches long.

Pests and Diseases

Regular pruning thwarts most problems because you remove infected and infested canes and let light and air in among the remaining canes. Discolored spots or lesions on canes are symptoms of one of a few cane diseases, such as spur blight and anthracnose. Remove infected canes as you prune. A cane that partially dies back may have a resident insect, a cane borer, which you can kill by cutting off and destroying the cane 6 inches below the point of entry (marked by a swelling). Dig out and destroy whole plants of black or purple raspberries if they show symptoms of orange rust: bright orange pustules on the undersides of the leaves.

Dieback of whole canes can be traced to a number of causes, including such horrible-sounding afflictions as verticillium wilt, crown gall, root rot, or cane borers. Dig out and destroy plants that fall victim to these pests and diseases. Avoid such problems in the first place by planting disease-free plants (certified as such from nurseries), ideally in soil that is also free from disease; that is, where

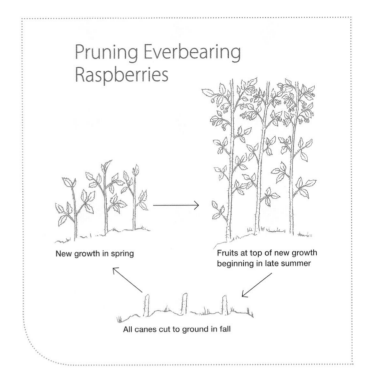

Pruning Everbearing Raspberries

New growth in spring

Fruits at top of new growth beginning in late summer

All canes cut to ground in fall

raspberries or other hosts to their diseases have not recently grown.

Fruit rots are common in wet weather, morphing the jewel-like fruits into balls of gray fuzz. Pick and dispose of those fuzzy balls into your compost pile to limit disease spread.

Eventually, pests and diseases make inroads into any raspberry patch and send it into decline. Although raspberries are technically perennial, plan on planting a new patch at a new location with new plants after a decade or less. I plant a fresh patch a year before grubbing out an old patch to make sure I don't go a season bereft of raspberries.

Harvesting

Raspberries are fragile when ripe and spoil quickly. At the height of the season, especially in hot weather, pick raspberries daily or every other day, harvesting only those fully colored berries that drop from the plant into your hand with just the slightest coaxing. For peak flavor, leave the rest on the bush until they reach this point. Underripe berries will not ripen at all after being harvested.

'Canby' raspberry is tops in flavor.

'Fallgold' raspberry is everbearing, with golden fruits that have a delicate, sweet flavor.

Selection of Plants and Varieties

BLACK RASPBERRY

'Allen' Fruits are firm, juicy, and sweet; plants are fairly disease resistant; moderately cold hardy; ripens over a short period early to midseason.

'Bristol' Large, sweet fruits; moderately cold hardy; upright canes; ripens early.

'Munger' Large, plump, firm, and not very seedy fruits; some disease resistance; well-adapted to Pacific Northwest; moderately cold hardy; ripens midseason.

RED RASPBERRY

'Autumn Bliss' Everbearing; large, very tasty fruits; canes are semi-erect with few spines; productive; cold hardy; ripens early.

'Bababerry' Everbearing; large, tangy, firm fruits; originated in southern California and adapted to regions with hot summers and mild winters; canes are sprawling and very vigorous, with small, soft prickles.

'Boyne' Summerbearing; dark red, medium, sweet fruits; very cold hardy and productive; upright canes; ripens early season.

'Canby' Summerbearing; bright red fruits with excellent flavor; sprawling plants are vigorous but not particularly disease resistant; thornless; thrives in cool summers, such as in the Pacific Northwest; not very cold hardy; ripens early to midseason.

'Caroline' Everbearing; large berries with excellent flavor; vigorous canes are cold hardy, upright, and widely adapted; ripens early.

'Heritage' Everbearing; mediocre flavor; canes are upright; cold hardy and widely available and adapted; ripens late season.

'Latham' Summerbearing; older variety of raspberry that yields large, deep red fruits with good flavor; productive, disease resistant, and very cold hardy; ripens late season.

'Lauren' Summerbearing; fruits are very large with good flavor; productive; moderately cold hardy; ripens early to midseason with long fruiting period.

'Meeker' Summerbearing; large, sweet fruits; only moderately cold hardy; well adapted to Pacific northwest; productive, with long, willowy canes; ripens early to midseason, yielding fruit over a long period.

'Taylor' Summerbearing; fruits are large, with superb flavor; sturdy, vigorous, and productive canes; moderately cold hardy; ripens late season.

PURPLE RASPBERRY

'Brandywine' Large, tangy raspberries; vigorous, semi-erect, and cold hardy; ripens mid- to late season.

'Royalty' Fruits are very large and tangy, although sweeter than 'Brandywine'; very cold hardy; ripens late season.

YELLOW RASPBERRY

'Fallgold' Everbearing; very sweet, flavorful fruits sure to elicit a "Wow!" from anyone who tastes them; productive, upright, cold-hardy canes; ripens early season.

Seaberry

Hippophae rhamnoides

GROWTH HABIT
Suckering, rounded shrub, 6 feet to 12 feet tall

POLLINATION
Male pollinator needed to pollinate females

LIGHT REQUIREMENT
Full sunlight

CLIMATE
USDA Hardiness Zones 3–8; AHS Heat Zones 8–1

REGIONS
Seaberry grows well throughout the climate zones to which it is adapted

Seaberry's gray-green leaves are the perfect foil for the bright orange fruits.

Pluck ripe seaberries from the plant and you're likely to say "ouch;" pop them in your mouth and you're likely to wrinkle your nose. The berries press close to stems that are heavily armed with thorns, and their flavor is very tart. Once you pass that "ouch" and wrinkled-nose stage, though, you'll enjoy a very rich flavor suggesting orange and passionfruit. Not what you'd expect to taste from a plant native to Russia, China, and northern Europe, a fruit that's also been called "Siberian pineapple." (I'm going with orange and passionfruit, but the flavor is nonetheless tropical.)

Seaberry is a newcomer beyond its native haunts, one that's been planted as much for its beauty (in New York City's Battery Park, for instance) as for its fruit. The willowy, silvery gray leaves create the perfect backdrop for the profusion of bright orange berries.

Where the plant is native, the berries have a long history of medicinal use as, among other things, an anti-inflammatory, an anti-microbial, and a pain reliever. The fruit has been called "among the most nutritious found in the plant kingdom" (Thomas S. C. Li, Agriculture and Agri-food Canada, Pacific Agri-Food Research Centre). Its botanical name comes from the Latin, meaning "shining horse." The leaves make good animal fodder and were said to make horses so healthy that their coats shined.

Growing

Besides a suitable climate, seaberry needs only two things: abundant sunlight and well-drained soil. Like other plants with silvery leaves, seaberry tolerates dry conditions as well as salt in soil or the air, which you probably guessed from the name *sea*berry. The plants tolerate infertile soils because a microorganism (*Frankia*, an actinomycete) associated with their roots takes nitrogen from the air and changes it into a form that the plant can use.

POLLINATION

If you want fruit, a seaberry female also needs a male plant nearby. A single male can sire six to eight females. Seaberry is wind pollinated, so keep males and females no more than about 20 feet apart, with the females downwind from the males, thus ensuring that enough pollen gets to those females for a good crop.

Pruning

Pruning needs are minimal. Flowers and fruits are borne on 2-year-old wood, so make some heading cuts (see p. 37) each winter to stimulate some new growth to bear fruit the season after the next. The shrub suckers, so it benefits from having old stems removed to make way for younger stems. Also remove any stems that crowd each other, look diseased, or are generally out of place (especially important for a shrub that's planted as an ornamental as well as for its fruit).

Pests and Diseases

Especially in a home setting, seaberry has no particular pests worth noting.

Harvesting

Here's the bugaboo in enjoying seaberries: Pressed tightly against stems that are heavily armed with thorns, the berries are tedious and painful to pick. Compounding the problem, the berries are generally processed into juice, so lots are needed.

Some people have sufficient patience to pluck the berries off one by one. I don't. Fortunately, there's a quick and painless way to harvest. Cut off whole berry-laden branches in 1-foot-long sections and put them into a plastic tub with a tightly fitting lid, leaving enough elbow room for the stems to move around. When the tub is filled, into the freezer it goes. Once the berries and branches are well frozen take the tub in hand and, with the lid still on, shake it. A lot. The berries will fall off and settle to the bottom of the tub, and the stems can be quickly picked up and out—with a gloved hand because they're still thorny. The final cleaning away of small twigs and leaves is easily done by winnowing; that is, in front of a fan, pour the frozen berries slowly so that the wind blows the twigs away and only the berries fall into a waiting bowl.

To juice the berries, use a hand-cranked "squeeze juicer" or simmer them in a pot with a little water, mash with a potato masher, and strain. Sweetened and diluted with water (½ cup each water and sugar per quart of seaberries is a good place to start), then chilled, the juice is delicious and looks very elegant in apéritif glasses.

Selection of Plants and Varieties

The wide geographic range to which seaberries are native is home to various types that sometimes have been split into separate species. Varieties developed in Germany generally tend to grow very vigorously and tolerate a wide range of soils, including wet soils; their berries tend to be more acidic than other types. Varieties from Buryatia (south central Russia) are dwarf, free of thorns, and have excellent quality, even for fresh eating; these varieties don't seem to grow well in heavier soils that remain wet. Yet another group of varieties has been developed by breeders in Moscow, varieties that are vigorous, early ripening, and tolerant of a wide range of soil and climatic conditions. These last kinds of seaberries are notable for their high oil content, brilliant color, and lower acidity compared to the German varieties. Other sorts have been introduced from other research and breeding stations in Canada, northern Europe, and Russia. Some of the most flavorful juices are made by combining various kinds of seaberries.

Many, many varieties have been developed of this up-and-coming fruit. Here is a mere sampling of some of the varieties.

'Askola' Developed in Germany, fruits have a deep orange color and are notable for being very high in vitamins C and E; bush is upright, 10 feet to 12 feet tall; ripens midseason.

'Baikal' ('Ayaganga') From Buryatia, fruits are bright orange with unusually sweet flavor and notably high in vitamins A, C, and E; bush is compact, 5 feet to 6 feet tall.

'Botanica' ('Botanicheskaya') From Moscow; fruits are very large, richly flavored, and bright orange; ripens early.

'Garden's Gift' ('Podarok Sada') From Moscow, fruits are large and dark orange, with a rich flavor; ripens early.

'Klims Prize' ('Malish') These Buryatian fruits are large and bright orange with a sweet flavor that is good fresh or juiced; bush is compact, growing 6 feet tall.

'Leikora' Developed in Germany, fruits are bright orange and tart, very ornamental; bush is 10 feet tall; ripens late and over a long period.

'Novostj Altaja' From Moscow, fruits are orange, medium, and less acidic than most other varieties; bush has few thorns.

'Titan' ('Trofimovskaya') Developed in Moscow, fruits are very large and bright orange; bush grows 10 feet tall with darker green leaves than most other varieties; ripens early.

Shipova

× *Sorbopyrus auricularis*

GROWTH HABIT
Pyramidal tree grows to 20 feet or taller; on a dwarf rootstock, tree grows to 8 feet tall

POLLINATION
Most likely self-fruitful

LIGHT REQUIREMENT
Full sunlight

CLIMATE
USDA Hardiness Zones 4–9; AHS Heat Zones 8–3

REGIONS
Most likely widely adaptable, with few pest problems

In spring, each shipova flowerbud opens to a cluster of as many as 20 blossoms.

Shipova is as obscure in name as it is in fruit. Few people know this fruit, but more should, and you can. Poor flavor can't account for the fruit's obscurity because it is delicious; it's something like a small, sweet, and flavorful pear with a satisfyingly meaty texture—the kind of fruit you fill your pockets with before going for an afternoon walk in early autumn.

Shipova is something of an oddity in being a hybrid of two plants of different genera. Such hybrids are relatively rare. A few—including the cama, a hybrid of camel (*Camelus* spp.) and llama (*Lama glama*)—are known in the animal kingdom. The plant kingdom, especially orchids, houses a few more. Shipova's probable parents are common whitebeam, *Sorbus aria*, which gives the hybrid the *Sorbo* part of its botanical name, and European pear, *Pyrus communis*, which gives the hybrid the *pyrus* part of its botanical name. As with the fruit, the plant represents the best of both parents, with large clusters of white flowers that bloom in spring followed by leaves that unfold with a downy whiteness, and good, spreading limb structure.

Shipova has been around a long time, since before 1610 in Europe, and was introduced into America in the early part of the 20th century. Let's get to know it better.

Growing

Because shipova has been so little grown, much of its needs can only be inferred with a nod to its parents. Give it full sun in well-drained soil of moderate fertility.

My two criticisms of shipova are its large size and its procrastination in bearing fruit. The size is forgivable if the tree is planted in a suitable location. At some sacrifice of longevity, a related plant, aronia, dwarfs the tree when used as a rootstock and induces precocity, taking care of its other problem: Standard-size trees typically take about eight years before bearing their first fruit. Except for using a dwarfing rootstock, none of the other usual techniques for coaxing a tree to bear more quickly, such as branch bending, has any effect on shipova.

Pruning

With excellent, natural form, the plant needs little training when young beyond removal of excess branches. A mature tree similarly needs little pruning because it bears fruit on spurs.

Pests and Diseases

Shipova would be expected to share the pest problems of its parents, both of which commonly grow free of pest problems.

Harvesting

Shipovas are ripe at about the same time as early to midseason pears. Look for the fruits to turn yellowish and detach easily from branches by their stems. Left longer, the fruits begin to drop. For longer-term storage, harvest when slightly underripe, although shipova does not seem to store well in any case.

Selection of Plants and Varieties

Shipova is a variety name. There is one other variety of the × *Sorbopyrus auricularis* hybrid, introduced into America from Romania as 'Baciu'. 'Baciu' is very similar to shipova, except its fruits are more pear shaped and much smaller.

Strawberry

Garden strawberry: *Fragaria × ananassa*
Alpine strawberry: *F. vesca*
Musk strawberry: *F. moschata*

GROWTH HABIT
Mounded, herbaceous perennial; garden and musk strawberries spread by runners at the ends of which grow new plants that root and spread farther

POLLINATION
Self-fruitful except for musk strawberry, which needs separate male pollinator plants

LIGHT REQUIREMENT
Full sunlight

CLIMATE
USDA Hardiness Zones 3–9; AHS Heat Zones 10–1

REGIONS
Strawberries are an easy home-grown fruit with some varieties best adapted to certain regions

"Doubtless God could have made a better berry, but doubtless God never did," wrote a Dr. Boteler about the strawberry (as quoted in Izaak Walton's 17th-century classic *The Compleat Angler*). And at that time, no one had experienced the large, sweet garden strawberry of today. Walton's and Boteler's berries were probably alpine strawberries (also called *fraises de bois*) and musk strawberries (also called *hautbois* strawberries), both occasionally still cultivated today for their smaller, highly aromatic fruits. Today's garden strawberry arrived on the scene in the last 200 years, the result of a chance mating—in Europe—of two American species, one from the east coast of North America and the other from the west coasts of North and South America.

Because of their large size, garden strawberries became a favorite, and a slew of tasty varieties soon reflected breeders' deft handiwork. Today, you can choose varieties from among three kinds of garden strawberries. The first are junebearing strawberries, yielding one crop per season, in spring or early summer. The second are so-called everbearing strawberries, developed early in the 20th century. I write "so-called" because these varieties actually bear only twice each season, first in spring and again beginning in late summer and on into autumn. The third kind of garden strawberries, day-neutral strawberries, appeared around 1980. Whereas other types of strawberries flower and fruit in response to the length of the day, day-neutrals, as their name implies, are unaffected by day length and so flower and fruit all summer long. Day-neutrals are truly everbearing, although scorching summer days can slow them down by interfering with flower fertilization. Some nursery

TOP: Alpine strawberries have been enjoyed by humans since ancient times.

BOTTOM: Potted alpine strawberry plants provide flavorful morsels all summer long and on into fall.

Grow It Naturally

- Plant in well-drained soil; preferably where strawberries, tomatoes, peppers, eggplants, or potatoes have not grown recently.

- Renovate annually (except everbearing and alpine strawberries).

- Harvest daily or every other day during warm weather, picking off and disposing of diseased fruits while doing so.

Strawberry Plant

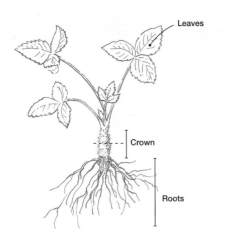

Leaves

Crown

Roots

Strawberry Plant and Runner

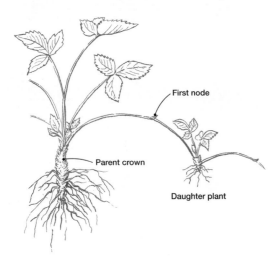

First node

Parent crown

Daughter plant

Strawberry Planting Depth

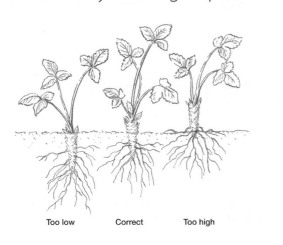

Too low   Correct   Too high

catalogs lump day-neutral strawberries and the older type of everbearing (two-crop) strawberries together on their pages as everbearing strawberries. Besides bearing all season long, everbearing strawberries (of either type) bear their first fruits the season they are planted. Junebearing strawberries bear their first crop the year after planting.

Old-fashioned alpine and musk strawberries—the ones that Dr. Boteler knew and loved—are not for stocking your freezer or even heaping into bowls. Their fruits are small and yields are low compared to garden strawberries. But grow them for a flavor treat. Alpines have a flavor of strawberry commingled with pineapple and bear fruit continuously as long as warmth, moisture, and fertility permit. In musk strawberries, the flavor of very ripe raspberry melds with that of strawberry. Musks are one-crop berries that bear in spring or early summer.

Growing

Strawberries will fruit over a broad range of climates, and perform at their best when given full sunlight, good soil, and ample water. Grow strawberries as annuals in regions with high summer heat and lack of winter cold. In these areas, junebearing varieties shipped from northern locations are planted in late summer or fall, plants flower and fruits are harvested through winter, and then plants are dug up and discarded. Do not expect high yields under these conditions.

PREPARING TO PLANT

"Good soil" for a strawberry plant is fertile, rich in organic matter, and slightly acidic. Before you plant, apply plenty of organic matter, fertilize if needed (as indicated by poor growth of existing vegetation), and rid the plot of weeds, especially perennial weeds. If drainage is less than perfect, grow plants in raised beds 6 inches tall and 2 feet to 3 feet wide.

To delay the onset of disease problems, plant certified disease-free plants from a nursery rather than a generous neighbor's extra plants. Ideally, choose a site where strawberries or other plants having pests in common with strawberries (tomato, pepper, eggplant, potato, and raspberry) have not recently grown.

Garden strawberry plants are sold in bundles of bare-root plants. Each plant will look like little more than a crown, which is a stubby stem with some roots attached at one end and, perhaps, a few leaves at the other end. The crown is just like a long stem, one that has been telescoped down so one leaf arises right above the other, forming a tight whorl of leaves. As the plants grow, runners form, which are leafless, wiry shoots along and at the ends of which form new strawberry plants, which can take root and eventually give rise to yet more runners and plants. The crown grows only a fraction of an inch longer each year.

Take that bundle of strawberry plants you got from the nursery, grab a pair of scissors, and give the roots a haircut to shorten lanky ones and make plants easier to handle. Then separate the plants and put them in a pan or bucket of water to keep the roots wet while you plant. In prepared ground, planting entails nothing more than jabbing a trowel into the ground, pulling the handle toward you, fanning out and inserting the roots into the waiting slit, removing the trowel, and firming the ground against the roots—all of which takes longer to write than to do! Soil should cover all the roots and the lower portion of the crown. Set too shallow and the plants dry out; set too deep, they suffocate.

LAYING OUT A STRAWBERRY BED
Choose from one of three methods of laying out a strawberry bed.

For the first method, the "matted row system," set plants 18 inches to 24 inches apart in rows that are 4 feet apart, and let runners fill in the bare spaces between mother plants. Rein in the matted row by cutting off any runners escaping beyond into a swathe greater than 18 inch wide.

The second planting method, the "hill system," yields a larger first harvest but requires more plants and initial maintenance. Set plants in a double row with 1 foot between plants and 1 foot between the rows. Pinch off all runners that form because more plants in the bed will lead to overcrowding. If you plant more than one double row, allow 4 feet from one double row to the next. The hill system is best suited to alpine strawberries; day-neutral strawberries; and junebearing strawberries, such as 'Darrow', 'Chandler', and 'Canoga', which make few or no runners.

A third option in planting strawberries is the "spaced plant system," a hybrid of the other two systems. Set plants 2 feet apart in rows 3 feet apart and allow only four well-placed runners to form around each mother plant.

Using pruning shears or scissors to shear strawberry roots to a convenient length before planting.

pine needles, and oak or any other nonmatting leaves. In summer, aside from their usual benefits, mulches keep ripening strawberry fruits clean. In regions where winters get colder than about 15°F, cover the tops of the plants with a fluffy mulch to fend off cold and to prevent frost from heaving the plants up and out of the soil. Wait to cover the tops of the plants with this "winter mulch" until the soil has frozen to a depth of 1 inch. Peek under the mulch in late winter or spring, and pull it aside just as new growth begins.

Be alert to spring frost when your strawberries are flowering. If frost threatens, pull mulch back over the plants, or throw a blanket over the bed.

POST-PLANTING

Strawberry blossoms appear soon after planting. The usual recommendation is to pinch off those blossoms (for the first six weeks on everbearing strawberries) to let the plants put energy into root and leaf growth. Let's be realistic: No one is going to take all that trouble just so that they *don't* get fruit. Go ahead and leave at least a few blossoms.

Mulch your strawberry bed right after planting and maintain it year-round. Straw is ideal, as are wood chips,

RENOVATING A STRAWBERRY BED

After a couple of years, a garden or musk strawberry bed will need annual renovation to prevent overcrowding, limit diseases and weeds, and maintain a population of young, fruitful plants. Renovate immediately after harvest, by first cutting off all your strawberries' leaves with hand clippers, a scythe, or a mower set high, and then raking up the debris. Then dig out old plants and thin out young plants so each remaining young plant enjoys its own square foot of space. For plants in a matted row, narrow the row to 18 inches wide. Mulch with compost 1 inch deep; top that with straw, pine needles, wood

Strawberry Planting Plans

MATTED ROW SYSTEM

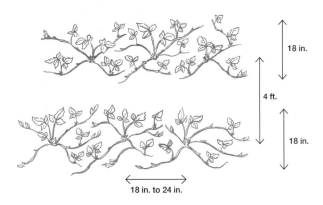

18 in.

4 ft.

18 in.

18 in. to 24 in.

Note: Distances are not to scale.

HILL SYSTEM

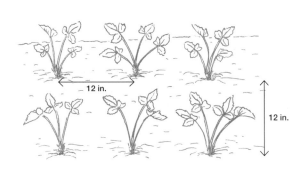

12 in.

12 in.

chips, or oak leaves; and water the bed—your plants will soon start growing again and getting ready for a big crop the next year. If sufficient compost is unavailable, spread fertilizer, such as soybean meal, at 2 pounds per 100 square feet of planted area, then top with mulch.

Do not renovate beds of everbearing strawberries, day-neutral strawberries, or alpine strawberries. Just replant them when they grow old and nonproductive. Alpine strawberries do not develop any runners. If you have patience, start new plants from seeds sown six weeks to eight weeks before the average date of the last spring frost in your area. Seed-grown plants bear their first summer. Partial renovation of everbearing or day-neutral strawberries, without sacrificing any crop, might be done by digging out old plants and thinning out young plants in spring. A full-scale renovation, as described for june-bearing strawberries, would sacrifice the early crop.

After 5 years to 10 years, a strawberry bed declines as weeds, pests, and diseases get the upper hand. Keep yourself in strawberrydom by starting a new bed in a new location the year before your old bed has to be replaced.

GROWING STRAWBERRIES IN CONTAINERS

All kinds of strawberries do well in pots. I have fruited alpine strawberries on a windowsill in only 4-inch-

Straw mulch keeps the soil moist and ripening berries free of dirt.

diameter pots. Certain everbearing varieties, such as 'Tristar' and 'Quinault', bear not only on mother plants but also on runners—even before the runners have rooted. Such a plant can look very decorative and luscious in a container with fruiting plantlets along and on the ends of runners draped over the edge.

Pests and Diseases

With good growing conditions and annual renovation, your strawberries' major pest will be birds. The only sure way to thwart them is to cover the bed with netting tacked high enough above plants so they cannot peck through at the fruits.

In moist weather, fruits also may be attacked by slugs, which work at night but leave telltale shiny trails. Trap slugs in shallow pans of beer (they are attracted to it and drown) or with a commercial product such as Sluggo®, or keep them from entering the bed in the first place with barriers of copper flashing.

In wet weather, you also may find rotting fruits. Mulch, adequate plant spacing, and avoiding over-fertilization (and resulting excess shade from overly lush leaf growth)

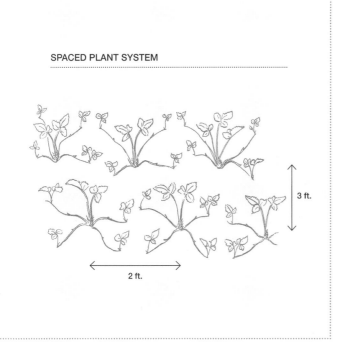

SPACED PLANT SYSTEM

3 ft.

2 ft.

lessens this problem. To prevent further spread of disease, pick off rotten berries and place them into a separate container for disposal while you harvest.

If whole plants decline, suspect root problems. Blackened roots or rat-tailed roots (no side roots) are problems associated with poor drainage, in which case you should replant at a better-draining site, with new plants.

Wilting plants with no evidence of root damage may have verticillium disease, for which there is no cure except to replant at a clean site, or you can try to avoid it altogether by planting a verticillium-resistant variety, such as 'Catskill', 'Sunrise', or 'Surecrop'. Many plants, including raspberry, tomato, pepper, eggplant, and potato, can also host verticillium, so avoid planting where these plants or other strawberry plants recently grew.

Red stele is a disease that causes roots to rot and their center cores—their steles—to turn red. Good drainage and resistant varieties avoid this disease.

A number of diseases potentially attack strawberry leaves. Annual renovation of a strawberry bed and resistant varieties avert these diseases, for a few years, at least.

Last, ripe strawberries, rather than being well-formed cones, sometimes become catfaced—misshapen with scars or holes. Frost damage or incomplete pollination because of cool weather can cause catfacing. The lygus bug is another catfacing culprit. Weeding in and near your strawberry bed, besides having other benefits, helps control this insect.

Harvesting

Garden strawberries generally are fully colored before they develop full flavor and sweetness. Give that thoroughly red fruit a slight tug and, if it resists, leave it for

Renovating a Strawberry Bed

1. Using a scythe, a mower set high, or hand shears, cut off and rake off all leaves right after fruiting finishes in spring or early summer.

2. Dig out old plants and excess young plants so that each remaining plant has about 1 square foot of space.

3. Shovel compost or some other organic material onto the bed. Sprinkle fertilizer before adding the organic material if it is not decomposed—autumn leaves for example.

another day or more, until the berry and its cap separate from the fruit stalk with a satisfying click. The first strawberries of the season are the best in that they are the first strawberries of the season; they're also the worst because who can help but pick those first berries before they are 100-percent ripe? It's a funny thing about garden strawberries, but even after the harvest is underway, a planting of a single variety yields berries of variable quality.

Harvesting alpine and musk strawberries at their peaks of perfection is easy because you can home in on ripe berries from their strong, delightful aromas. At that point, white alpine strawberries are creamy white with dark seeds. Ripe musk strawberries rarely are uniformly red, but they are very soft and what red they have is on the purple side. Ripe alpine and musk strawberries separate easily from their fruit stalks and caps when ripe.

Wire hoops and a net fend birds off strawberries.

4. Spread the compost or other organic material over the whole bed.

5. In a few weeks, plants will come out of their rest and sprout new leaves. More mulch can be added at that time to keep next year's fruit off the ground and clean, to conserve soil moisture, and to suppress weeds.

Strawberries can be grown in a variety of settings and containers, but keep them close at hand for frequent picking.

Selection of Plants and Varieties

New strawberry varieties are constantly being developed, and there are varieties specifically suited to certain regions. Contact your local Cooperative Extension office for names of varieties best suited for your garden. The following is a selection of some of the more popular varieties and, where appropriate, their regions of adaptation.

A few varieties of alpine strawberries exist, some with red fruits and others with white fruits. I once grew as many varieties of alpine strawberries as I could get, and found that all the red-fruited varieties tasted about the same and all the white-fruited varieties tasted the same, but the red-fruited varieties tasted different from the white-fruited ones. I prefer the white ones, both for their flavor and because birds ignore them.

In the wild, musk strawberries are dioecious; many cultivated varieties are perfect-flowered and at least partially self-fruitful. Two excellent varieties are 'Capron'

and 'Profumata di Tortona', the latter having been grown commercially in Italy as recently as the middle of the 20th century. It's as enjoyable to speak the name as it is to eat the fruits. Best yields probably come with planting both varieties together for cross-pollination. 'Capron' fruits are larger and the plants produce more runners. Both are delectable.

DAY-NEUTRAL STRAWBERRIES

'Aromas' Large fruit; high yielding; adapted to southern regions; moderately disease resistant, but not to some root diseases.

'Mara des Bois' Bred in Europe specifically for its excellent and unique flavor; berries are soft and small; vigorous plant produces many runners.

'Tristar' Small to medium fruit with very good flavor; adapted everywhere except far north and far south; plants are moderately resistant to many diseases.

'Chandler' strawberries are large and flavorful, and can be grown almost everywhere.

Musk strawberry fruits are ugly, small and very soft but have a most delectable flavor that is a smooth blend of strawberry and raspberry.

EVERBEARING STRAWBERRIES

'Ozark Beauty' Berries are large, sweet, bright red; very good flavor.

'Quinault' Very large, soft berries with good flavor; plants produce many runners; disease resistant; fruits can form on unrooted runners.

JUNEBEARING STRAWBERRIES

'Allstar' Large fruit with good flavor; productive; disease resistant; ripens midseason.

'Cabot' Large fruit, pale and sometimes misshapen; very good flavor; moderate yields; resistant to red stele; few runners; adapted to northern regions; ripens late season.

'Chandler' Very large fruits with good flavor; very high yields; widely adapted; long ripening season beginning early.

'Earliglo' Medium to large fruits with excellent flavor; moderate yields; very disease resistant; widely adapted except far north and far south; ripens very early season.

'Hood' Large berries with excellent flavor; moderate yields; disease resistant; especially adapted to Northwest; ripens early.

'Jewel' Berries are large and firm with very good flavor; moderate yields; resistant to leaf and fruit diseases but susceptible to root diseases; ripens late season.

'Sparkle' Medium, soft berries with excellent flavor; high yields; resistant to red stele disease; ripen mid- to late season.

'Surecrop' Large, glossy red fruits with good flavor; disease resistant; ripens early season.

'Sweet Charlie' Light red, medium fruits with good flavor; high yields; great variety for southern regions; short fruiting season; ripens very early season.

'Totem' Medium fruit with excellent flavor; moderate yields; adapted to the Northwest; ripens late midseason.

USDA Hardiness Zone Map

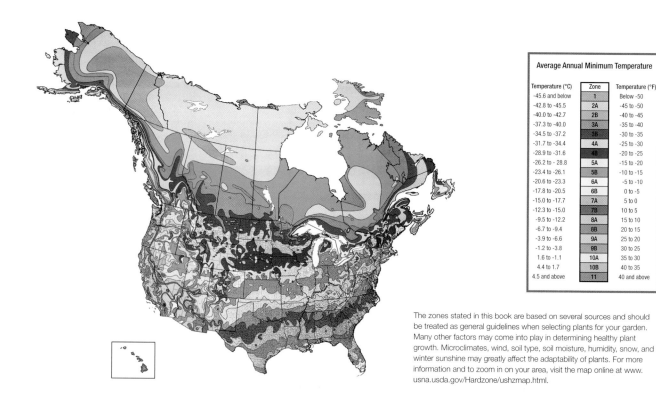

Average Annual Minimum Temperature

Temperature (°C)	Zone	Temperature (°F)
-45.6 and below	1	Below -50
-42.8 to -45.5	2A	-45 to -50
-40.0 to -42.7	2B	-40 to -45
-37.3 to -40.0	3A	-35 to -40
-34.5 to -37.2	3B	-30 to -35
-31.7 to -34.4	4A	-25 to -30
-28.9 to -31.6	4B	-20 to -25
-26.2 to -28.8	5A	-15 to -20
-23.4 to -26.1	5B	-10 to -15
-20.6 to -23.3	6A	-5 to -10
-17.8 to -20.5	6B	0 to -5
-15.0 to -17.7	7A	5 to 0
-12.3 to -15.0	7B	10 to 5
-9.5 to -12.2	8A	15 to 10
-6.7 to -9.4	8B	20 to 15
-3.9 to -6.6	9A	25 to 20
-1.2 to -3.8	9B	30 to 25
1.6 to -1.1	10A	35 to 30
4.4 to 1.7	10B	40 to 35
4.5 and above	11	40 and above

The zones stated in this book are based on several sources and should be treated as general guidelines when selecting plants for your garden. Many other factors may come into play in determining healthy plant growth. Microclimates, wind, soil type, soil moisture, humidity, snow, and winter sunshine may greatly affect the adaptability of plants. For more information and to zoom in on your area, visit the map online at www. usna.usda.gov/Hardzone/ushzmap.html.

AHS Plant Heat Zone Map

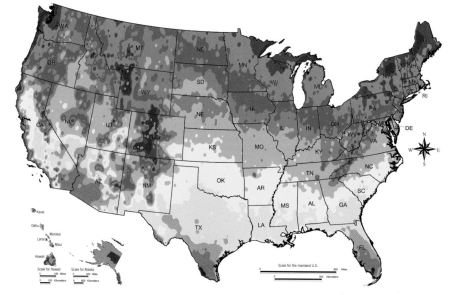

American Horticultural Society
7931 East Boulevard Drive
Alexandria, VA 22308 U.S.A.
(703) 768-5700 Fax (703) 768-8700

Coordinated by:
Dr. H. Marc Cathey, President Emeritus

Compiled by:
Meteorological Evaluation Services Co., Inc.

Underwriting by:
American Horticultural Society
Goldsmith Seed Company
Horticultural Research Institute of the American
 Nursery and Landscape Association
Monrovia
Time Life Inc.

Copyright ©1997 by the American Horticultural Society

Reproduced with permission of the American Horticultural
Society (www.ahs.org)

Average Number of Days per Year Above 86° F (30°C)

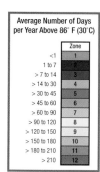

	Zone
<1	1
1 to 7	2
> 7 to 14	3
> 14 to 30	4
> 30 to 45	5
> 45 to 60	6
> 60 to 90	7
> 90 to 120	8
> 120 to 150	9
> 150 to 180	10
> 180 to 210	11
> 210	12

Resources

Nurseries

ADAMS COUNTY NURSERY
26 Nursery Rd.
P.O. Box 108
Aspers, PA 17304
717-677-8105
acnursery.com
Good selection of many varieties of common fruit trees.

BAY LAUREL NURSERY
2500 El Camino Real
Atascadero, CA 93422
805-466-3406
baylaurelnursery.com
Good selection of temperate and sub-tropical fruits, and some fruit-growing supplies.

BIG HORSE CREEK FARM
P.O. Box 70
Lansing, NC 28643
bighorsecreekfarm.com
Specializing in antique and heirloom apple trees, hundreds of varieties; custom grafted, so you get your tree in fall.

BRITE LEAF CITRUS NURSERY
480 CR 416 S
Lake Panasoffkee, FL 33538
352-793-6861
briteleaf.com
Specializing in citrus; offers a very large selection of kinds and varieties.

BURNT RIDGE NURSERY
432 Burnt Ridge Rd.
Onalaska, WA 98570
360-985-2873
burntridgenursery.com
Wide selection of common and un-common fruits for temperate and subtropical climates.

CUMMINS NURSERY
1408 Trumansburg Rd.
Ithaca, NY 14456
607-592-2801
cumminsnursery.com
Good selection of many varieties of common fruit trees and good selection of fruit-related books.

DURIO NURSERY
5853 Highway 182
Opelousas, LA 70570
337-948-3696
durionursery.biz
Very good selection of figs, pomegran-ates, bananas, and citrus.

EDIBLE LANDSCAPING
361 Spirit Ridge Ln.
Afton, VA 22920
800-524-4156
ediblelandscaping.com
Wide selection of common and uncommon fruits from temperate, subtropical, and tropical climates.

FEDCO CO-OP GARDEN SUPPLIES
P.O. Box 520
Waterville, ME 04903
207-873-7333
fedcoseeds.com
Good selection of hardy fruit trees, bushes, and vines; also good selection of fruit-growing supplies and gardening books.

FOUR WINDS GROWERS
P.O. Box 3373, Sackett Ln.
Winters, CA 95694
877-449-4637
fourwindsgrowers.com
Many subtropical and temperate zone fruits; specialize in dwarf and full-size citrus; mail-order nationally or, in Cali-fornia, through local nurseries.

GREENMANTLE NURSERY
3010 Ettersburg Rd.
Garberville, CA 95542
707-986-7504
greenmantlenursery.com
Temperate zone fruits and figs, espe-cially varieties best adapted to Califor-nia and the Pacific Northwest (west of the Cascades).

HARTMANN'S PLANT COMPANY
P.O.Box 100
Lacota, MI 49063-0100
269-253-4281
hartmannsplantcompany.com
Specializes in blueberries, but also offers many other berries and larger fruits as well as bird netting and a few other fruit-growing supplies.

HIDDEN SPRINGS NURSERY
170 Hidden Springs Ln.
Cookeville, TN 38501
931-268-2592
hiddenspringsnursery.com
Wide selection of common and uncommon fruits from temperate climates.

INDIANA BERRY
2811 US 31
Plymouth, IN 46563
800-295-2226
indianaberry.com
Offers a wide selection of kinds and varieties of berries; also some fruit-growing supplies, including bird netting.

ISON'S NURSERY
6855 Newnan Highway
Brooks, GA 30205
800-733-0324
isons.com
Offers a wide selection of fruits, and specializes in muscadine grapes.

JOHNSON NURSERY
1352 Big Creek Rd.
Ellijay, GA 30536
888-276-3187
johnsonnursery.com
Offers a wide selection of fruits and fruit-growing supplies.

JUST FRUITS AND EXOTICS
30 St. Frances St.
Crawfordville, FL 32327
850-926-5644
justfruitsandexotics.com
Offers a wide selection of temperate, subtropical, and tropical fruits.

LOGEE'S TROPICAL PLANTS
141 North St.
Danielson, CT 06239
888-330-8038
logees.com
Offers a wide selection of ornamental and tropical and subtropical fruiting plants for growing in pots.

NOURSE FARMS
41 River Road South
Deerfield, MA 01373
413-665-2658
noursefarms.com
Offers a wide selection of kinds and
varieties of berries.

ONE GREEN WORLD
28696 S. Cramer Rd.
Molalla, OR 97038-8576
877-353-4028
onegreenworld.com
Offers a wide selection of common and
uncommon fruits from temperate and
subtropical climates, and some fruit-
growing supplies.

**PEACEFUL VALLEY FARM &
GARDEN SUPPLY**
P.O. Box 2209, 125 Clydesdale Ct.
Grass Valley, CA 95945
888-784-1722
groworganic.com
Offers a wide selection of fruits from
temperate and subtropical climates;
gardening supplies.

RAINTREE NURSERY
391 Butts Rd.
Morton, WA 98356
800-391-8892
raintreenursery.com
Offers a wide selection of common
and uncommon fruits from temperate
and subtropical climates, and some
fruit-growing supplies, including bird
netting.

ROGER AND SHIRLEY MEYER
16531 Mt. Shelly Circle
Fountain Valley, CA 92708
714-839-0796
E-MAIL: xotcfruit@yahoo.com
Specializes in jujubes, kiwifruits, and
other unusual subtropical fruits.

ST. LAWRENCE NURSERIES
325 State Highway 345
Potsdam, NY 13676
315-265-6739
sln.potsdam.ny.us
Specializes in fruit trees, vines,
and shrubs, and nut trees, for cold
climates.

**STARK BRO'S NURSERIES &
ORCHARDS CO.**
P.O. Box 1800
Louisiana, MO 63353
800-325-4180
starkbros.com
Offers a wide selection of common and
uncommon fruits from temperate and
subtropical climates.

THE STRAWBERRY STORE
107 Wellington Way
Middletown, DE 19709
302-378-3633
thestrawberrystore.com
Specializes in strawberries, including
musk and alpine, and rare varieties.

TREES OF ANTIQUITY
20 Wellsona Rd.
Paso Robles, CA 93446
805-467-9909
treesofantiquity.com
Offers a wide selection of common and
uncommon fruits from temperate and
subtropical climates.

TRUE VINE RANCH
15014 Kreider Rd.
Bonner Springs, KS 66012
913-441-0005
truevineranch.com
Offers four varieties of blueberries in
various fruiting sizes, potted.

WHITMAN FARMS
3995 Gibson Rd. NW
Salem, OR 97304
503-585-8728
whitmanfarms.com
Offers many berries; has an especially
large selection of currants, gooseberries, and mulberries.

WILLIS ORCHARD CO.
P.O. Box 119
Berlin, GA 31722
866-586-6283
willisorchards.com
Offers many subtropical and temperate
zone fruits.

Fruit-Growing Supplies

**A. M. LEONARD HORTICULTURAL
TOOL & SUPPLY CO.**
241 Fox Dr.
Piqua, OH 45356-0816
amleo.com
Garden tools, safety wear, growing
supplies.

BENNER'S GARDENS
1100 Schell Ln., Suite 1
Phoenixville, PA 19460
800-769-9722
bennersgardens.com
Offers deer and rodent fencing and
bird netting.

CONTECH ENTERPRISES INC.
Unit 115, - 19 Dallas Rd.
Victoria, BC V8V 5A6
Canada
800-767-8658
contech-inc.com
Pest control products.

DRIPWORKS, INC.
190 Sanhedrin Circle
Willits, CA 95490
800-522-37470
dripworksusa.com
Irrigation supplies.

**FEDCO CO-OP GARDEN
SUPPLIES**
P.O. Box 520
Waterville, ME 04903
207-873-7333
fedcoseeds.com
Seeds, plants, garden tools, pest con-
trol, irrigation supplies.

GARDENER'S SUPPLY
Garden Center
128 Intervale Rd.
Burlington, VT 05401
802-660-3505
gardeners.com
Garden tools, pest control, irrigation
supplies.

GARDENS ALIVE!
5100 Schenley Pl.
Lawrenceburg, IN 47025
513-354-1482
gardensalive.com
Pest control, fertilizers, tools.

GEMPLER'S
P.O. Box 44993
Madison, WI 53744-4993
800-382-8473
gemplers.com
Garden tools, workwear, pest control.

HARMONY FARM SUPPLY &
NURSERY
3244 Highway 116 North
Sebastopol, CA 95472
707-823-9125
harmonyfarm.com
Irrigation supplies, pest control,
garden tools, seeds.

LEE VALLEY TOOLS
P.O. Box 1780
Ogdensburg, NY 13669
U.S.: 800-871-8158
Canada: 800-267-8767
leevalley.com
Wide selection of gardening tools and
supplies, especially pruning tools.

NEEM RESOURCE
The Ahimsa Alternative, Inc.
Bloomington, MN 55437
877-873-6336
neemresource.com
Offers unpurified neem oil.

NYLON NET COMPANY
845 North Main St.
Memphis, TN 38107
800-238-7529
nylonnet.com
Offers a wide selection of netting,
some of which can be used to keep
animals at bay.

OESCA, INC.
P.O. Box 540, Route 116
Conway, MA 01341
800-634-5557
oescoinc.com
Offers a wide selection of tools,
pest controls, and equipment for
orcharding.

THE URBAN FARMER STORE
2833 Vicente St.
San Francisco, CA 94116
415-661-2204
urbanfarmerstore.com
Irrigation supplies.

Biological Control Suppliers

GREEN SPOT LTD./GREEN
METHODS
The Green Spot Ltd.
93 Priest Rd.
Nottingham, NH 03290-6204
603-942-8925
GreenMethods.com

HARMONY FARM SUPPLY &
NURSERY
3244 Highway 116 North
Sebastopol, CA 95472
707-823-9125
harmonyfarm.com

IPM LABORATORIES, INC.
P.O. Box 300
980 Main St.
Locke, NY 13092-0300
315-497-2063
ipmlabs.com

KOPPERT BIOLOGICAL SYSTEMS
28465 Beverly Rd.
Romulus, MI 48174
800-928-8827
koppertonline.com/home.asp

NATURAL PEST CONTROLS
8864 Little Creek Dr.
Orangevale, CA 95662
916-726-0855
natpestco.com

NATURE'S CONTROL
3960 Jacksonville Highway
P.O. Box 35
Medford, OR 97501
541-245-6033
naturescontrol.com

PEACEFUL VALLEY FARM SUPPLY
P.O. 2209
Grass Valley, CA 95945
Questions: 530-272-4769
Orders: 888-784-1722
groworganic.com

PLANET NATURAL
1612 Gold Ave.
Bozeman, MT 59715
800-289-6656
planetnatural.com

RINCON-VITOVA
INSECTARIES, INC.
P.O. Box 1555
Ventura, CA 930221555
800-248-2847
rinconvitova.com

Organizations

AMERICAN POMOLOGICAL
SOCIETY
Dr. Robert Crassweller
102 Tysons Building
University Park, PA 16802
americanpomological.org

CALIFORNIA RARE FRUIT
GROWERS (CRFG)
66 Farragut Ave.
San Francisco, CA 94112-4050
crfg.org
Fruit Gardener magazine (six times per
year); a diverse and fun-loving group
of fruit enthusiasts looking for the best
varieties of mostly tropical and subtropical fruits; fruit specialist consul-
tants; annual festival of fruit.

HOME ORCHARD SOCIETY
P.O. Box 230192
Tigard, OR 97281-0192
homeorchardsociety.org
Newsletter, arboretum, library,
events, tours.

MIDWEST FRUIT EXPLORERS
(MIDFEX)
P.O. Box 93
Markham, IL 60428-0093
midfex.org
Workshops, information, tours; based
mostly in Chicago area.

MIDWEST ORGANIC TREE FRUIT
GROWERS NETWORK
P.O. Box 339
Spring Valley, WI 54767
715-778-5775
mosesorganic.org/treefruit/intro.htm
Fruit component of Midwest Organic
Sustainable and Education Service
(MOSES), which serves farmers striv-
ing to produce high-quality, healthful
food using organic and sustainable
techniques and offers workshops and
educational literature and an annual
conference.

NATIONAL CENTER FOR APPROPRIATE TECHNOLOGY
NCAT Sustainable Agriculture Project
P.O. Box 3838
Butte, MT 59702
**attra.ncat.org/horticultural.
html#Fruits**
This arm of the U.S. Department of Agriculture offers the latest information in sustainable agriculture and organic farming news, events, and funding opportunities, in addition to in-depth publications on production practices, innovative marketing, organic certification, and highlights of local, regional, and USDA and other federal sustainable agriculture activities.

NATIONAL PLANT GERMPLASM SYSTEM (NPGS)
ars-grin.gov/npgs
ars-grin.gov/npgs/rephomepgs.html
This arm of the U.S. Department of Agriculture has repositories at 26 locations throughout the United States; houses site-appropriate collections of varieties and species of agricultural plants; limited quantities of propagating material (not whole plants) are available; website also provides valuable links to other organizations with similar missions around the world.

NORTH AMERICAN FRUIT EXPLORERS (NAFEX)
nafex.org
Pomona magazine (four times per year); a diverse and fun-loving group of fruit enthusiasts looking for the best varieties of mostly temperate and some subtropical fruits; access to experts on all fruit types; private library access; annual summer conference.

Books, Some Useful References

Ashton, R. *The Incredible Pomegranate*. Tempe: Third Millenium Publishing, 2006.

_____. *Plums of North America*. Tempe: Third Millenium Publishing, 2008.

Beach, S. *The Apples of New York*. Albany: J. B. Lyons Co., 1905.

Bradley, F., B. Ellis, and D. Martin, eds. *The Organic Gardener's Handbook of Natural Pest and Disease Control*. Emmaus: Rodale, 2009.

Bunyard, E. *The Anatomy of Dessert: With a Few Notes on Wine*. New York: Modern Library, 2006.

Burford, T. *Apples: A Catalog of International Varieties*. Greenville: Burford Brothers, 1998.

Card, Fred W. *Bush-Fruits*. New York: Macmillan, 1925.

Chandler, W. *Evergreen Orchards*. Philadelphia: Lea & Febiger, 1958.

Condit, I. *The Fig*. Waltham: Chronica Botanica, 1947.

Darrow, G. *The Strawberry: History, Breeding, and Physiology*. Austin: Holt, Rinehart, and Winston, 1966.

Downing, A. J. *The Fruits and Fruit Trees of America*. New York: Wiley & Putnam, 1845.

Eck, P. and N. Childers, eds. *Blueberry Culture*. New Brunswick: Rutgers University Press, 1966.

Ferree, D., and I. Warrington, eds. *Apples: Botany, Production and Uses*. Oxfordshire, UK: CABI Publishing, 2003.

Hartmann, H., and D. Kester. *Plant Propagation: Principles and Practices*. Upper Saddle River: Prentice-Hall, 1983

Hedrick, U. *The Grapes of New York*. Albany: J. B. Lyons Co, 1908.

_____. *The Pears of New York*. Albany: J. B. Lyons Co., 1921.

_____. *The Small Fruits of New York*. Albany: J. B. Lyons Co., 1925.

Himelrick, D. and G. Galleta. *Small Fruit Crop Management*. Upper Saddle River: Prentice-Hall, 1990.

Ingels, C., P. Geisel, and M. Norton. *The Home Orchard*. Davis: University of California Agriculture & Natural Resources, 2007.

Janick, J., and J. Moore, eds. *Advances in Fruit Breeding*. West Lafayette: Purdue University Press, 1975.

Morton, J. *Fruits of Warm Climates*. Boynton Beach: Florida Flair Books, 1987.

Phillips, M. *The Apple Grower*. White River Junction: Chelsea Green Publishing, 2005.

Reich, L. *Landscaping with Fruit*. North Adams: Storey Publishing, 2009.

_____. *The Pruning Book*. Newtown: Taunton Press, 2010.

_____. *Uncommon Fruits for Every Garden*. Portland: Timber Press, 2004.

Rombough, L. *The Grape Grower*. White River Junction: Chelsea Green Publishing, 2002.

Shrock, D., ed. *Ortho All About Citrus & Subtropical Fruits*. Des Moines: Meredith Publishing, 2008.

Thomas, John J. *The American Fruit Culturalist*. New York: Orange Judd Co., 1909.

Tukey, H. *Dwarfed Fruit Trees for Orchard, Garden, and Home: With Special Reference to the Control of Tree Size and Fruiting in Commercial Fruit Production*. New York: Macmillan Company, 1964.

Waldheim, L. *Citrus: Complete Guide to Selecting & Growing More Than 100 Varieties for California, Arizona, Texas, The Gulf Coast of Florida*. Tucson: Ironwood Press, 1996.

Westcott, C. *The Gardener's Bug Book*. New York: Doubleday & Co., 1973

_____. *Westcott's Plant Disease Handbook*. Revised by R. K. Hoest. New York: Van Nostrand Reinhold Company, 1979.

Westwood, M. *Temperate Zone Pomology*. Portland: Timber Press, 1993.

Winkler, A., J. Cook, W. Kliewer, and L. Lider. *General Viticulture*. Davis: University of California Press, 1974.

Glossary

Alternate bearing: The tendency of a fruit plant to bear heavy and light crops in alternate years.

Anther: The male parts of a flower on which pollen is borne.

Aril: An accessory seed covering that is typically colored and hairy or fleshy to attract animals and aid seed dispersal.

Biodiversity: The degree of variation of life forms, including plants, insects, and animals as well as microorganisms, in the world or a particular habitat.

Biological control: The use of beneficial plants, animals, and microorganisms to control plant pests and diseases by natural means such as predation, parasitism, and exclusion.

Bud sport: A mutation in a growing point on a plant—and hence all shoots originating from that point—that results in a slight change, perhaps an improvement (from a human stand-point, at least) from which new plants can be propagated.

Cane: *Cane* has many meanings; in fruit growing, it generally signifies a one-year-old stem off which fruits are borne.

Central leader: In tree training, the central leader is the leading, most vertical shoot of the plant.

Chill: Temperature that is cool, not cold, typically between 30°F and 40° F, under which changes occur in plant physiology, such as sprouting of hardy seeds or flower bud development.

Clay: The smallest mineral particles in the soil; by one standard they are particles with diameters less than 0.002mm.

Clone: A group of plants, animals, or other organisms that are genetically identical.

Cordon: A permanent arm of a woody plant off of which grow temporary shoots.

Cross-pollination: The transfer of pollen from the anther of a flower of one plant to the stigma of a flower of another plant.

Cross-unfruitful: Varieties that will not set fruit when pollen is transferred between their flowers.

Crown: The compact stem off of which grows a whorl of leaves at the base of an herbaceous plant; or the limbs and branches of a tree.

Deciduous plant: A woody plant that sheds its leaves every year.

Dioecious plant: Literally meaning "two houses," a species in which male and female flowers are borne on separate plants.

Drip irrigation: Irrigation by dripping water near a plant, ideally at a rate approximating that at which a plant transpires water.

Espalier: The training of a plant to an orderly form, often two-dimensional, in which the tracery of the branches is prominent.

Fruit thinning: The deliberate removal of some fruits to increase size and flavor of remaining fruits and to promote a good crop the following year.

Fruiting spur: A short stem on which fruit is borne; the spur might be naturally short, as with apple and pear, or could be a stem cut back to a couple of buds, as with grape.

Germplasm: A collection of genetic resources—living plants, seeds, or cells of varieties or species—of a plant.

Graft: The bringing together, and subsequent growing together, of plant parts; grafts might occur naturally or by human intervention.

Gypsum: A soft mineral that is a hydrated form of calcium sulfate.

Heading cut: A pruning cut that removes only a portion of a stem.

Hill: In gardening, a cluster or group of plants growing close together.

Interstem: A piece of stem grafted between the scion and root-stock; useful when there is a graft incompatibility between the rootstock and the scion or when the interstem variety, if used as a rootstock, would not have the desired root properties.

Intersterile: See *cross-unfruitful*.

June drop: The tendency of many fruit plants to naturally shed a portion of fruits a few weeks after they have set, typically in June.

Leader: The main vertical shoot of a developing tree; it becomes the trunk and central leader.

Loam: A soil that contains a mix of clay, silt, and sand in proportions that give it a good spectrum of pore sizes for movement and retention of air and water.

Microclimate: The climate of a very small or restricted area that because of its elevation, aspect, nearby structures, or other factors, differs from the more general climate of a region.

Micronutrient: Nutrients that are necessary but are needed in very small amounts.

Monoecious plant: Literally meaning "single house," a species having separate male and female flowers on the same plant.

Organic matter: Living and once-living plants and animals in various states of decomposition in the soil.

Parthenocarpy: The development of fruits without fertilization of the flowers.

Perfect flower: A flower having both male and female parts.

pH: A measure of acidity or its inverse, alkalinity, expressed on a scale of 0 to 14, with the lower half denoting acidity, pH 7 denoting neutrality, and the upper half denoting alkalinity.

Pheromone: A chemical substance released by an animal that is detected by and influences related animals.

Pollenizer (pollinizer): A plant species or variety that provides pollen.

Pollen-sterile: A plant whose pollen is nonviable so its flowers cannot pollinate other plants or itself.

Pollination: The transfer of pollen from where it was formed (anther) to a receptive surface (stigma).

Pollinator: An agent (bees, insects, people) of pollen transfer.

Rootstock: The root portion of a grafted plant.

Runner: A stem that grows horizontally along the ground taking root at various points along its length.

Sand: Mineral particles in the soil with size ranges, by one standard, of 0.05mm to 2.00mm.

Scion: A piece of detached twig or a shoot that is grafted on a rootstock; the whole plant beyond the graft is the scion variety.

Seedling: A plant grown from a seed, contrasted with a clone, which generally is propagated asexually.

Self-fruitful (self-fertile): A plant that has the ability to set fruit or seeds with its own pollen.

Self-pollination: The transfer of pollen from the male flower parts of a plant to the same plant's, or a clone's, female flower parts.

Self-unfruitful (self-sterile): A plant that lacks the ability to produce seeds or fruits with its own pollen.

Silt: Mineral particles in the soil with size ranges, by one standard, of 0.002mm to 0.05mm.

Sport: See *Bud sport*.

Spur: See *Fruiting spur*.

Standard: *Standard* has two meanings. The first denotes a full-size tree. The second denotes a normally bushy plant that is trained to a trunk capped by a head of branches so it looks like a miniature tree.

Stenospermocarpy: Fruit that is seedless because the seed aborts subsequent to fertilization.

Root sucker (sucker): A shoot arising at the base of a plant.

Stigma: The female part of a flower that receives pollen.

Temperate zone: Climate zone that is colder than subtropical and warmer than polar, having an annual well-defined cool or cold winter and a warm or hot summer.

Thinning cut: A pruning cut that removes a branch completely.

Tip layering: The rooting of some plants that occurs where the tip of a stem touches the ground; once roots have developed at the stem tip, the stem can be severed from the mother plant to become an independent plant.

Watersprout: A vigorously growing, upright shoot.

Whip: A young, unbranched tree from a nursery.

Credits

All photos by Lee Reich, except as listed below.

FRONTISPIECE   © Andrea Jones

p. 3   © Saxon Holt

CHAPTER 1

p. 6   iStockphoto.com/Cameron Whitman

p. 15   (left) © Rosalind Creasy; (center) © Andrea Jones; (right) © Rosalind Creasy

CHAPTER 4

p. 56   © Rosalind Creasy

CHAPTER 5

p. 64   © Andrea Jones

p. 65   Les Jorgensen

p. 66   from The Apples of New York by S. A. Beach, J. B. Lyons Company, 1905

PART 2

p. 68   © Andrea Jones

p. 69   © Saxon Holt

p. 82   iStockphoto.com/lillisphotography

p. 85   iStockphoto.com/Zuki

p. 86   iStockphoto.com/David T. Gomez

p. 88   Carl Stucky

p. 86   iStockphoto.com/Melissa Carroll

p. 90   (top) iStockphoto.com/Sylvie Lebchek; (bottom) iStockphoto.com/Pixhook

p. 106   © Saxon Holt

p. 107   © Saxon Holt

p. 108   © Andrea Jones

p. 109   © Saxon Holt

pp. 110-111   © Saxon Holt

pp. 112-113   © Saxon Holt

p. 124   iStockphoto.com/Krzysztof Slusarczyk

p. 129   Archives of the Arnold Arboretum

p. 138   (top) Michael McConkey

p. 140   iStockphoto.com/seraficus

p. 145   © Saxon Holt

p. 149   (bottom) © Andrea Jones

p. 150   iStockphoto.com/Dennis Tokarzewski

p. 154   iStockphoto.com/Roger Whiteway

p. 155   David Karp

p. 156   © Andrea Jones

p. 159   iStockphoto.com/Joakim Leroy

p. 161   iStockphoto.com/Ilona Budzbon

p. 165   iStockphoto.com/David T. Gomez

p. 178   © Saxon Holt

p. 180   © Saxon Holt

p. 183   © Saxon Holt

p. 184   (right) © Rosalind Creasy

pp. 192-193   © Jerry Pavia

pp. 194-195   © Saxon Holt

p. 196   © Saxon Holt

p. 197   © Dierdre Larkin

p. 200   © Dierdre Larkin

p. 201   iStockphoto.com/Cathleen Abers-Kimball

p. 209   iStockphoto.com/lek

p. 214   Matthew Benson

p. 215   (top) © Andrea Jones

p. 222   © Andrea Jones

p. 223   © Jerry Pavia

Index